Freedom and the Fifth Commandment

Manchester University Press

Freedom and the Fifth Commandment

Catholic priests and political violence in Ireland, 1919-21

Brian Heffernan

Manchester University Press

Copyright © Brian Heffernan 2014

The right of Brian Heffernan to be identified as the author of this work has been asserted by him in accordance with the Copyright, Designs and Patents Act 1988.

Published by Manchester University Press
Altrincham Street, Manchester M1 7JA, UK
www.manchesteruniversitypress.co.uk

British Library Cataloguing-in-Publication Data is available

Library of Congress Cataloging-in-Publication Data is available

ISBN 978 1 5261 0652 0 *paperback*

First published by Manchester University Press in hardback 2014

This edition first published 2016

The publisher has no responsibility for the persistence or accuracy of URLs for any external or third-party internet websites referred to in this book, and does not guarantee that any content on such websites is, or will remain, accurate or appropriate.

Printed by Lightning Source

To my parents,
Jim and Annelies Heffernan

Contents

List of figures and tables	page ix
Acknowledgements	x
List of abbreviations and note on spelling	xii
Map: Ecclesiastical provinces and dioceses of Ireland, 1919–21	xiv

Introduction	1

I OBEYING THE LAW OF GOD

1	In the old groove: traditional political alignments	15
2	The Fifth Commandment and the brand of Cain: condemnation from the pulpit	35
3	Interfering where they shouldn't: interaction with republicans	65

II REPUBLICAN PRIESTS

4	Sinn Féin priests: support for Sinn Féin, the Dáil and local IRA units	97
5	Aiding and abetting: priests involved in the IRA campaign	122
6	Troublesome priests: responses to clerical support for republicanism	151

III THE CLERGY AND THE CROWN

7 Priest and victim: British measures against the clergy   179
8 The reign of frightfulness: clerical responses to the British campaign   208
9 Preserving the peace: mediation, relief work and political activism   226

Epilogue   240

Appendices   247
Bibliography   265
Index   279

Figures and tables

Figures

2.1. Reported instances of clerical denunciation and non-agrarian indictable offences, January 1919 – July 1921   39

Tables

7.1. Charges preferred against arrested clerics, January 1919 – July 1921   185
7.2. Results of arrests of clerics, January 1919 – July 1921   185

Acknowledgements

This book has its origins in a PhD thesis completed in 2011 at the National University of Ireland, Maynooth. It was funded by the university and by what was then still the Irish Research Council for the Humanities and Social Sciences. To both institutions I owe an important debt of gratitude.

The book has benefited immensely from the assistance of a number of persons. Foremost among them is Professor Vincent Comerford. I was very fortunate in having him as my PhD supervisor in Maynooth, and I am particularly grateful to him for investing time and effort in this project even after his retirement. His advice and feedback – always subtle and always to the point – have been simply indispensable, and his constant kind encouragement has been very important to me. My thanks are also due to Dr Joost Augusteijn, a generous mentor from whose teaching and writing I have learnt many of the things that enabled me to write this book. Professor Charles Townshend, Dr Thomas O'Connor and a number of anonymous reviewers all offered most valuable advice. Any remaining errors of fact or judgement are, of course, entirely my own.

I would also like to thank the following people for their valued help: Margaret de Brún; Damien Burke; Joseph Canning; Gerard Chestnutt; the late Professor Patrick J. Corish; Dr Edward Daly; Bernie Deasy; Gerard Dolan; Noelle Dowling; Margaret Doyle; Thomas Doyle; Martin Fagan; Ignatius Fennessy, OFM; Hugh Fenning, OP; Carole Jacquet; David Kelly, OSA; Professor Dermot Keogh; Tom Kilgarriff; Dr Brian Kirby; Dr John Kirby; Professor Brendan McConvery, CSsR; Joseph Mac Loughlin, CSsR; Clement Mac Mánuis CSsR; Laura Magnier; Fintan Monahan; Dr William Murphy; the late Patrick O'Donnell, CSsR; Fergus O'Donoghue,

SJ; Paul Ryan; Joseph Somerville; Professor Frans Vosman and Kieran Waldron. I am very grateful to the team at Manchester University Press for all their work on this book and to Dr Fiona Little for the copyediting.

Many thanks also to the following holders of copyright who kindly permitted me to quote from material from their archives or databases: the archbishops of Armagh, Dublin and Tuam, the bishops of Clonfert, Cork and Ross, Elphin, Galway, Kerry and Killaloe, the diocesan archivist of Kildare and Leighlin, the provincials of the Irish Jesuit and Capuchin provinces, the rector of the Pontifical Irish College, Rome, the director of the Centre Culturel Irlandais, Paris, the rector of Clonard Redemptorist Monastery, Belfast, and the Irish Newspaper Archives for quotations from the *Irish Independent*, the *Freeman's Journal* and the *Nenagh Guardian*.

I thank Drs Caroline Gallagher, Marta Ramón and Pierre Ranger for sharing their academic expertise with me, for their help on many an occasion and for their good friendship. I am, as always, grateful to Mary Heffernan for her generous encouragement. John Heffernan and Claire Conway I thank for ever-stimulating conversation and for their extraordinary hospitality, which made Ireland a home away from home. Above all, I am grateful to Etienne Chéreau for his patience, support and unfailing good humour.

My greatest debt is to my parents, Jim and Annelies Heffernan. Their constant support in good times and bad has meant much more to me than they realise. To them I affectionately dedicate this book.

Abbreviations and note on spelling

Abbreviations

ADA	Armagh Diocesan Archives, Armagh
AICP	Archives of the Irish College, Paris
AICR	Archives of the Pontifical Irish College, Rome
BMH	Bureau of Military History
CD	contemporary document
CDA	Cork and Ross Diocesan Archives, Cork
CIC	*Codex iuris canonici* (*Code of Canon Law*)
CMA	Clonard Redemptorist Monastery Domestic Archive, Belfast
CO	Colonial Office: Dublin Castle records
CPA	Capuchin Provincial Archives, Dublin
CtDA	Clonfert Diocesan Archives, Loughrea
DDA	Dublin Diocesan Archives, Dublin
EDA	Elphin Diocesan Archives, Sligo
GDA	Galway Diocesan Archives, Galway
ICD	*Irish Catholic Directory*
IGMR	Inspector general's monthly confidential report
IJA	Irish Jesuit Archives, Dublin
IRA	Irish Republican Army
KDA	Killaloe Diocesan Archives, Ennis
KyDA	Kerry Diocesan Archives, Killarney
MA	Military Archives, Dublin
NLI	National Library of Ireland, Dublin
PP	parish priest
RIC	Royal Irish Constabulary
TD	*Teachta Dála* (member of the Dáil)
TDA	Tuam Diocesan Archives, Tuam
TNA	The National Archives, Kew

UCDA   University College Dublin Archives, Dublin
WO   War Office: Army of Ireland: Administrative and Easter rising records
WS   witness statement

Note on spelling

Quotations have been tacitly edited to conform with the capitalisation style used in the rest of the book.

Map: Ecclesiastical provinces and dioceses of Ireland, 1919–21

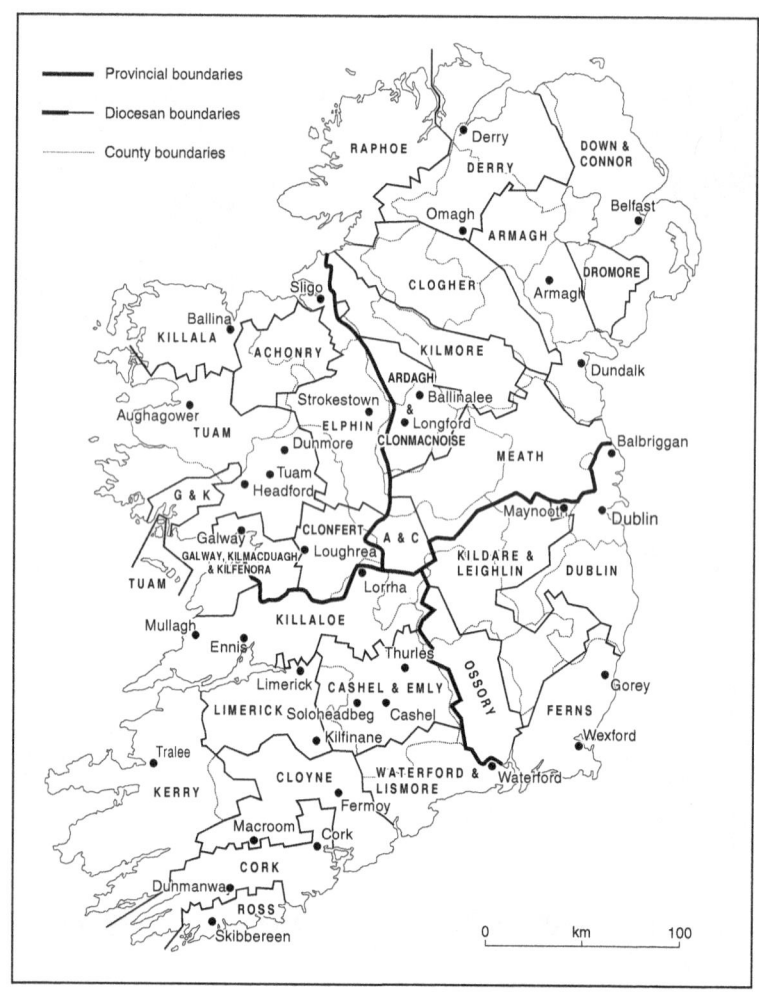

Introduction

The nineteenth century saw the rise of modern nations in Europe, the 'imagined communities' of those who shared the same culture and recognised each other as fellow members.[1] When cultural conceptions of the nation merged with the liberal idea of representative government, nationalism became one of the most important mobilising forces in European politics.[2] Nationalists strove to establish states for their nations, or, if these existed already, to turn them into true nation states. In order to achieve this goal they tried to bring about an awakening of the national idea among the masses. However, formulating the precise contents of the nationalist message – of what it meant to be Italian, or Polish or Irish – was a controversial affair, and different rivals competed for the right to define national identity.

In many parts of Europe, the Catholic church was a formidable contender for this task. Catholicism had emerged from its skirmishes with *ancien régime* monarchs and its life-or-death combat with revolution to undergo a remoulding that was very similar to modern nation building. As Peter Raedts has observed, the transformation of the church in the nineteenth century 'can be described in exactly the same terms as the transformation from traditional

---

1 See Benedict Anderson, *Imagined Communities. Reflections on the Origin and Spread of Nationalism* (revised edn; London and New York: Verso, 1991), pp. 5–7, and Ernest Gellner, *Nations and Nationalism* (2nd edn; Ithaca, NY: Cornell University Press, 2008), pp. 6–7.
2 Joost Augusteijn, 'The origins of Irish nationalism in a European context', in Brian Heffernan *et al.* (eds), *Life on the Fringe? Ireland and Europe, 1800–1922* (Dublin and Portland, OR: Irish Academic Press, 2012), pp. 15–38, at p. 26.

states into nation states', involving as it did 'bureaucratisation, mass mobilisation and cultural homogenisation'.[3] The ultramontane church that was the result of this process staked a strong claim to its members' loyalty, very similar to the demands made by the nation and the nation state.

Even though Europeans were capable of dividing their allegiances according to the different spheres of modern life, there was the risk of a clash.[4] Not content with being relegated to the domain of private religious conviction, Catholicism dealt with the challenge by 'writing itself into the script' of nationalism.[5] This strategy had varying degrees of success, depending on the level and nature of the opposition it encountered in each particular nation. Urs Altermatt has distinguished a number of ways in which Catholic identity interacted with European nationalities, ranging from 'traditional opposition' to 'cultural symbiosis'.[6] He has contended that Ireland was an example of the latter model, Catholicism having become, in Sean Connolly's words, 'the basis of a communal identity opposed to the state'.[7] The validity of this interpretation is not negated by the enduring existence of a minority tradition that imagined the Irish nation in purely secular terms.

The opposition to the state sponsored by the Catholic church was of the constitutional type. When it took the form

---

3 Peter Raedts, 'The church as nation state. A new look at ultramontane Catholicism (1850–1900)', *Dutch Review of Church History*, 84 (2004), pp. 476–96, at p. 484.

4 E. J. Hobsbawm, *Nations and Nationalism since 1780. Programme, Myth, Reality* (2nd edn; Cambridge: Cambridge University Press, 1992), p. 123.

5 Raedts, 'Nation state', p. 481.

6 Urs Altermatt, 'Katholizismus und Nation. Vier Modelle in europäisch-vergleichender Perspektive', in Urs Altermatt and Franziska Metzger (eds), *Religion und Nation. Katholizismen im Europa des 19. und 20. Jahrhunderts* (Stuttgart: W. Kohlhammer, 2007), pp. 15–33.

7 Sean J. Connolly, 'Religion and Nationality in Ireland. An Unstable Relationship', in Urs Altermatt and Franziska Metzger (eds), *Religion und Nation. Katholizismen im Europa des 19. und 20. Jahrhunderts* (Stuttgart: W. Kohlhammer, 2007), pp. 119–34, at p. 125. See also Emmet Larkin, *The Historical Dimensions of Irish Catholicism* (Washington, DC, and Dublin: Catholic University of America Press and Four Courts Press, 1984), pp. 91–130.

of republicanism, with secret societies plotting armed rebellion, it was firmly repudiated by bishops and priests alike. Whatever common bonds tied Irish separatists to the church, the violent means they used from time to time were never endorsed by the majority of the clergy. On the contrary, violence was the most important bone of contention between republicans and Catholic churchmen, forcefully summarised in 1867 by the bishop of Kerry's famous dictum that hell was not hot enough, nor eternity long enough to punish the Fenian leaders.[8] This antagonism arose from the church's instinctive distrust of secret movements that conspired to undermine order in society and were impervious to elite control. As David Miller has pointed out, it also gave the bishops bargaining power vis-à-vis the British government.[9] The church's opposition helped to contain the 'physical force' tradition of Irish republicanism throughout much of the nineteenth century, with home rule remaining the dominant nationalist aspiration. In the meantime, Catholicism continued to shape Irish national identity, with Catholic themes featuring very strongly in the discourse of Gaelic revivalists. Moreover, clerical influence loomed large over the organisations of the Gaelic revival and over the Irish Parliamentary Party.

This situation changed in the wake of the 1916 Easter rising. The republican party Sinn Féin began its rise to victory and replaced the Irish Parliamentary Party as the main vehicle of Irish nationalist politics. There were signs of a rapprochement between republicanism and the church during the 1918 anti-conscription campaign as Sinn Féin and the clergy joined forces against the British government.[10] But as Joost Augusteijn has shown, a section of the republican movement became radicalised after Sinn Féin's

8   E. R. Norman, *The Catholic Church and Ireland in the Age of Rebellion 1859–1873* (Ithaca, NY: Cornell University Press, 1965), p. 117.
9   David W. Miller, *Church, State and Nation in Ireland 1898–1921* (Dublin and Pittsburgh, PA: Gill and Macmillan and University of Pittsburgh Press, 1973), p. 4.
10 Pauric Travers, 'The priest in politics. The case of conscription', in Oliver MacDonagh, W. F. Mandle and Pauric Travers (eds), *Irish Culture and Nationalism, 1750–1950* (London, Basingstoke and Canberra: The Macmillan Press and Humanities Research Centre, Australian National University, 1983), pp. 161–81, at p. 161.

December 1918 election victory, turning from public defiance to guerrilla warfare.[11] This process placed a strain on the relationship. Irish Volunteers, soon styling themselves the Irish Republican Army (hereafter IRA), began attacking the servants of the crown, with the struggle developing into full-blown guerrilla war in 1920. What made this violence particularly poignant from a clerical point of view was the fact that many of the combatants on either side were Catholics, including the majority of the largest police force, the Royal Irish Constabulary (hereafter RIC).[12]

This book examines how Catholic priests responded to the campaign of political violence during the 1919–21 War of Independence. It looks at the stresses which this campaign caused on the relationship between republicans and the church, and analyses how these were eventually resolved, or, more accurately, endured.

In doing so, the book focuses on priests at a local level, rather than on the 'high politics' of the bishops and their dealings with national republican leaders.[13] This approach is not inspired by the conviction that either bishops or republican leaders were unimportant, but by the desire to contribute to newer trends in the historiography both of religion and of the Irish War of Independence. If church historians' main concern in the past was the functioning of the institutional church and the official formulation of its theology, nowadays it is 'the place of religion within the community, ... facets of daily Christian life and the impact of social and cultural factors upon pious practice'.[14] Examining the attempts of priests to shape social and political behaviour can contribute to this approach. And in a comparable development, the attention of historians of the War

---

11 Joost Augusteijn, *From Public Defiance to Guerrilla Warfare. The Experience of Ordinary Volunteers in the Irish War of Independence 1916–1921* (London and Portland, OR: Irish Academic Press, 1996).
12 Peter Cottrell, *The Anglo-Irish War. The Troubles of 1913–1922* (Oxford: Osprey Publishing, 2006), p. 20.
13 Emmet Larkin, *The Roman Catholic Church and the Emergence of the Modern Irish Political System, 1874–1878* (Dublin and Washington, DC: Four Courts Press and Catholic University of America Press, 1996), p. viii.
14 R. V. Comerford et al. (eds), *Religion, Conflict and Coexistence in Ireland. Essays Presented to Monsignor Patrick J. Corish* (Dublin: Gill and Macmillan, 1990), p. 3.

of Independence has also shifted since the 1970s to participants at a local level, and indeed to the perspective of non-participants.[15] Groups whose involvement in the struggle was previously regarded as irrelevant have begun to be investigated. In order to place the conflict in its proper context, the experiences of 'ordinary Volunteers' need to be examined, as well as those of women, members of the crown forces, home rule supporters, Protestants, Irish First World War veterans and Catholic unionists.[16] Looking at clerical perspectives will similarly contribute to an understanding of the conflict that does not privilege one group's account over another's.

Although these new approaches have been implemented very fruitfully in Irish history, they have not yet inspired much research of the religious history of the revolutionary period. In 1978, John Newsinger explored the religiosity of the Volunteers, and in 2000 Patrick Murray published an outstanding book on the Catholic church and Irish politics between 1922 and 1937.[17] But there is only one study devoted to Catholic priests and the War of Independence, an article published by Tomás Ó Fiaich in a *Capuchin Annual* edition to mark the conflict's fiftieth anniversary.[18] It appeared alongside articles by veterans such as Tom Barry and Seán MacEoin in a feature intended to 'extol the generation that suffered unto victory'.[19] Ó Fiaich, then professor of modern history in Maynooth and subsequently cardinal-archbishop of Armagh, wrote it at a time when the civil rights movement in Northern Ireland had just begun. Although well documented and eschewing crassly partisan conclusions, the article was nonetheless

15 The classic example is David Fitzpatrick, *Politics and Irish Life 1913–1921. Provincial Experience of War and Revolution* (Dublin: Gill and Macmillan, 1977).
16 For an example of a study of the 'experience of ordinary Volunteers', see Augusteijn, *Defiance*.
17 John Newsinger, '"I bring not peace but a sword". The religious motif in the Irish War of Independence', *Journal of Contemporary History*, 13 (1978), pp. 609–28; Patrick Murray, *Oracles of God. The Roman Catholic Church and Irish Politics, 1922–37* (Dublin: University College Dublin Press, 2000).
18 Tomás Ó Fiaich, 'The Catholic clergy and the independence movement', *The Capuchin Annual* (1970), pp. 480–502.
19 *The Capuchin Annual* (1970), pp. 225–6.

designed to highlight the clergy's involvement in the independence movement.[20] Its conclusions need reassessment, all the more so because much new source material has become available since 1970. Some recent works on the War of Independence also contain references to priests, and while their conclusions are important, their primary focus has been on other aspects of the conflict.[21] Studies of the Irish church at this time have tended to focus on the traditional 'church and state' theme and rarely discuss parish-level developments.[22] This book aims to fill the gap.

As its subtitle announces, the book proposes to discuss Catholic priests and political violence in Ireland between 1919 and 1921. The three parts of this sentence – Catholic priests, political violence and the 1919–21 time frame – are in need of some further clarification. It was not so much the rise of Sinn Féin as the IRA's use of guerrilla tactics that caused the clergy concern. Therefore the narrative in this book begins with the Soloheadbeg ambush in January 1919, an event commonly reckoned to mark the start of the guerrilla phase of the 'Irish revolution'.[23] Similarly, since guerrilla fighting more or less stopped after the Anglo-Irish truce of 11 July 1921, which opened the way to peace negotiations between the republican and British governments, the narrative takes this date as its *terminus ad quem*. There certainly was violence before Soloheadbeg, most notably at Easter 1916. But the moral and practical difficulties associated with guerrilla tactics differed considerably from those connected with the open rebellion of the

20 Ó Fiaich, 'Clergy', p. 480.
21 For example Augusteijn, *Defiance*, pp. 301–9; Marie Coleman, *County Longford and the Irish Revolution 1910–1923* (Dublin and Portland, OR: Irish Academic Press, 2003), pp. 157–9, and D. M. Leeson, *The Black and Tans. British Police and Auxiliaries in the Irish War of Independence, 1920–1921* (Oxford: Oxford University Press, 2011), pp. 51–2, 164.
22 For two able examples see Miller, *Church, State* and Dermot Keogh, *The Vatican, the Bishops and Irish Politics 1919–39* (Cambridge: Cambridge University Press, 1986).
23 Michael Hopkinson, 'Negotiation. The Anglo-Irish War and the revolution', in Joost Augusteijn (ed.), *The Irish Revolution, 1913–1923* (Basingstoke: Palgrave, 2002), pp. 121–34, at p. 130. See also Peter Hart, 'Definition. Defining the Irish revolution', in *ibid.*, pp. 17–33, at p. 24.

Easter rising, and this justifies the 1919 *terminus a quo*. A similar argument accounts for the exclusion of violence after the truce, notably that during the Civil War of 1922–23. In the eyes of the bishops and a majority of the priests, the crucial issue of the new government's legitimacy had been resolved in 1922, and this meant that the dynamics of clerical involvement in the Civil War differed much from those in the War of Independence. Patrick Murray has observed that the bishops found the moral dilemmas during the second conflict 'much clearer and less ambiguous' than those that existed during the first.[24] The hierarchy consequently assumed a much more definite position during the Civil War than it did during the War of Independence, creating an entirely different ecclesiastical context for priests at parish level. This has motivated the decision to choose July 1921 as the end point of this study. There is, moreover, an important historiographical reason, as Murray's book provides an account of the clergy's role during the Civil War that leaves little to be desired.[25]

The term 'political violence' has been used here to mean any exercise or threat of physical force against persons or property carried out to further a political goal. This definition allows for the inclusion of acts both by the IRA and by the crown forces, the former's professed objective being the removal of a foreign occupying force from Irish soil and the latter's being the suppression of rebellion against the crown. The inclusiveness of the term is important, because it will be argued that the British counterinsurgency campaign was crucial in shaping the response of Catholic priests to republican violence. As Charles Townshend has pointed out, the term is an abstraction, imputing as it does an overriding political motive to acts of violence that could have been caused by any one of a 'mass of obscure local determinants'.[26] Of course history writing would lose much of its meaning if all such abstractions were to be abjured, but it is important to be alert to the possibility that violence in any given case was motivated by other than political goals. Thus Chapter 3 will discuss the issue of sectarian violence. A different term that has been favoured recently, 'terror', is less

---

24 Murray, *Oracles*, p. 409.
25 *Ibid.*, pp. 11–136.
26 Charles Townshend, *Political Violence in Ireland. Government and Resistance since 1848* (Oxford: Clarendon Press, 1983), p. ix.

successful than 'political violence' in achieving value neutrality.[27] However, it has the benefit of highlighting the psychological effects of physical force, which was intended to 'create an acute fear of violence': to terrify as much as to destroy.[28] It has been used occasionally in this book, as have the terms 'guerrilla', 'guerrilla war' and 'guerrilla warfare', which, according to the *Oxford English Dictionary*, mean 'an irregular war carried on by small bodies of men acting independently'.[29] If 'acting independently' is taken somewhat loosely, so as not to preclude the existence of a national command attempting to impose central control, 'guerrilla' is an accurate term for the IRA campaign.

The period between 1919 and 1921 is often described in this book as the 'War of Independence'. This name is unfortunate, as the term 'war' conjures up images of a coordinated campaign of one army against another, which is hardly an adequate description of the conflict. But to the extent that any guerrilla struggle can be called a war, the Irish War of Independence was one too. This name has been used here because it is at least better than other descriptions. 'Anglo-Irish War' does not address the issue at stake – Ireland's independence – and even more strongly than 'War of Independence' suggests the existence of two warring sovereign states. And 'Tan War' is too much associated with Civil War rhetoric to be useful in a work of historical scholarship. 'IRA campaign', 'British campaign', 'struggle' and 'conflict' also feature as less problematic if vaguer alternatives. The belligerents of this conflict on the republican side are referred to as the 'Irish Volunteers' up to 1919 and as 'IRA' thenceforth, with members of this organisation described throughout as 'Volunteers'. The belligerents on the other side are referred to by the generic term of 'crown forces', which is

---

27 See Brian Hanley, 'Terror in twentieth-century Ireland', in David Fitzpatrick (ed.), *Terror in Ireland 1916–1923. Trinity History Workshop* (Dublin: Lilliput Press, 2012), pp. 10–25, at p. 10.
28 David Fitzpatrick, 'Introduction', in David Fitzpatrick (ed.), *Terror in Ireland 1916–1923. Trinity History Workshop* (Dublin: Lilliput Press, 2012), pp. 1–9, at p. 5. See also Anne Dolan, '"The shadow of a great fear". Terror and revolutionary Ireland', in *ibid.*, pp. 26–38.
29 *The Oxford English Dictionary* (2nd edn; Oxford: Oxford University Press, 1989).

intended to include both the army and the different types of constabulary active in Ireland at the time.

The subject of this book is the Catholic clergy. The terms 'church' and 'Catholic church' have been avoided as much as possible, except when referring to buildings. As the Second Vatican Council has emphasised, 'the church' in Catholic theology means the collectivity of all believers who hold the Catholic faith.[30] However, journalists and historians almost invariably use it as a synecdoche for the ordained ministers of the church, or even for the 'hierarchy', meaning the pope and the bishops. This book has attempted to avoid confusion by indicating which specific subsection of the church is at issue in each given place. Although the primary focus is on priests, bishops make very frequent appearances, all the more inevitably on account of Ireland's exceptionally high ratio of bishops per capita.[31] It is impossible to write a history of priestly attitudes to political violence without discussing episcopal attitudes. The term 'Catholic' has been used throughout to mean 'Roman Catholic', not just for reasons of brevity, but also because it was the most common self-descriptor used by Roman Catholics themselves. It implies no judgement on the claims of other Christian denominations to this particular note of the church.

This is a study of men rather than women. A number of women do feature, but they are much in the minority. The reason and only justification for this regrettable imbalance is, of course, the Catholic custom of ordaining only men to the priesthood. The decision to focus on the Catholic priesthood is motivated by the simple hypothesis that most of the civilians engaged in political violence between 1919 and 1921 were Catholics. This means that Catholic priests were confronted with the matter in a way unique to them, one very different from the way in which Protestant clergy – or Protestants in general – had to deal with the issue. This distinction

---

30 Second Vatican Council, *Dogmatic Constitution on the Church* (Lumen gentium), 21 November 1964, no. 14, in *Vatican Council II. The Basic Sixteen Documents: Constitutions, Decrees, Declarations*, ed. Austin Flannery (Northport, NY, and Dublin: Costello Publishing and Dominican Publications, 1996), p. 20.
31 See Appendix 8 for a list of Irish Catholic bishops between 1919 and 1921.

justifies making Catholic priests the specific focus of a separate study.

The material used to construct this book's narrative has been derived from five categories of sources. The first of these consists of religious archives, including diocesan archives from all four provinces of Ireland, college archives, provincial archives of religious orders and the domestic archives of religious houses. These collections vary in size and organisation, and some of the smaller repositories have not been used much by historians of this period before. Despite frequent assurances by modest archivists that their collections contained little of relevance, many of these smaller archives yielded excellent new material. The second category consists of British archives, specifically the War Office's Army of Ireland records and the Colonial Office's Dublin Castle records in The National Archives in Kew. These yielded a considerable amount of material about raids, prosecutions and evidence of seditious activities gathered against priests.

The third category is made up of archives containing republican papers. The main collection consists of the Bureau of Military History's witness statements in the Military Archives in Dublin, but it also includes papers held in the National Library of Ireland and in University College Dublin Archives. The witness statements provided a veritable mine of new material, especially since the Military Archives made them available online in August 2012. This has allowed a systematic search of the entire database, yielding hundreds of hits, many of them very useful. Diarmaid Ferriter has argued that 'the attitude of the Catholic church to the crisis … deserves reassessment on the basis of these statements'.[32] It is hoped that this book will achieve precisely that.

The fourth category consists of newspapers and periodicals. Special attention was given to the two main Catholic publications of the day, the *Irish Catholic* and the *Catholic Bulletin and Book Review*, and every issue of these two publications for the duration of the conflict was consulted. The weekly *Irish Catholic* described itself in 1920 as 'broadly national in tone' but upholding 'in political as in all other matters the principles of the Catholic faith', and

---

32 Diarmaid Ferriter, '"In such deadly earnest"', *The Dublin Review*, 12 (2003), pp. 36–64, at p. 48.

claimed to treat all such matters 'from that standpoint alone'.³³ To judge by its political commentary, it catered to a conservative readership. The strongly republican monthly *Catholic Bulletin* has provided insight into the other side of the political spectrum of early twentieth-century Catholic Ireland.³⁴ In addition to these specifically Catholic journals, one of the most widely read national daily newspapers was consulted: the *Irish Independent*. Politically, this newspaper stood more or less half-way between the conservatism of the *Irish Catholic* and the republicanism of the *Catholic Bulletin*. It became closely allied with Sinn Féin and the Dáil and critical of the British and the crown forces, although it opposed the use of violence by republicans.³⁵

The *Irish Independent* was not the only national daily at the time, the *Irish Times* and the *Freeman's Journal* traditionally being two competitors. Although these two newspapers were also incidentally consulted, as well as a number of regional newspapers, the *Irish Independent* was nonetheless selected for particular scrutiny. The *Irish Times* was then still a Protestant newspaper. This quality makes its perspective on the Catholic clergy's attitude towards republican violence an interesting subject in its own right, but the *Irish Independent's* unofficial alignment with Catholicism made it better suited as a source for this book. And the *Freeman's Journal's* longstanding association with the Irish Parliamentary Party, although repudiated by the end of 1919, caused it to lose ground to the *Irish Independent*.³⁶ The *Independent* was, in short, more Catholic than the *Irish Times*, and more radical than the *Freeman's Journal*, qualities making it the most suitable national newspaper for present purposes. Every issue of the *Irish Independent* during the period was consulted through the medium of the online search facility

---

33 *Irish Catholic*, 2 October 1920.
34 For a sympathetic characterisation of the *Catholic Bulletin*, see Brian P. Murphy, 'J. J. O'Kelly, the Catholic Bulletin and contemporary Irish cultural historians', *Archivium Hibernicum*, 44 (1989), pp. 71–88, and Brian P. Murphy, *The Catholic Bulletin and Republican Ireland with Special Reference to J. J. O'Kelly ('Sceilg')* (Belfast and London: Athol Books, 2005).
35 Ian Kenneally, *The Paper Wall. Newspapers and Propaganda in Ireland 1919–1921* (Cork: Collins Press, 2008), p. 118.
36 *Ibid.*, p. 78.

provided by the Irish Newspaper Archives.[37] The fifth category of sources, finally, consists of published material, such as the memoirs of veterans, fictional representations of clerical responses to the guerrilla war and other sources. Some official publications were also used, mainly those emanating from ecclesiastical authorities, as well as articles published in theological journals.

This book consists of three parts. The first, entitled 'Obeying the law of God', considers clerical opposition to republican violence. It looks at the enduring presence of a politically conservative section among the clergy that continued to oppose Sinn Féin. It also examines the phenomenon of clerical denunciation, its prevalence, chronological and spatial distribution and contents. It analyses how this particular clerical attitude was received by republicans and how the clergy responded to the issue of sectarian violence. The second part of the book considers the different guises of the 'republican priest': from sympathisers of Sinn Féin to sympathisers of the IRA. It distinguishes between different forms of support for the republican movement, up to and including 'aiding and abetting' active Volunteers in the guerrilla struggle. It weighs the significance of these phenomena and their impact on republicans and attempts a quantitative analysis. The third and final part of the book, entitled 'The clergy and the crown', looks at the way in which the British campaign in Ireland impinged on the Catholic clergy, and examines how the counterinsurgency measures affected clerical attitudes towards republican violence. It also looks at non-partisan ways in which priests responded to violence. The Epilogue, finally, assesses the legacy of the clergy's attitude to the struggle and evaluates by way of conclusion how priests negotiated the conflicting demands of freedom and the Fifth Commandment.

---

37 Irish Newspaper Archives, www.irishnewsarchive.com (accessed 29 July 2010).

I
Obeying the law of God

1

In the old groove: traditional political alignments

By the beginning of 1919, the Irish Parliamentary Party had all but vanished from the political stage. At the outbreak of war in 1914, John Redmond's party had just succeeded in securing home rule. The implementation of the new law was shelved for the duration of hostilities, mainly because the Ulster question needed to be resolved first. But for Redmond, the prize had been won, and he could see only benefits for the nationalist militia, the Irish National Volunteers, in joining the imperial army. Although many churchmen shared this point of view and there was effective support in some quarters for the recruitment drive, enthusiasm soon waned.[1] The deferring of home rule caused unease and the army's privileging of Ulster unionists over Irish nationalists caused irritation. In any case Pope Benedict XV's peace appeals of 1915 provided a convenient pretext for opposition to the war. Bishops such as Edward O'Dwyer of Limerick and Michael Fogarty of Killaloe criticised the war effort and distanced themselves from Redmond. Jérôme aan de Wiel has shown that by April 1916, the Redmondite clergy had become 'practically voiceless'.[2]

The Easter rising received no official comment from the bishops, but the insurrectionists soon had a few defenders among them, and in any case the subsequent executions of the republican leaders had the same effect on the clergy as on the population at large.[3] In May 1916, O'Dwyer refused to discipline two of his priests at the behest

1 Jérôme aan de Wiel, *The Catholic Church in Ireland 1914–1918. War and Politics* (Dublin and Portland, OR: Irish Academic Press, 2003), pp. 1–41.
2 *Ibid.*, p. 41.
3 *Ibid.*, pp. 89–104. See also Edward P. O'Callaghan, 'Correspondence

of the military governor, General John Maxwell, publicly aligning the church with the separatists and against the British government.[4] In September O'Dwyer declared himself a supporter of Sinn Féin, and in May 1917 Archbishop William Walsh of Dublin gave the party's candidate his implicit endorsement at the South Longford by-election.[5] When the government announced its intention to introduce the draft in Ireland to boost lagging recruitment figures in 1918, the entire spectrum of Irish nationalism united to form an anti-conscription campaign. The campaign gained the support of the hierarchy, who declared that the people might oppose conscription 'by every means consonant with the law of God'.[6] At the December 1918 elections, Walsh revealed that he was voting for the republican candidate.[7] In David Miller's words, Sinn Féin had received a *nihil obstat*.[8]

This did not imply, however, that there had been a wholesale conversion of the body of the clergy to the principles of republicanism. The Irish Parliamentary Party had applauded the fact that many parish priests became chairmen of the local anti-conscription committees in 1918 precisely because it had prevented the domination of these bodies by Sinn Féin.[9] Sentiments critical of Sinn Féin remained strong among priests, especially during 1919, and Ó Fiaich has suggested that 'the swing in opinion towards Sinn Féin, ... seems to have been a slower process among the clergy than among the flocks'.[10] However, the contingent of home rulers among the clergy declined in number throughout 1919 and 1920 as the conflict developed and the inexorable demise of the Irish Parliamentary Party became clear. Moreover, the British counter-insurgency campaign of 1920 and 1921 dampened these priests' nostalgia for the days of home rule politics. But even then they

---

between Bishop O'Dwyer and Bishop Foley on the Dublin rising, 1916–17', *Collectanea Hibernica*, 18–19 (1976–77), pp. 184–212.
4   Aan de Wiel, *Church*, pp. 104–14.
5   O'Dwyer: *ibid.*, p. 113; Walsh: Thomas J. Morrissey, *William J. Walsh. Archbishop of Dublin, 1841–1921. No Uncertain Voice* (Dublin: Four Courts Press, 2000), p. 301.
6   Miller, *Church, State*, p. 405.
7   Morrissey, *Walsh*, p. 316.
8   Miller, *Church, State*, p. 391. See also Travers, 'Priest', p. 177.
9   Travers, 'Priest', p. 174.
10 Ó Fiaich, 'Clergy', p. 500.

were not a spent force entirely. The revival towards the end of the conflict of clerical support for political compromise solutions such as 'dominion home rule' is testimony to the enduring influence they exercised over their fellow churchmen. The current chapter examines this group and analyses how its attitudes developed under the pressure of political reality. It also assesses the impact that these priests had on general clerical opinion.

Wild ideas and irresponsible young men

One IRA veteran recalled that 'notwithstanding the verdict of the 1918 election and the sweeping victories in every field of endeavour', Sinn Féin and the IRA continued to have their opponents 'in the person of an odd old P.P. here and there who thundered, threatened and condemned "secret societies"'.[11] These priests were the clerical equivalent of the 'moderate nationalists' identified by Paul Bew, whose 'strong intellectual tradition' continued to assert that home rule was the 'obvious basis for a peaceful settlement of the Anglo-Irish conflict', or the 'lost creatures whose instincts called them back to constitutionalism' described by David Fitzpatrick.[12] Some had relatives in the British army abroad or in the colonial service. A nephew of Bishop Patrick Foley of Kildare and Leighlin was a lieutenant in the army serving in Egypt.[13] And the brother of Monsignor Bartholomew Fitzpatrick, parish priest of St Kevin's, Harrington Street, Dublin, was a former lieutenant-governor of the Punjab and a member of the Council of India.[14]

Others were former army chaplains. The *Irish Catholic Directory* for 1919 listed a total of fifty-eight diocesan priests who were serving as chaplains to the British army at the beginning of that year and another sixty-four religious priests, their total number falling to

---

11 Military Archives, Dublin (hereafter MA), Bureau of Military History (hereafter BMH), witness statement (hereafter WS) 1219, Sean O'Neill, p. 67.
12 Paul Bew, 'Moderate nationalism and the Irish revolution, 1916–1923', *The Historical Journal*, 42:3 (1999), pp. 729–49, at pp. 729–30; David Fitzpatrick, *Politics and Irish Life 1913–1921. Provincial Experience of War and Revolution* (reprint; Cork: Cork University Press, 1998), p. 99.
13 *Irish Independent*, 31 May 1919.
14 *Irish Catholic*, 29 May 1920.

no more than five in 1921.[15] Although some of the most republican priests had also been British army chaplains during the First World War, those priests who were still serving as such between 1919 and 1921 were likely to feel loyalty to the army and the empire. One of these was the Dominican Father J. T. Crotty, chaplain to the Royal Dublin Fusiliers. Crotty attended a 'welcome home' dinner in Dublin in January 1919 at which hundreds of soldiers were feted upon their return. At the dinner, Crotty said that he had been asked by many people what had 'bound together the men under him in their fervent and assiduous attendance to their religious duties'. Crotty replied that they 'had been what Irishmen and Irish Catholics should be – proud of their religion and true to their faith and country'.[16] This was Irish nationalism in Redmond's style.

For these priests Sinn Féin's 1918 election victory spelt an ill fate for the country's future. Bishop Denis Kelly of the tiny southern diocese of Ross wrote in early January 1919 to the rector of the Irish College in Paris that at the elections 'all Ireland has declared itself Sinn Fein. Their present policy is ... to resist English law in Ireland. This means constant collision with police and military – arrests, trials, possibly bloodshed.' This caused him concern as the government was less inclined to compromise than it had been for a long time: 'we had not so strong an old Tory government for a century. They will stand no humbug from Sinn Fein.'[17] Clerics like Kelly had swift confirmation of their fears on 21 January, when nine IRA members killed two constables during an ambush at Soloheadbeg in County Tipperary. Although Sinn Féin was not implicated, conservatives saw the 'spirit of Sinn Féin' at work in the attack.

A few days after the ambush, Michael Canon O'Donnell, parish priest of Rathkeale, County Limerick, wrote to the rector of the Irish College in Rome, the republican sympathiser Michael O'Riordan. In an earlier letter to O'Donnell, O'Riordan had attempted to

---

15 *The Irish Catholic Directory and Almanac for 1919 with Complete Directory in English* (Dublin: James Duffy, 1919) and *The Irish Catholic Directory and Almanac for 1921 with Complete Directory in English* (Dublin: James Duffy, 1921).
16 *Irish Independent*, 22 January 1919. I am grateful to Rev. Hugh Fenning, OP, for information about Fr Crotty.
17 Archives of the Irish College, Paris (hereafter AICP), Collège papers, A2.h108, Kelly to Boyle, 6 January 1919.

assuage the canon's fears about republicanism by arguing that Sinn Féin could not be held responsible for violent excesses by individuals, just as the land league of the 1880s and 1890s should not be blamed for the violence of its followers. O'Donnell responded:

> Such outrages, you say, follow [outside the intention] of leaders ... as happened in the land league days. With all respect, I deny the parity. The land league leaders did not go in for physical force ... . Very different now. The spirit of Sinn Feinism is active resistance, and very active and aggressive, even to attacking barracks and shooting soldiers and policemen. And the leaders did not stop at words but set the example by their own deeds.[18]

This 'spirit of Sinn Feinism' was, according to O'Donnell, a 'delirium', a 'spirit of unrest in the country'.

Bishop Kelly entertained the same suspicion that Sinn Féin leaders themselves were intentionally aiming for the use of violence. In a sermon at Skibbereen pro-cathedral on Palm Sunday 1919 he complained that 'several elected members of parliament [had] held up to admiration the actions of the people in Russia and Hungary' in the Dáil. Kelly had paid no attention to the 'wild ideas' of Madame Markievicz, who had 'proclaimed the doctrine twelve months ago of backing up the revolution', because he had thought she stood alone. But now he found 'in his newspapers on Saturday that these ideas were also held by responsible men – members of parliament and some officials of the new "government"', and this was cause of great concern to him. He warned the congregation that 'if these ideas were spread amongst them, if they were picked up, the faith of St. Patrick would not stand'.[19] These views were shared by Kelly's colleague of Ardagh and Clonmacnoise, Joseph Hoare, who warned that revolutionary action would not only make the Irish people 'the prey of their enemies', but would also lead to 'what has taken place in France, Portugal, Mexico, and Russia. Secret societies and revolution did not bring the rebirth of nations, but their devastation and destruction.'[20]

Kelly's statements were a recurring source of irritation to the

---

18 Archives of the Pontifical Irish College, Rome (hereafter AICR), O'Riordan papers, 19/190/4, O'Donnell to O'Riordan, 30 January 1919. The original reads *praeter intentionem* for 'outside the intention'.
19 *Irish Catholic*, 19 April 1919.
20 *Ibid.*, 8 March 1919.

republican *Catholic Bulletin*, which had taken upon itself the mission of rooting out and exposing clerical as well as lay offenders against the new political orthodoxy. With regard to his Palm Sunday sermon, the *Catholic Bulletin* complained that Kelly had uncritically accepted reports of Dáil proceedings in the censored newspapers: 'the faith of Patrick has more to fear in one day from bishops who base their sermons on such reports than from all that has been said under the auspices of Sinn Fein and the Dail during the whole course of their existence'.[21] A few weeks later, Kelly refused to allow prayers in the pro-cathedral for the repose of the soul of the Sinn Féiner and Irish Volunteer leader Pierce McCan who had died in prison in March. 'Perhaps', the *Catholic Bulletin* asked, 'His Lordship wishes to be recognised as a willing instrument of English tyranny.'[22]

Liturgical events such as the reciting of public prayers at the death of republican heroes were symbolically charged moments that could easily turn into show-downs between conservative priests and Sinn Féiners. This was also the case with Sinn Féin meetings planned on church property. Thus the parish priest of Aughrim, County Wicklow, forbade a Sinn Féin meeting scheduled to be held near his church in March 1919, causing the organisers to move the venue to elsewhere in the village.[23] On the same day, a Sinn Féin meeting was held in the market square of nearby Tinahely to protest against the imprisonment of a number of local men for making threats. Speakers at the meeting called the police the 'curse of society in this country', and said that local 'bobbies' were 'accessory' to the imprisonment of the local men. The parish priest, John Canon Dunne, was more conciliatory than his Aughrim colleague. He addressed the meeting, saying he was no Sinn Féiner and did not support Sinn Féin's programme, but that he sympathised with the object of demanding the release of the prisoners and declared that he would 'do anything which was not against the moral law' to help them.[24] Michael Cardinal Logue, the archbishop of Armagh,

---

21 *Catholic Bulletin*, 9:5 (May 1919), p. 218.
22 *Ibid.*
23 The National Archives, Kew (hereafter TNA), War Office: Army of Ireland: Administrative and Easter rising records (hereafter WO), 35/104.
24 *Ibid.*

had meetings like these in mind when he warned Archbishop Walsh in the same month that 'the Sinn Feiners would like to use the priests' to get them to organise meetings for their own purposes.[25]

According to conservative clerics, the wild ideas which Sinn Féin leaders were proclaiming at such meetings had dangerous effects on irresponsible young men with too much time on their hands. Responding to the Soloheadbeg killings, Father John Slattery, administrator of the local parish, denounced the shooting and deplored 'the habit of many young fellows, without much sense or education or steadiness of character, of carrying loaded firearms'. This was especially dangerous considering 'the temptation that so easily arises from possession of firearms'. Slattery therefore advocated that 'due restriction on the right of all men to carry firearms was demanded as their contribution to real Irish liberty'.[26] In his Lenten pastoral of 1919, Logue echoed this view of IRA members as young men up to no good. He asked the Catholics of his diocese not to expose themselves to trouble by attending 'needless assemblies, gatherings, or other practices which serve no useful purpose'. He singled out drilling as a case in point – '"tomfoolery," as a learned judge lately termed it. They might practice the goose-step to the Greek kalends, and it would never bring them one step nearer to freedom.'[27] Similarly, somewhat later in the conflict, Father Peter Kelly, parish priest of Carnaross, County Meath, called a Volunteer a 'blackguard' when he came to show the priest a threatening notice he had received from the Black and Tans. He told the young man 'to go home and behave [him]self and no one would shoot [him]'.[28]

Roman soundings

An excellent source for the political views of Irish priests during the summer of 1919 is the archive of the Pontifical Irish College in Rome. As Dermot Keogh has shown, this institution became a centre for republican-minded Irish clerics, mainly on account of

---

25 Dublin Diocesan Archives, Dublin (hereafter DDA), William Walsh papers, 386/5, Logue to Walsh, 14 March 1919.
26 *Irish Catholic*, 1 February 1919.
27 *Ibid.*, 8 March 1919.
28 MA, BMH, WS1734, Seán Farrelly, p. 17.

its two rectors, Michael O'Riordan (1905–19) and John Hagan (1919–30).[29] O'Riordan's and Hagan's diplomatic endeavours to neutralise the preponderance of English influence at the Holy See were quite successful, and as Jérôme aan de Wiel has demonstrated, they managed to forge a new relationship between republican Ireland and the Vatican.[30] The two men's early enthusiasm for Sinn Féin put them at odds with the conservative strand among the Irish clergy, and ensured that the college became a focal point for clerics of advanced political views.

Hagan not only kept in touch with like-minded priests; he actively solicited information about potential opponents. In the summer of 1919 a former student of the college, Father Edward Rawlins, was in expectation of an appointment in Newfoundland. While waiting for the assignment, he toured the country to report verbatim to Hagan what colleagues had told him about their political views. A lay correspondent of Hagan's, Patrick Keohane, wrote that he had found Rawlins 'good timber', saying that if the young man acted on Keohane's advice and 'be not as *definite* in giving his own convictions too open expression to *everyone* he will be able to give you some true accounts of the *condition* of *mind* of certain curates and inscrutable "P.Ps" here and there'.[31] Hagan paid for Rawlins's expenses, making this a very deliberate fact-finding mission.

In his first letter Rawlins explained his tactics to Hagan:

> Since my arrival here I have met several priests and had some very amusing while at the same time interesting conversations. It is very hard to restrain oneself at times here, however, one easily succeeds by making sure he himself never becomes the centre of the conversation.[32]

Conversations that Rawlins had with two priests at St Andrew's parish, Westland Row, Dublin, show that curates living in the same

29 Keogh, *Vatican*, pp. 13–14.
30 Jérôme aan de Wiel, 'Monsignor O'Riordan, Bishop O'Dwyer and the shaping of new relations between nationalist Ireland and the Vatican during World War One', *Archivium Hibernicum*, 53 (1999), pp. 95–106, and Aan de Wiel, *Church*, pp. 256–303.
31 AICR, Hagan papers, HAG1/1919/184, Keohane to Hagan, 1 July 1919. Italics in the original.
32 AICR, Hagan papers, HAG1/1919/154, Rawlins to Hagan, 12 June 1919.

presbytery could hold different political views without even being aware of each other's position. Father Thomas Ryan told Rawlins that he was 'sorry to know [he] was a Sinn Feiner and that [he] had received such a narrow education', and then said that there were no Sinn Féin supporters among the eight priests attached to the parish. Father Richard Fleming, Ryan's colleague, 'gave his attentions to the language rather than to politics'.[33] However, Fleming turned out to be much more of a republican than his colleague gave him credit for. When Rawlins told him what Ryan had said, Fleming 'threw up his hands [and] said, – why he's not a Sinn Feiner, he's a conservative. He added also that F[ather] Ryan's policy was absurd today.'[34]

The same divisions existed in Dunleer, County Louth, where Rawlins was the guest of one of the curates, a Sinn Féin supporter. The parish priest, Father John Byrne, had quite different views, however: 'two minutes conversation showed me he was no Sinn Feiner. Consequently our meeting was short. There was no love lost.' Rawlins fared no better with the senior curate, Father Peter Coherane: 'a few hot words on politics' exchanged with him convinced Rawlins that he 'also was a fierce anti-Sinn Feiner'.[35] A month later, Rawlins was in County Wexford, attending a concert in the presence of Father Thomas Quigley, parish priest of Blackwater. At the end of the recital, Quigley said during a speech that the cause of Ireland's difficulties was the fact that 'Irishmen could never agree'. 'This language of the enemy rose my blood', Rawlins told Hagan, and 'as a result I made a horrible mistake'. He stood up and told the audience: 'Well now ladies [and] gentlemen, I said, ... it's a damn lie. Needless to say the cheering was fierce [and] F[ather] Quigley was as mad as could be.' Although the other priests present appeared delighted, there was only one curate in the presbytery who was 'willing to stand or fall by S[inn] F[éin]'.[36] Rawlins feared that many priests who supported Sinn Féin were beginning to lose

---

33 *Ibid.*
34 AICR, Hagan papers, HAG1/1919/176, Rawlins to Hagan, 25 June 1919.
35 *Ibid.* The *Irish Catholic Directory* (hereafter *ICD*) for 1919 has Coherane as 'Corcoran', p. 136.
36 AICR, Hagan papers, HAG1/1919/233, Rawlins to Hagan, 25 July 1919.

confidence in the party because its emphasis on an appeal to the Paris peace conference was not paying off.

Keohane told Hagan that he was not surprised by the prevalence of anti-Sinn Féin ideas among the clergy. A senior Augustinian of Irish extraction, Father Canice O'Gorman, had visited Dublin some days previously. Keohane reported that O'Gorman

> will return with really wrong impressions about the condition of the country generally from a political standpoint; and through no fault of his. ... He met of course ... many of the notabilities with whom perhaps he found himself in general agreement on deep theological questions, and no doubt they regaled him with tales of atrocities sufficient to shake the faith of any man less or perhaps more robust in sympathy with us than he is.[37]

This had already had its effect on O'Gorman. Another of Hagan's correspondents had noted that the Augustinian had been 'going around denouncing red ruin [and] revolution in all moods [and] tenses at his visitations'.[38] Other correspondence provides even more evidence for the strength of the conservative faction. The republican sympathiser Father J. P. Conry of Ballyhaunis, County Mayo, wrote in August: 'I am astonished at the number of priests I meet [in the diocese of Tuam] who do not think our way. So many of them are in the old groove. These simply laugh at us.'[39]

Priests' views were determined not simply by political conviction, but also by internal clerical power struggles. Rector O'Riordan died in the summer of 1919, and Vice-Rector Hagan was an important contender for the vacant post. Archbishop Walsh's secretary Father Michael Curran wrote to him with the latest gossip about his chances. Curran mentioned the existence of an animus against Hagan among a group of Dublin priests. A number of alumni of the college had returned to Dublin a few years previously complaining about O'Riordan's and Hagan's regime while they had been students there. 'Political opponents' in the Dublin diocesan seminary,

---

37 AICR, Hagan papers, HAG1/1919/184, Keohane to Hagan, 1 July 1919.
38 AICR, Hagan papers, HAG1/1919/106, Curran to Hagan, 11 May 1919.
39 AICR, Hagan papers, HAG1/1919/293, Conry to Hagan, 27 August 1919.

Clonliffe College – meaning mainly the president, John Canon Waters – had taken up these grievances and used them to discredit the late rector and his vice-rector, whose republican views they disliked.[40] This anti-O'Riordan party among the Dublin clergy now opposed Hagan's candidature: ineffectively, as it happened, because Hagan was appointed. But Curran's letter shows that conservative senior priests, as clerical power brokers, could exert considerable influence over younger colleagues, and that political divisions sometimes reflected ecclesiastical factionalism.

Somewhat outspoken against the Sinn Féiners

If the Irish College in Rome was a hotbed of clerical republicanism, a much more conservative atmosphere prevailed in the Irish College in Paris. Bishop Kelly was a frequent correspondent of the rector, the Lazarist Father Patrick Boyle. Kelly felt free to vent his frustration not only at Sinn Féin – something he did in public too – but also at brother bishops and priests who had proved too weak to resist the strong republican current of the day. In August 1919 he wrote that 'the world is so upset that I ... don't know what to do beyond trying to save my soul, and preach to others the *defined* truths of religion – even the latter are now doubted'.[41]

Other conservatives also expressed bewilderment at the perceived sliding moral scale of Irish Catholics as the number of attacks on RIC men and barracks began to increase. Discouraging a congregation in Clonmel, County Tipperary, from taking the law into their own hands, Bishop Bernard Hackett of Waterford and Lismore pointed out that 'the affairs of the nations are in the hands of God, whose loving providence directs all things. It should, therefore, be the duty of the people to realise that the future is in God's hands ...'.[42] And Father John Gleeson of Lorrha, County Tipperary, responded to the killing of an RIC sergeant in his parish in September by asking:

---

40 AICR, Hagan papers, HAG1/1919/389, Curran to Hagan, 14 September 1919.
41 AICP, Collège papers, A2.h108, Kelly to Boyle, 14 August 1919. Italics in the original.
42 *Irish Catholic*, 7 June 1919.

Who has authorised a small band of unknown, ignorant persons ... to decide that the life of a fellow-being may be lawfully taken? The Irish people did not consider this question at the general election. It was not put before them, and if it had been, it would have been rejected with horror.[43]

If the ascendancy of Sinn Féin meant violence, then it was 'better for Ireland to wait on than to place power in the hands of men who would work out their ends by the weapons of the tyrant'.[44] Similarly, Bishop Lawrence Gaughran of Meath asked a congregation in Mullingar in November 1919: 'what benefit could come to the country from crimes that are representing Irishmen to be as savage and uncultivated as the bushmen of the forest?'[45]

Paul Bew has shown that many in the Irish Parliamentary Party had come to accept by 1918 that partition of the island into two separate home rule entities was the only way to accommodate the demands both of Irish nationalism and of Ulster unionism.[46] This view received little support from republican priests, and none at all in Ulster presbyteries, but conservative clerics elsewhere were among its advocates in 1919. Father Nicholas Lawless, parish priest of Kilcurry, County Louth, presided at a meeting of delegates of the United Irish League and the Ancient Order of Hibernians in November, saying that an Ulster parliament should be accepted 'as an admission of the home rule principle'.[47] And Father Walter McDonald, professor at Maynooth College, argued for it in his 1919 book *Some Ethical Questions of Peace and War*:

> Were Ireland made a republic fully independent of Great Britain, it seems to me that she would be bound to allow home rule to the northeast corner; on the principles that underlie the claim we make for home rule in the United Kingdom, which I regard as well-founded.[48]

Some of these priests played out the ideals of the Gaelic revival against those of republicanism, such as Father John Carr, parish

---

43 *Ibid.*, 13 September 1919.
44 *Ibid.*
45 *Ibid.*, 8 November 1919.
46 Bew, 'Nationalism', p. 733.
47 *Irish Independent*, 11 November 1919.
48 Walter McDonald, *Some Ethical Questions of Peace and War with Special Reference to Ireland* (reprint; Dublin: University College Dublin Press, 1998), p. 70.

priest of Lehane, County Galway. He told his parishioners in January 1920 that people would be doing their country a service by taking up the study of Irish instead of carrying out arms raids and committing larceny.[49]

Hagan's republican friend Keohane asserted that the influence of such conservative clerics was declining, not only in politics, but even in the church. 'The people are becoming tired of priests who hanker after what is called "society".' People regarded them 'with almost as much indifference as they did the parson in my early days'.[50] And in his September 1919 letter to Hagan, Curran wrote that 'nobody minded' the anti-republican party among the Dublin clergy anymore.[51] These statements were accurate to the extent that conservatives were powerless to halt the tide of republicanism. But the home rulers among the clergy could still make their presence felt. Their public displays of hostility towards Sinn Féin continued to be a source of irritation and embarrassment to republican colleagues well into 1920.

The rector of the Jesuit Crescent College, Limerick, Father Lawrence Potter, complained to his provincial in February 1920 that one of the members of staff, a priest by the name of Robert Dillon-Kelly, was 'somewhat outspoken against the Sinn Feiners'. Since 'Limerick at present is almost completely dominated by Sinn Fein', this did Father Dillon-Kelly no favours in the eyes of students and parents.[52] The recent student plays which he had been directing had consequently been box office flops. Joost Augusteijn has mentioned a priest from Tuam who wrote to a local newspaper in March 1920 that Sinn Féin politicians were 'upstarts who imagine that they are the alpha and omega of nationality here' even though they were all 'corner boys without any business'.[53] Bishop Kelly also continued to fulminate against the new party. In July 1920 he wrote to Boyle that a priest they both knew had told

---

49 *Irish Catholic*, 31 January 1920.
50 AICR, Hagan papers, HAG1/1919/184, Keohane to Hagan, 1 July 1919.
51 AICR, Hagan papers, HAG1/1919/389, Curran to Hagan, 14 September 1919.
52 Irish Jesuit Archives, Dublin (hereafter IJA), Crescent College papers, SC/CRES/57, Potter to Nolan, 17 February 1920.
53 Augusteijn, *Defiance*, p. 308.

him that 'the *active* movement in Cork is pure communism – *les rouges de Paris* in 1871'.[54] Two months later, he mentioned the Paris commune again, this time revealing something of the background to his anti-republicanism: 'the rouges in Paris in 1871 were sound in doctrine as compared to pious Irish today. That same 1871 has saved the cardinal, myself and others – a pity more of us did not go through it.'[55] Kelly and Logue had been at the Irish College in Paris during the 1871 rising, and it was an experience that had moulded their outlook permanently.

While Terence MacSwiney's hunger-strike was delivering a propaganda blow for Sinn Féin in September 1920, James Canon Dunne, parish priest of Donnybrook, refused to allow any public show of support for the martyr-to-be in his church, despite pressure and complaints from parishioners. While the hunger-strike was ongoing, a number of republican parishioners complained to Archbishop Walsh that Dunne had 'flatly refused' their request to have mass said for MacSwiney's intentions in Donnybrook church. The canon's actions were not simply inspired by intellectual doubts as to the morality of the hunger-strike, which had been the subject of scholarly debate among Catholic theologians for some years.[56] Dunne had also caused 'grievous pain to his interviewers by the manner and words of his refusal'. Moreover, the parishioners recalled that his inaction during the anti-conscription campaign had 'pained many of our people' and that he had offended parents by showing 'hostility to the teaching of the Irish language in the schools'.[57] Walsh dodged the political implications and pretended that it was a matter of Dunne's private opinions on 'a matter in dispute among theologians', which he was unwilling to challenge. The correspondents agreed to let the issue rest, but not without saying that they felt 'keenly the manifestations of hostility shown

---

54 AICP, Collège papers, A2.h108, Kelly to Boyle, 10 July 1919. Italics in the original. 'Les rouges de Paris' were the activists of the Paris Commune.
55 AICP, Collège papers, A2.h108, Kelly to Boyle, 16 September 1919.
56 Pádraig Corkery, 'Bishop Daniel Cohalan of Cork on republican resistance and hunger strikes. A theological note', *Irish Theological Quarterly*, 67 (2002), pp. 113–24, at p. 120.
57 DDA, Walsh papers, 380/4, O'Connor *et al.* to Walsh, 10 September 1920.

by our parish priest to the national and patriotic aspirations of our people'.[58]

In the absence of a realistic political substitute for the Sinn Féin policy, the alternatives which priests such as Dunne suggested amounted to a pietistic retreat from politics. They demonstrate to what extent they had lost touch with the political ideas and motivations of the day. The example of passive endurance which Christ provided on the cross was a much-quoted theme. Archbishop Thomas Gilmartin of Tuam, speaking in September 1920, admonished his congregation to

> Fix your minds to-day, you who are maltreated, on the suffering Christ. He was captured in the night-time, he was terrorised as far as he allowed it, he was scourged and he opened not his mouth. He was murdered with the most shocking cruelty, but all this was the greatest triumph of human history. In the patience of Christ you shall win.[59]

Gilmartin also called upon his priests to 'put religion above all politics and all human strategy, and to preach, in season and out of season, the great commandment of God'.[60] Similarly, in November, Father Philip Callery, parish priest of Tullamore, King's County, advised his parishioners that 'freedom, like the thrones of heaven, by suffering virtue, must be won'.[61] And John Canon McMahon, parish priest of Nenagh, County Tipperary, advised mourners attending the funeral of one of the victims of the crown forces that 'all should be in their homes in proper time to pray God for peace and unity amongst all'.[62]

The notion that violence was due to a few 'miscreants' became less and less tenable as the months went by, and clerical insistence on the adverse political effects of the republican campaign became stronger. A common theme was the assertion that the republican drive was damaging Ireland's prospects of gaining autonomy. A typical exponent, John Canon Walsh, parish priest of Ballymurn, County Wexford, had said in November 1919 during a meeting of the local United Irish League branch that the 'physical force

---

58 DDA, Walsh papers, 380/5, O'Connor to Walsh, 15 September 1920.
59 *Irish Catholic*, 2 October 1920.
60 *Ibid.*, 25 September 1920.
61 *Ibid.*, 13 November 1920.
62 *Ibid.*, 4 December 1920.

movement, and ... crime and outrage, instead of helping the Irish cause, only covered it with dishonour and disgrace'. A resolution that was passed condemned 'the cowardly and brutal murders committed in several parts of the country as being not only forbidden by divine and human law, but inflicting a stain on the national character'.[63] Jesuit Father William Delaney, in a letter to Archbishop Walsh a year later, deplored the 'abominable assassinations' that had recently taken place in the capital, which were 'furnishing our enemies with such taking arguments for our unfitness for self-government'.[64] And in private correspondence with Rector Boyle in Paris, Bishop Kelly complained that 'there is no security of life, liberty or property. In train, on street, in your house, your life may go at any moment between the IRA and the English forces'. Responsible for it all were the young men who were active Sinn Féiners, and they were everywhere: 'our universities, colleges and schools are chock-full of youths – there is now, and will be, no room for them, and they are a veritable power-house of mischief'.[65]

Attainable goals

Father Rawlins had written to Hagan in June 1919 that he had met a priest in Kingstown, County Dublin, who was a 'true blue', and 'who hated Sinn Feiners simply [and] solely because de Valera had said they wouldn't accept anything less than independence'.[66] The parish priest of Termoneeny, County Derry, was of the same disposition and told Hagan in October 1919 that 'an Irish republic is unattainable'.[67] As the conflict turned more violent from the autumn of 1920 onwards, priests in their public pronouncements began to concentrate more on the evils of British atrocities. However, those conservative priests who still ventured an opinion on the merits of the republican movement insisted that

---

63 *Ibid.*, 22 November 1919.
64 DDA, Walsh papers, 380/3, Delaney to Walsh, 27 November 1920.
65 AICP, Collège papers, A2.h108, Kelly to Boyle, 5 May 1921.
66 AICR, Hagan papers, HAG1/1919/154, Rawlins to Hagan, 12 June 1919.
67 AICR, Hagan papers, HAG1/1919/467, O'Neill to Hagan, 18 October 1919. This theme seems to have been initiated by Cardinal Logue in November 1917: Travers, 'Priest', p. 173.

Sinn Féin's goals were unrealistic. During the first year and a half after the party's election victory in December 1918 their fears of guerrilla warfare – 'arrests, trials, possibly bloodshed' as Kelly had written – had all materialised. These priests believed that it could end quickly if Sinn Féin would give up its intransigence in holding out for a republic. To the frustration of republican leaders, conservative clerics started to claim that a home rule arrangement short of a republic would also satisfy the Irish people. Bishop Patrick Morrisroe of Achonry, in a public letter to the parish priest of Tobercurry, County Sligo, in October 1920, argued for a 'sane political outlook that will enable true statesmanship to look straight at the facts ... and, putting aside the impossible and unattainable, work for ends that it is possible to achieve'. He contended that 'the fostering during these latter years of ideals clearly impossible of attainment has done much to unsettle the mind of our youth ... We must not look for miracles in the political sphere as we might not expect them in other spheres either without very good reason.'[68]

Morrisroe found allies among his fellow bishops, including Archbishop Gilmartin.[69] Gilmartin declared in December 1920 that the great majority of the Irish people 'would be willing to accept what is called dominion home rule, including full fiscal control'.[70] Others pointed out the obvious discrepancy in military strength between the IRA and the forces of the British empire. Father J. F. Enright, curate in Miltown Malbay, County Clare, told a congregation in October 1920 that 'it is folly to make an attempt to overthrow the power of the British government .... The murder of a few policemen ... will not overthrow the power of the government, and it is absolute insanity to think so.'[71] Similarly, Bishop Daniel Cohalan of Cork, previously a cautious supporter of Sinn Féin, asserted in his Lenten pastoral of 1921 that

---

68 *Irish Catholic*, 16 October 1920.
69 Brian Heffernan, '"It is for a nation of martyrs to cultivate constant self-restraint." The Irish Catholic bishops' attitude to the IRA campaign, 1919–21', *Leidschrift. Historisch Tijdschrift*, 23:1 (2008), pp. 151–69, at pp. 159–60.
70 *The Irish Catholic Directory and Almanac for 1922 with Complete Directory in English* (Dublin: James Duffy, 1922), p. 503.
71 *Irish Catholic*, 30 October 1920.

everything depends on whether a republican status is attainable or not. Suppose it is unattainable, who then stultifies himself – the man who is in favour of keeping the country in turmoil and crime looking for an unattainable object, or the man who accepts provisionally a less perfect settlement?[72]

Gilmartin echoed this view some months later when he assured an audience at Knock, County Mayo, that 'he had no doubt about the bravery of the Irish boys, and he did not want to say anything against them; they were a magnificent body of men, but no matter how good they were they were not equal to the forces against them'.[73]

Understandably, these statements were a source of annoyance to republican clerics. In July 1920, Curran told Hagan that he had received a letter from Archbishop Michael Kelly of Sydney, who had just returned to Australia after a visit to Ireland. Kelly had written that all the clergy he had met would welcome a genuine home rule act. Curran commented acidly: 'Enough said, except to add that he says he has been with old friends in Dublin [and] Ossory. The "*old*" might help to explain matters.'[74] And in a letter sent in September 1921, Bishop Kelly of Ross told Boyle that Bishop Fogarty of Killaloe had 'complained that Paris priests were no patriots'. According to Kelly, a number of Killaloe priests – alumni of the college – had been 'thorns' for Fogarty, while Kelly himself 'of course [was] the Coryphaeus of non-patriots'. The upshot of Fogarty's complaint was that he had suggested that the college be abolished as a seminary; 'young priests having got the true faith in Maynooth should go there for a high course'. Kelly was attempting to frustrate this plan by having the impending visitation of the college by Fogarty and the bishops of Clogher and Kerry deferred until the next year. He contended that 'the temperature of Sinn Fein is rapidly falling' and that the visitors – whom he described as 'mad on politics' – were likely to be 'more reasonable' in May 1922 than in November 1921, which was the original date for the visitation.[75]

72 *Freeman's Journal*, 7 February 1921.
73 *Irish Catholic*, 7 May 1921.
74 AICR, Hagan papers, HAG1/1920/346, Curran to Hagan, 15 July 1920. Italics in the original.
75 AICP, Collège papers, A2.h108, Kelly to Boyle, 28 September 1921.

In Kelly's mind, Fogarty's plan for the college was similar to Sinn Féin's usual *modus operandi*: 'Sinn Fein has a mania for smashing up, and does not count the cost, nor the power of reconstructing.'[76] Kelly was not simply protecting the college from interference, but was actively engaged in strengthening its political colour. When the Anglo-Irish treaty was put before the Dáil in December 1921, he assured Boyle that 'through the country the opinion in favour of the treaty seems to be general. In Dublin and among the TDs, opinion seems strongly divided'. Determined that the students at the Parisian college would not be misinformed by republicans about the political situation at home, he then asked the rector to 'kindly convey these facts to the students'.[77]

The Kelly–Boyle correspondence – like the Rawlins–Hagan correspondence – demonstrates the continued existence of clerical opposition to Sinn Féin, as well as the determination of republican-minded priests to outmanoeuvre their conservative colleagues. The realities of the prevailing new order meant that the latter had suddenly found themselves in the political rearguard. Keohane's and Curran's judgement that 'nobody minded' them any more was true to the extent that their political lead was no longer followed. But they still included such senior priests as Father O'Gorman in Rome and Canons O'Donnell, Dunne and Waters, who wielded power within the ecclesiastical establishment. If they were no longer a political force to be reckoned with, at least their presence acted as a counterweight to the republican sympathies of many of their colleagues. It is testimony to this that some bishops and priests began to argue towards the end of the conflict for 'dominion home rule'. Certainly the conservatives stiffened their moderate republican colleagues' opposition to violence.

For the conservatives, the foundation of the Irish Free State in 1922 was equivalent to the reaching of dry ground again, and they were quick to join moderate republicans in recognising the legitimacy of the new government. The strength of the church's support for the treaty and for the Free State during the Civil War is a measure of this. As soon as there was a Free State government,

76 *Ibid.*
77 AICP, Collège papers, A2.h108, Kelly to Boyle, 14 December 1921.

Sinn Féin priests and anti-Sinn Féin priests alike eased back into their familiar role of upholders of legitimate authority. This was not the case in Ulster, where bishops and priests viewed the new government with hostility. As will be seen, this was an attitude they had learnt during the War of Independence.

2

The Fifth Commandment and the brand of Cain: condemnation from the pulpit

It is no surprise that priests who continued to think 'in the old groove' condemned the IRA campaign. But denunciation was not limited to this group. Many clerics who sympathised with Sinn Féin and who wished to see Ireland an independent republic were nonetheless vociferous in condemning IRA violence. The same 'long-standing traditions' that governed clerical involvement in politics also governed clerical responses to republican violence.[1] According to David Miller, the bishops had traditionally recognised the British state and discouraged the use of physical force by republicans in return for the protection of their interests in education.[2] The discouragement of violence was thus an important aspect of the clergy's traditional political alignment. This goal was pursued principally by exerting moral pressure on Irish Catholics through condemnation, although from time to time it was also served by forming alliances with radical republicans in order to exert a mitigating influence.[3] Clerical opposition to violence was inspired not only by political calculation. James O'Shea, in his study of clerical politics in County Tipperary between 1850 and 1891, has pointed also to the fact that as 'sons of well-off tenant farmers', it 'was bred in the priests to dislike revolution'.[4] Nor did their politically conservative seminary training teach them otherwise.

1 Mary N. Harris, 'The Catholic church from Parnell to partition', in Brendan Bradshaw and Dáire Keogh (eds), *Christianity in Ireland. Revisiting the Story* (Blackrock: Columba Press, 2002), pp. 205–19, at p. 205.
2 Miller, *Church, State*, pp. 1–14.
3 Travers, 'Priest', pp. 171, 176–7.
4 James O'Shea, *Priest, Politics and Society in Post-Famine Ireland. A Study*

Thus by 1919, condemnation was already a standard clerical response to revolutionary violence. During the two and a half years of guerrilla warfare that followed, there were serious challenges to this tradition. It is not necessary to hold that Sinn Féin's 1918 election victory gave a democratic mandate to the IRA campaign to acknowledge that the latter could count on greater popular support than Irish insurrections had ever had before. The risk that priests by their condemnation might alienate not only the fighting men themselves, but a substantial section of the Catholic population was considerable. This gives some weight to the question of how often and in what terms priests denounced republican violence. It also explains the increasingly important role which clerical denunciation of the British government and the crown forces came to play during the conflict, as this could serve as a pretext for silence on the morality of republican violence. This chapter examines public clerical condemnation of the IRA campaign. It looks first at its incidence, then analyses the means by which clerics communicated their message and subsequently examines the contents of this message.

Quantifying clerical condemnations

Quantifying historical attitudes is always a precarious exercise, and it is futile to aspire to a precise figure of priests who condemned IRA violence. It is possible, however, to provide a minimum number by compiling press reports of denunciations. Newspapers carried many reports of clerical comments on the IRA campaign. Invariably, these were condemnations. The Irish press was under wartime censorship until August 1919, and continued afterwards to be subject to the stringent emergency regulations of the Defence of the Realm Act (1914) and the Restoration of Order in Ireland Act (1920).[5] Because of this, it was practically impossible for newspapers to publish anything other than denunciations when reporting on clerical responses to IRA violence. This bias must be taken into account in assessing the usefulness of newspaper sources, which shed light only on one particular form of clerical response. Chapter 5, which investigates clerical support, will look elsewhere for its source material.

---

of County Tipperary 1850–1891 (Dublin and Atlantic Highlands, NJ: Wolfhound Press, 1983), pp. 177, 14.

5 Kenneally, *Paper*, pp. 5–42.

How did clerical condemnations find their way into the newspapers? In the event of a major IRA attack, journalists travelled to the town or area in question to gather material for their report.[6] Interviewing the local priest or taking notes of clerical comments in sermons at subsequent masses was a standard part of their work on the ground. However, as Ian Kenneally has shown, government interference hampered free journalistic inquiry.[7] Correspondents were sometimes barred from entering towns after reprisals had taken place. In these cases, the official reports prepared by a propaganda bureau set up by Dublin Castle in mid-1920 were left as the only available account of events. These reports keenly included clerical condemnations of IRA violence, often in an unashamedly propagandistic manner. Kenneally has mentioned two instances of articles emitting from the Castle's propaganda bureau which alleged that local priests had placed curses on Volunteers. He has dismissed these articles as 'drivel ... designed to play on the minds of the supposedly superstitious Irish'.[8] As this chapter will show, however, priests did in fact talk about curses, and at least one of the instances Kenneally mentions had a basis in fact. The cleric in question had said that IRA killers 'could not expect good luck even in this world'.[9] As will be seen, when misfortune befell the killers' relatives, parishioners interpreted this comment as a curse.[10] Official reports served a clear propaganda purpose, but that does not make them entirely redundant as sources for clerical attitudes. As long as they are used cautiously and in combination with other source material, these reports can yield useful material.

Pulpit commentary on IRA violence outside the context of a major attack in the locality was much less likely to come to the attention of the press. Bishops and priests sometimes spontaneously sent their own comments to newspaper editors. Chapter 3 will show

---

6 See for instance *Irish Catholic*, 6 November 1920.
7 Kenneally, *Paper*, pp. 19, 38–42.
8 *Ibid.*, pp. 33–4.
9 TNA, Colonial Office: Dublin Castle records (hereafter CO), 904/115, Inspector general's monthly confidential report (hereafter IGMR), May 1921.
10 For an anthropological account of magical powers attributed to Irish priests, see Lawrence J. Taylor, *Occasions of Faith. An Anthropology of Irish Catholics* (Dublin: Lilliput Press, 1995), pp. 102–66.

that the IRA was keen to avoid publicity for pulpit condemnations, and in one instance punished a lay parishioner who had sent notes of a sermon to the press.[11] An analysis of press reports must take into account the fact that newspapers were under pressure from two sides, with Dublin Castle eager to see as many, and the IRA as few, reports of clerical condemnation as possible. Although the possibility of false reports resulting from Castle propaganda is real, it is nonetheless more likely that newspaper reports underestimated the number of clerical condemnations. Journalists came to report a sermon only when a major event had taken place, and copy about denunciations at other times was rare and haphazard. What a quantitative analysis of press reports of clerical comments achieves, therefore, is to give a minimum figure of denunciations. This figure does, however, include clerical comments on all of the most important IRA operations.

In order to obtain an indication of the frequency and geographical distribution of these denunciations, it is helpful to examine reports of them in two national newspapers. Both the conservative weekly *Irish Catholic* and the increasingly Sinn Féin-oriented daily *Irish Independent* took a keen interest in the views of the clergy and covered the entire country. When each issue of these papers is perused for the period beginning in January 1919 and ending at the truce in July 1921, and double reports of the same comments are taken into account, there are 243 instances of reported comments, made by a total of 149 priests and bishops.[12] Of a total of approximately 3,700 priests, 149 represents about 4 per cent.[13] It also stands to reason to assume that many more denunciations are likely to have been uttered, and also that many priests in parishes simply tried to ignore the matter as much as possible.

11 MA, BMH, WS1250, John O'Driscoll, p. 3.
12 Based on perusal of each issue of the *Irish Catholic* for this period and on a systematic search of each issue of the *Irish Independent* through the Irish Newspaper Archives, www.irishnewsarchive.com, using the search terms 'priest', 'Father', 'Fr', 'Rev' and 'Canon'. Any further instances found in other sources have also been included. See Appendix 1.
13 There were 3,689 priests in Ireland in 1911 and 3,836 in 1926. Jeremiah Newman, 'The priests of Ireland. A socio-religious survey. I. Numbers and distribution', *The Irish Ecclesiastical Record*, 98 (1962), pp. 1–27, at p. 6.

THE FIFTH COMMANDMENT AND THE BRAND OF CAIN

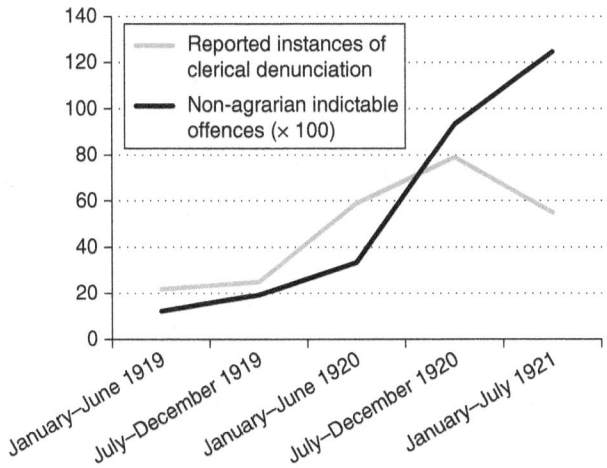

Figure 2.1 Reported instances of clerical denunciation and non-agrarian indictable offences, January 1919 – July 1921

Note: The RIC figures are from Charles Townshend, *The British Campaign in Ireland, 1919–21. The Development of Political and Military Policies* (Oxford: Oxford University Press, 1975), p. 213. The slump in the growth of non-agrarian indictable offences in the first half of 1920 is probably due to the fact that records are missing for March and April 1920. For the figures for clerical condemnation, see Appendix 1.

Keeping these caveats in mind, it is instructive to compare the pattern that emerges from a chronological break-down of the available figure with the chronological development of IRA violence. This has been done in Figure 2.1, which takes the number of non-agrarian indictable offences recorded by the RIC as indicative of levels of IRA violence during the war. These figures are not precise, but for present purposes they can serve as a rough indicator of the chronological spread of violence.[14] When the two sets of figures are compared, a

---

14 See for reflections on the RIC figures David Fitzpatrick, 'The geography of Irish nationalism 1910–1921', *Past and Present*, 78 (1978), pp. 113–44, at p. 115, and Augusteijn, *Defiance*, pp. 14–15. It is hoped that Professor Eunan O'Halpin's 'The dead of the Irish revolution' project will provide more precise data soon: Eunan O'Halpin, 'Counting terror. Bloody Sunday and *The Dead of the Irish Revolution*', in David

roughly similar chronological trend becomes visible up to the last quarter of 1920, followed by diverging trends after that period.

There were generally low instances of offences and denunciations until the end of 1919, when both began to rise sharply. Up to the last quarter of 1920, clerics condemned IRA violence more often as it became more frequent. At the end of 1920, however, the figure for offences overtook that for denunciations, which actually began to decline in the first half of 1921. The fact that this trend is visible in both newspapers examined indicates that it was not due to a change in editorial policy, but rather to a change in the pattern of clerical behaviour. From the last quarter of 1920 on, clerics condemned IRA violence less often even as it was becoming more frequent.[15] Thus the last three months of 1920 are an important turning point in the history of clerical condemnations. As will be seen, the cause of these developments was the rise in violence by the crown forces rather than any change in appreciation of IRA violence itself.

An analysis of the geographical distribution of these condemnations yields an equally important result. Nationally, 4 per cent of priests condemned IRA violence, but this figure fluctuated considerably by region. Appendix 3 shows the geographical spread of percentages per county. In Longford, a county with high levels of IRA violence, the percentage of priests who denounced was more than twice the national figure at 9.3 per cent, and other violent counties such as Cork and Tipperary also had much higher numbers. Peter Hart has provided figures for IRA violence per 10,000 people per county for this period.[16] If these figures are compared with the different county percentages of priests who condemned, a positive correlation (0.59) emerges. Thus high levels of violence in a county often went together with a high percentage of priests who condemned it. This is an important conclusion. The recent historiography of the conflict has emphasised that fighting was 'patchy and heavily localised', with most of it limited to Dublin and parts of

---

Fitzpatrick (ed.), *Terror in Ireland 1916–1923. Trinity History Workshop* (Dublin: Lilliput Press, 2012), pp. 141–57.

15 Ó Fiaich, 'Clergy', pp. 484–5, reached a similar conclusion.

16 See Appendix 3 for the figures. Peter Hart, 'The geography of revolution in Ireland 1917–1923', *Past and Present*, 155 (1997), pp. 147–54, at p. 147. I have used Hart's figures for 1920–21, even though the clerical figures also include 1919 and exclude 1921 from July onwards.

Munster.[17] The calculation performed here shows that geographical location was also a determinant of clerical responses. Priests in quiet areas were unconcerned about the matter, while priests in 'hot' areas were much more vocal in condemning violence.

Parish priests and curates

All priests were not equal. There were differences arising from canon law, such as those between diocesan and religious clergy, between parish priests and curates, and also between those senior priests who participated in the government of a diocese and those who did not. There were, moreover, unofficial distinctions based on the wealth or poverty of the parish to which priests were appointed, age, educational achievements, willingness to tow the political or theological line favoured by the bishop and socio-economic background. These differentiating factors – especially age, and the concomitant distinction between parish priests and curates – are relevant to the role of priests in politics.

In 1921, seventy-seven of the total number of 305 secular priests in the diocese of Dublin were parish priests, forming a relatively small elite.[18] Parish priests had typically served as curates themselves first before being appointed, but judging by the relatively high number of secular clergy in the diocese compared with the number of parishes, only a minority of curates could hope to be appointed parish priest at some stage.[19] The distinction between parish priests and curates was a substantial one and not just a matter of honour. The church's brand-new statute book, the 1917 *Codex iuris canonici* or *Code of Canon Law*, stipulated that the parish priest was a priest 'to whom a parish has been entrusted in his own name, with the cure of souls, which is to be exercised under the authority of the local ordinary'.[20] The curate, on the contrary, was 'subordinate

---

17 Hopkinson, 'Negotiation', p. 122.
18 *ICD 1921*, p. 208.
19 In smaller dioceses the ratio of priests to parishes was lower and the chances for curates of becoming a parish priest were therefore better.
20 *Codex iuris canonici Pii X Pontificis Maximi iussu digestus, Benedicti Papae XV auctoritate promulgatus* (Rome: Typus Polyglottis Vaticanis, 1918) (hereafter *CIC*), canon 451, par. 1. The 'ordinary' was normally the diocesan bishop.

to the parish priest, who must instruct him in a fatherly manner, direct him in the cure of souls, keep watch over him and report to the ordinary about him at least once a year'.[21] Full responsibility for pastoral care in a parish lay with the parish priest, who entrusted certain aspects of it to his curates at his leisure. Similarly, the parish priest received almost all of the revenue from his parish and the curates depended on him for most of their income.

A clear hypothesis emerges from the historiography that the generation gap between older and younger priests also found expression in the political field, with the latter being more inclined to support the republican movement than the former.[22] The question is whether a stronger tendency among curates to support Sinn Féin also meant that they were more accepting than parish priests of IRA violence. The figures of condemnations based on *Irish Catholic* and *Irish Independent* reports show that clerics who condemned were indeed more likely to be senior clergy: of the 144 clerics counted whose status could be determined, 67 per cent were senior and 33 per cent junior clergy.[23] Given that curates outnumbered parish priests by approximately two to one, this means that senior clergy were considerably overrepresented among clerics who condemned.[24] But it would involve an argument from silence to conclude that curates were more sympathetic than parish priests

---

21 *Ibid.*, canon 476, par. 7.
22 See for example John A. Murphy, 'Priests and people in modern history', *Christus Rex. Journal of Sociology*, 23:4 (1969), pp. 235–59, at p. 257; Miller, *Church, State*, pp. 221–2; Sheridan Gilley, 'The Catholic church and revolution', in D. G. Boyce (ed.), *The Revolution in Ireland, 1879–1923* (Dublin: Gill and Macmillan, 1988), pp. 157–72, at p. 170, and Murray, *Oracles*, p. 12.
23 Ninety-six were senior and forty-eight were junior priests. 'Senior priests' includes bishops, parish priests, administrators and priors of religious houses. 'Junior priests' includes curates and members non-priors of religious communities.
24 There were 1,115 parishes in 1911 and 3,027 diocesan priests. In 1926 these numbers were 1,116 and 3,082 respectively. Newman, 'Priests', p. 6. If we assume that each parish had a parish priest or administrator then the figure of two curates for each parish priest is more or less justified. This figure does not take into account any diocesan priests not employed in a parish or any religious priests. The latter accounted for very few condemnations.

to republican violence. Much of the imbalance in the figures is likely to have been due to the newspapers' greater interest in the views of senior clergy. And, as Chapter 5 will demonstrate, parish priests were more or less proportionately represented in the figures indicating active support for the IRA. Although it is true that senior clergy were most likely to be the source of public condemnations as they appeared in the press, it must not be concluded that curates were generally more accepting of IRA violence.

Soloheadbeg

Irish Volunteer branches had made several attempts to disarm constables during 1918, but the first time such an attempt caused fatalities was on 21 January 1919 at Soloheadbeg, County Tipperary, causing the incident to go down in history as the start of the War of Independence. Two constables were shot dead when they refused to hand over gelignite to Volunteers of the South Tipperary brigade.[25] For all the belligerent language that had been used by republicans ever since the Easter rising, the incident came as a shock, and the strongly worded clerical denunciation that followed it probably reflected widespread popular feeling.[26] The clergy's criticism was all the stronger because the victims were Catholics like most of their colleagues.[27]

The priests of Soloheadbeg parish condemned the crime from the pulpit at the following Sunday's masses. The administrator, Father John Slattery, said that he did not believe that anyone in the parish had had any part in it, and that the 'most shocking feature of the sad affair was the thought that the perpetrators were actuated by what they considered a desire to further the cause of Ireland'. God never blessed a cause that 'sought to gain its end by criminal means'. His curates Fathers William Keogh and William Condon followed suit, with the former stating that none of the crimes of the bolsheviks in Russia had been worse than the 'frightful outrage'

---

25 Michael Hopkinson, *The Irish War of Independence* (Dublin: Gill and Macmillan, 2004), pp. 115–16.
26 *Ibid.*, and Augusteijn, *Defiance*, p. 87.
27 See for instance Keogh, *Vatican*, p. 24; Bew, 'Nationalism', p. 738; Robert Kee, *The Green Flag. A History of Irish Nationalism* (London: Penguin, 2000), p. 632.

that had been committed in the parish. Contrary to Slattery, Keogh did not believe that the perpetrators were members of the 'popular movement', whose leaders were 'far too logical and God-fearing to countenance such crimes'. Condon was no less emphatic when he said that 'persons who perpetrated such crimes would bring upon their country disgrace and on themselves the curse of God'.[28]

The same Sunday, the parish priest of nearby Tipperary, Arthur Canon Ryan, expressed similar views. During his sermon, he said that 'two of his flock' had been murdered 'while performing a public duty in protecting civilian property. These two men who were murdered were martyrs to duty.' He emphasised that the killing of the two constables could not be compared to the killing of soldiers in war or the execution of criminals:

> The soldier, before he faced the enemy's bullets, prepared himself for death. ... Even the murderer who paid the penalty of his crime on the scaffold, had the benefit of the ministrations of his clergyman. But the murderers with the blackened faces and blacker hearts gave their victims no such chance. They shot them as if there were no immortal souls within those poor bodies – as if there were no judgment to follow instant death.[29]

Moreover, because the ambush had happened in their neighbourhood, 'the deep sorrow and the deeper shame is ours'. There was an almost physical stain on the locality. Ryan quoted Lady Macbeth to make his point clear:

> How can we wash that stain away? Not merely by saying, like the murderess in the tragedy, 'Out, damned spot'. We must show our abhorrence of this inhuman act; we must denounce it and the cowardly miscreants who are guilty of it.[30]

He hoped and prayed that there were none among his parishioners who excused or justified the deed, because those who did were 'partakers in this crime, and the curse of Cain that has ever followed the murderer will rest on them, too'. Ryan concluded by exclaiming: 'It used to be said "where Tipperary leads, Ireland follows". God help poor Ireland if she follows this lead of blood!'[31] In Thurles

---

28 *Irish Catholic*, 1 February 1919.
29 *Ibid.*
30 *Ibid.*
31 *Ibid.*

cathedral, the archbishop of Cashel and Emly, John Mary Harty, was equally clear, if less florid: the crime was an 'offence against the laws of God' and 'against the fair name of our country'. He hoped that all 'without distinction of political party' looked with horror on the deed and expressed their 'deep sense of outrage that has been committed against Christian morals'. Harty asked for prayers for the victims and for 'the unhappy men who have this heavy crime on their consciences'.[32]

These comments from local clergy set the tone for clerical condemnations of IRA violence up to the last months of 1920, becoming set tropes of denunciation. There were assertions that local people had nothing to do with the crime, there were warnings that killings left a stain on the locality and betrayed the cause of Irish freedom, and that sympathy for them brought the 'curse of Cain'. There was also the contention that constables were good Catholics and Irishmen who were doing their duty, and that it was murder to kill them.

Speaking at mass on Sunday

The most common forum for such denunciations was the pulpit, and the most common format was the Sunday sermon: newspaper reports of clerical condemnations often began with the words 'speaking at mass on Sunday, …'. Until the rise of mass communication technology, sermons were one of relatively few means in society of getting a message across to a large audience. They have been the subject of some research by historians in recent years, although very little has been written about Catholic preaching in modern Ireland.[33] Inspired by Pope Pius X's rediscovery of the scriptural 'homily' rather than the catechetical instruction, the *Code of Canon Law* prescribed that the parish priest should 'with the customary sermon … proclaim the word of God to the people,

---

32 *Ibid.*
33 See for instance Robert H. Ellison (ed.), *A New History of the Sermon. The Nineteenth Century* (Leiden: Brill, 2010). Some attention has been given, however, to preaching during parish missions: Emmet Larkin, 'The parish mission movement, 1850–80', in Brendan Bradshaw and Dáire Keogh (eds), *Christianity in Ireland. Revisiting the Story* (Blackrock: Columba Press, 2002), pp. 195–204.

especially during the mass which is most frequented' each Sunday and holy day of obligation.[34] The sermon was intended primarily to expound those things 'which the faithful must believe and do for salvation', and preachers were exhorted to 'abstain from profane or abstruse arguments that exceed the common understanding of the audience'. In this way the *Code* hoped to ensure that the ministry of the word would not be exercised 'with persuasive words of human wisdom, nor with the profane lavishness and enticement of inane and ambitious eloquence'.[35]

Archbishop Gilmartin echoed these instructions during a sermon in Westport, County Mayo, in June 1919 when he said that

> a priest can have his views about [politics], but he is not to take an aggressive part on either side, because we belong to you and you are all belonging to us; and no priest should take any part in politics that would give offence to any section of his people, because he is the father of all his people.[36]

In practice neither the canonical injunction nor the archbishop's words prevented clerics from dwelling at length on the merits of republican or government policies during their sermons – including, incidentally, Gilmartin himself. It was a matter for interpretation where 'politics' ended and 'morality' began. Both the *Code* and Gilmartin's terms permitted preachers to comment on the morality of political violence, as that issue belonged to the realm of 'things necessary for salvation'. Sunday masses were not the only liturgical occasion when priests addressed this issue. Many reports exist of clerics using sermons at funerals – often of victims – or devotional speeches at other religious services such as benediction or at a parochial retreat or mission to the same end.[37]

Priests often made good use of oratorical effects. In January 1920, Constable Luke Finnegan was fatally shot in Thurles, and Father Michael K. Ryan, curate in the cathedral, condemned the act in a sermon at Sunday mass. He asked 'if anyone believed

---

34 Gottfried Bitter, 'Katholische Predigt der Neuzeit', in Horst Balz *et al.* (eds), *Theologische Realenzyklopädie*, 27 (Berlin and New York: Walter de Gruyter, 1997), pp. 262–96, at p. 280; *CIC*, canon 1344, par. 1.
35 *CIC*, canon 1347, pars. 1–2.
36 *Irish Catholic*, 14 June 1919.
37 See for examples *Irish Catholic*, 23 October 1920 and 26 March 1921.

he could dispense with God's commandment, "thou shalt not kill", or that he was justified in firing volley after volley into the body of a policeman?' Ryan used emotive imagery to associate approval of Finnegan's shooting with a deliberate and personal rejection of God: 'If anybody approved or taught it, let him come to Jesus Christ and say – "I tear your Fifth Commandment in your face, and throw it back to you".'[38] Similarly, Father John Burke, the parish priest of Menlough, County Galway, gave such fiery sermons attacking 'tin-pike soldiers who think they can beat England' that his masses became a popular attraction. According to one IRA veteran, local people thought it was 'as good as a pantomime' to hear Father Burke preach against the IRA. Even people from outside the parish used to come to Menlough church to hear him 'for the sport of it'.[39]

It happened frequently that the local bishop wrote a letter to the parish priest of a parish where violence had taken place, with the instruction to have it read from the pulpit at the masses on the subsequent Sunday.[40] These letters were sometimes addressed to all parishes in the locality or the diocese.[41] Such instructions could place priests in a difficult position if they believed that their bishop's comments were inopportune. When an RIC patrol was ambushed in Dundalk by the IRA in August 1920, Cardinal Logue wrote a public letter vigorously denouncing the outrage. However, before Father J. McKeone, the administrator, had a chance to read the letter on Sunday, crown forces carried out reprisals, and McKeone was concerned that Logue's letter might alienate the traumatised congregation. After having read it, he

> said the cardinal had addressed them on certain moral duties, and his words should be heard with respect and obeyed ... Had [Logue] known [of the reprisal] he would, of course, have condemned and repudiated it in the strongest possible terms, and he would have sympathised with the relatives of those who had lost their lives.[42]

---

38 *Irish Catholic*, 31 January 1920.
39 MA, BMH, WS1219, Sean O'Neill, pp. 67–8.
40 See *Irish Catholic*, 16 August 1919, 20 March 1920 and 19 February 1921.
41 See *Irish Catholic*, 12 June 1920, 2 October 1920 and 12 March 1921.
42 *Irish Catholic*, 4 September 1920.

Bishops' regular pastoral letters at the beginning of the seasons of Advent and Lent were also noted opportunities for them to condemn violence and disturbances in their dioceses, as were confirmation visits to parishes.[43]

On a number of occasions, parish priests convened ad hoc public meetings of Catholics in their parishes to pass a resolution condemning deeds of bloodshed or destruction. Thus the parish priest of Kilfenora, Father Francis Cassidy, presided over 'a hastily-summoned meeting' to denounce an ambush on the RIC in July 1919. The meeting passed a resolution which declared that it 'knew of no reason why any policeman in Kilfenora should be attacked' and asserted that

> Kilfenora, in common with Claremen generally, believe [sic] in fair-play. They do not think that the right of Ireland to self-determination can be helped by midnight assassins. The true friends of Ireland prize the honour of their native land too highly to have it stained by abominable crime.[44]

Similarly, the diocesan bishop sometimes convened a conference of local clergy to discuss events and issue a public statement. This happened in Lisdoonvarna, County Clare, in September 1920, when Bishop Thomas O'Dea of Galway and Kilmacduagh met the priests of the diocese of Kilfenora to condemn an ambush and reprisals in Rineen.[45] It also took place in Navan, County Meath, in the same month, when Bishop Gaughran met priests to denounce similar events in Trim.[46]

Killing policemen and soldiers

Several historians have observed that ostracism of the RIC by the local community was a necessary precondition for what Joost Augusteijn has called the radicalisation of Volunteers from public defiance to active guerrilla warfare.[47] Clerical denunciations of republican

43 See *ibid.*, 24 May 1919, 9 October 1920 and 4 June 1921.
44 *Ibid.*, 19 July 1919.
45 *Ibid.*, 2 October 1920.
46 *Ibid.*
47 Augusteijn, *Defiance, passim*. Ostracism: most recently Brian Hughes, 'Persecuting the Peelers', in David Fitzpatrick (ed.), *Terror in Ireland 1916–1923. Trinity History Workshop* (Dublin: Lilliput Press, 2012),

violence tried to counter this process by emphasising the humanity and exemplary Catholic virtues of the victims. The IRA campaign up to the summer of 1920 consisted mainly of attacks on constables and RIC barracks. The fact that many constables were Catholic Irishmen became an important argument against IRA violence in clerical condemnations. When Sergeant Philip Brady was killed in Lorrha, County Tipperary, in September 1919, a curate from Ulster wrote a letter to the *Irish Independent* to condemn the crime. Brady had previously been stationed in Father Thomas MacBrien's parish of Portadown, County Armagh, and MacBrien testified to Brady's excellent Catholic credentials. Brady 'attended daily mass, when he could. He was a weekly communicant. He never, through his own fault, missed benedictions or sodality meetings.' MacBrien described the dead man as 'a quiet, inoffensive man [who] was deeply respected in the district by all classes and creeds'.[48] A similar testimony came from Father J. Crowley, curate in Inishannon, County Cork, in April 1920. In the aftermath of an ambush at Upton, during which an RIC sergeant and constable were killed, Crowley said that he had never spoken to 'a better or more honest man or Catholic' than the dead constable, and that he felt his loss as he would the loss of a brother. Crowley 'regarded both the constable and the sergeant as two saints'.[49] And Philip Canon Murphy, parish priest of Castlemartyr, County Cork, provided another example in November, when two constables were killed on their way home from attending devotions in his parish church. In his sermon the following Sunday, Murphy recounted how he had attended one of the dying men:

> It is my duty ... to condemn in the strongest language that indefensible and odious outrage which has taken place in our midst in the killing of poor Constable Quinn and the wounding of Sergeant Curley ... It was pitiable to see poor Constable Quinn dragged, mortally wounded, by a woman from the street into a hallway, where I had to kneel in a pool of blood to hear his confession and speak words of prayer, encouragement, and hope into his dying ears.[50]

---

pp. 206–18. See also W. J. Lowe, 'The war against the R.I.C., 1919–21', *Éire-Ireland. An Interdisciplinary Journal of Irish Studies*, 37:3–4 (2002), pp. 79–117, at p. 85, and Augusteijn, *Defiance*, pp. 318–45 and 344.
48 *Irish Independent*, 15 September 1919.
49 *Ibid.*, 28 April 1920.
50 *Irish Catholic*, 4 December 1920.

This theme lost some of its effectiveness in early 1920, when constables began to carry out occasional reprisals. But it gained some currency again after the summer of 1920, when Auxiliaries and Black and Tans arrived, presenting themselves as suitable alternative subjects for the accusation of being 'conscienceless vindictive brutes', as one Galway Jesuit put it.[51] D. M. Leeson has argued that the coming of these British recruits was convenient for republicans, as it gave the crown forces a more English and less Irish aspect. This allowed republicans to 'bypass the RIC's inconvenient liminality' and to think of the conflict 'in properly binary terms'.[52] Priests opposed to IRA violence continued to claim Irish Catholic constables as belonging to their own community, but the arrival of the new recruits allowed them to project their rising frustration at the behaviour of the crown forces upon the latter's foreign element. Clerical assessment of the army was also initially quite positive, with military victims being described as innocent men who had been going about their duty. When the IRA killed a soldier in Fermoy in September 1919, Father John O'Donoghue, administrator of the parish, declared at mass that 'the law of almighty God had been violated, an innocent life had been taken, and he, in the discharge of his duty, publicly denounced and condemned this most hideous crime'.[53] His curate, Father John Nunan, said at a later mass that 'it was a most appalling tragedy, and every surrounding circumstance increased the enormity and wickedness. ... the authors ... had usurped in a flagrant manner the right that belongs to God alone.'[54]

Sudden and unprovided death

Another way of repudiating the IRA contention that it was lawful to kill servants of the crown was to assert that killings during an ambush were especially heinous because they left the victim without sufficient time to prepare for death. The history of Catholic spirituality had a long tradition of the 'good death', which not only

---

51 IJA, St Ignatius' College papers, SC/GALW/45, Foley to Nolan, September 1920.
52 Leeson, *Black and Tans*, p. 193.
53 *Irish Catholic*, 20 September 1919.
54 *Ibid*.

required the right spiritual disposition on the part of the dying person, but also the sacramental ministrations of a priest.[55] He would hear the dying person's confession, bestow a plenary indulgence in the form of apostolic benediction, administer the sacrament of extreme unction and give holy communion as *viaticum* or 'food for the journey'. The necessity and form of this ritualisation of death were communicated to the laity during the nineteenth and twentieth centuries through the medium of popular missals.[56] The moment of death was a particularly significant one with regard to the dying person's eternal fate, and a sudden death, without time to make peace with God, became the object of particular fear for many Catholics.

The faithful were encouraged to ask God and the saints for the grace of a happy death, and many prayers to obtain this favour were circulated in popular devotional texts. One such prayer was the pious ejaculation: 'From a sudden and unprovided death, deliver us, O Lord', derived from the litany of the saints. It was a recognised principle in theology, however, that God granted pardon for sins committed even without the sacramental ministry of a priest if people 'made an act of perfect contrition' in the moment of death. Thus the *Penny Catechism* explained that 'perfect contrition will reconcile us to God, and give us pardon of our sins' if 'we cannot go to confession soon after falling into mortal sin'.[57] Similarly, a handbook of moral theology used in a number of Irish seminaries in the early decades of the twentieth century, Jean-Pierre Gury's *Compendium theologiae moralis*, taught that 'perfect

---

55 See Lawrence J. Taylor, 'Bás i-nÉirinn. Cultural constructions of death in Ireland', *Anthropological Quarterly*, 62:4 (1989), pp. 175–87, at pp. 179–83 for a discussion of 'Catholic death' in Ireland.
56 For the emergence of these missals see André Haquin, 'The liturgical movement and Catholic ritual revision', in Geoffrey Wainwright and Karen B. Westerfield Tucker (eds), *The Oxford History of Christian Worship* (Oxford and New York: Oxford University Press, 2006), pp. 696–720.
57 *Catechism Ordered by the National Synod of Maynooth and Approved of by the Cardinal, the Archbishops and the Bishops of Ireland for General Use throughout the Irish Church* (reprint; Galway: Firinne Publications, n.d.), p. 24.

contrition justifies man by itself even outside of the sacrament of penance'.[58] Children were taught the text of an act of contrition in the *Penny Catechism*, not only so that they would know to use it during confession, but also so that they would be well prepared if some fatal danger were to come their way. Catholics who whispered the act of contrition into the ear of a person in danger of death were praised for their exemplary conduct.[59]

The horror of sudden and unprovided death was a frequent theme in clerical denunciations. Bishop O'Dea of Galway condemned the killing of two constables near Ennistymon in early August 1919 by observing that 'one of the victims has been mercilessly sent before his God without notice or preparation ... God grant that those who shot [him] may not themselves meet with such an unprovided death'.[60] After the Lorrha killing in September, the parish priest, Father John Gleeson, was shocked that the victim had not been given a chance to prepare for his death: 'he ... fell dead, without having time to say an act of contrition; but I believe he was fully prepared to die'.[61] And Bishop Morrisroe told the parish priest of Tobercurry in a public letter in October 1920 that he regretted that

> fine young fellows, so stainless and pure in most ways, ... will ... speed the bullet that leaves wife without husband, child without father, and that will, perhaps – most awful reflection of all – send a soul for which Christ died into the presence of its Maker without a moment's time for preparation.[62]

---

58 Ioannes Petrus Gury, *Compendium theologiae moralis* (Regensburg: Georg Joseph Manz, 1862), p. 510. For its use in Maynooth, see Patrick J. Corish, *Maynooth College 1795–1995* (Dublin: Gill and Macmillan, 1995), p. 209, and for Holy Cross College, Clonliffe, Dublin, see Richard Sherry, *Holy Cross College, Clonliffe, Dublin, 1859–1959. College History and Centenary Record* (Dublin: Holy Cross College, 1962), p. 77.
59 *Catechism*, p. 24. For whispering an act of contrition into the ears of victims of violence see *Irish Catholic*, 17 July 1920 and 12 March 1921.
60 *Irish Catholic*, 16 August 1919.
61 *Ibid.*, 13 September 1919.
62 *Ibid.*, 16 October 1920.

Tutored by local guides

The question of how much popular support the IRA campaign could muster has not only exercised the minds of subsequent historians. It also troubled contemporaries. Whenever an ambush took place somewhere, local clerics hastened to declare that their own parishioners had not been involved. Thus when arms raids were carried out in December 1919 and January 1920 in Tralee, the parish priest and dean of Kerry, Father David O'Leary, defended the reputation of his parishioners. He told a congregation at mass that

> he felt bound to repudiate in the name of the people of Tralee any connection, direct or indirect, with these attacks. It was acknowledged on all hands that their people had nothing whatever to do with these attacks, and had no interest in them.[63]

Bishop Joseph MacRory of Down and Connor condemned the killing of District Inspector Oswald Swanzy in Lisburn in August 1920 in an interview with a newspaper correspondent. When asked if he intended to send a public letter to the press denouncing the shooting, as he had done with the recent expulsion of Catholic workers from the Belfast shipyards, MacRory said that he did not, as 'he had no reason to think that any of his flock were concerned'. Were he to write a letter of condemnation, this might 'be taken to imply that he believed members of his own flock to be implicated, and this he was especially anxious to avoid'. MacRory then told the reporter that 'for all he … knew of the authors of the Lisburn tragedy they might be [atheists] or nihilists and not Catholics at all'.[64] Unlikely as it was that atheists or nihilists were responsible for the killing, these frequent clerical disclaimers of local involvement were not entirely without credibility. Augusteijn has shown that since IRA brigade areas extended across county boundaries, Volunteers often took part in operations outside their counties. Moreover, Volunteers sometimes also operated outside their brigade areas, and in some parts of the country this was standard practice.[65]

---

63 *Ibid.*, 17 January 1920.
64 *Ibid.*, 28 August 1920.
65 Joost Augusteijn, 'Accounting for the emergence of violent activism among Irish revolutionaries, 1916–21', *Irish Historical Studies*, 35:139 (2007), pp. 327–44, at pp. 331–2.

But none of this ruled out local help, much less local sympathy for the deeds. As the parish priest of Caherlistrane, County Galway, asked in January 1920, the question was whether the 'experts from a distance' who carried out ambushes had been 'tutored by local guides'.[66] Dean Innocent Ryan of Cashel complained that 'there was a loosening of principles which they considered a second nature of their race. Otherwise how explain those robberies they read of every day, or the horrible murders, formerly so rare, now, alas! so frequent'. Ryan blamed intimidation and peer pressure for the fact that few dared to contradict the advocates of physical force: 'Many people are afraid to raise their voices against wicked counsels and corrupt projects.' However, his argument also assumed that violence could count on a measure of popular acclaim: 'They go with the crowd, and, through fear or for popular applause, encourage the foolhardy.'[67]

This topic was the subject of a public dispute in the summer of 1920 between Archbishop Gilmartin and the highest military officer in Ireland, Sir Nevil Macready. Gilmartin wrote a public letter to Macready after crown forces carried out reprisals in Tuam following the killing of two constables. Referring to the shooting of the policemen, Gilmartin said: 'I am satisfied the good people of Tuam do reprobate this deed; but the sequel is calculated to seriously imperil the peace and good order of the town'.[68] Macready responded a few days later, observing that 'he would be only too ready to share His Grace's opinion that no large section of the people of Tuam have sympathy with crime; but the fact that a jury could not be found to inquire into the shootings of policemen proves that the people are at least indifferent'.[69] The archbishop replied to this rather compelling point by insisting that 'the assassination of two constables three miles from Tuam by unknown persons is no evidence that a large section, or even a small [section], of the people of the town have any sympathy with crime'.[70]

There was more than a little wishful thinking involved in such

---

66 *Irish Catholic*, 24 January 1920.
67 *Ibid.*, 7 February 1920.
68 *Ibid.*, 24 July 1920.
69 *Ibid.*, 31 July 1920.
70 *Ibid.*

assertions, and frequent clerical warnings that parishioners should not sympathise with crime are proof that many priests were aware that the opposite was the case. Canon Walsh of Ballymurn, County Wexford, contended in November 1919 that 'he who committed a crime or endorsed it, or countenanced it in any way, even remotely, was an enemy of Ireland'.[71] Two months later, Bishop Foley addressed a congregation in Carlow cathedral with the following telling warning:

> [In] the inflamed state of the popular mind, there may be grave danger of permitting to spring up in your hearts sentiments which, if indulged in, must partake of a murderous character. You must be on your guard against permitting yourselves to deliberately indulge in sentiments of approval of murder, no matter who may be the victim, or who the doer of the dastardly deed; ... Beware, then, of thoughts of your minds, and the feelings of your hearts.[72]

And Canon O'Donnell of Rathkeale said in early March 1920 after the killing of a sergeant in the parish that 'the people should nurture and stimulate healthy Catholic opinion, and no longer tolerate such unholy doings in their midst'.[73]

The brand of Cain

As Canon Ryan's invocation of the 'curse of Cain' in January 1919 has already shown, priests used more forceful means than mere condemnation to instil horror of bloodshed in their people.[74] This theme of the curse was taken up again in September 1919 by Father Gleeson after the Lorrha killing:

> The sin of Cain has been committed in the peaceable parish of Lorrha; ... The brand of Cain lies on the assassins, who, standing behind a wall, slew an innocent man, almost at our own doors, on Tuesday night, and the shadow of that crime will hang over this parish for many generations. The murderers ... will walk, like Cain, fugitives

71 *Ibid.*, 22 November 1919.
72 *Ibid.*, 3 January 1920.
73 *Ibid.*, 20 March 1920.
74 *Ibid.*, 1 February 1919.

on the earth. ... May the curse of Cain, the curse of the priest, and the curse of God fall on those who are guilty of this murder.[75]

Similarly, Father Denis O'Brien, curate in Thurles, said in January 1920 that the killer of a constable 'must have known and felt that ... he was imprinting on his own soul the brand of Cain, and staining it with blood which, as long as he lives, shall never cease to cry to heaven against him'.[76] This terminology – indelible stains of blood, the sin of Cain, the brand of Cain, the curse of Cain, the curse of the priest and of God – was quite different from the dispassionate language of moral disapproval that pulpit condemnations used so often. These concepts were alien to the handbooks of moral theology used in seminaries, but they were reminiscent of popular traditions about 'cursed' people and places.

The parishioners of Swanlinbar, County Cavan, took it very literally when their parish priest denounced an act of violence that had taken place in their parish in December 1920. Police had been ambushed in the town, with one constable killed and two others badly wounded. The local parish priest denounced the incident and told his congregation that 'the actual murderers [and] their relatives could not expect good luck even in this world'. According to the RIC county inspector for Cavan, it was well known locally that two brothers of a family named Leonard had been 'the chief instruments in bringing the ambush off'. The two brothers judiciously absconded. Within a month of the priest's denunciation two Leonard sisters, who up to that time had been the picture of health, suddenly 'pined away [and] died'. And when the Leonard parents were then also stricken by illness and were not expected to recover, the parish quickly made up its mind that these deeds were 'acts of vengeance from on high' in fulfilment of their parish priest's dire predictions. Nor did the incident miss its effect on the local IRA, and the inspector general reported in May 1921 that the district was still comparatively peaceful owing to the 'strange occurrence' that had taken place in December.[77]

The concept of the curse of Cain could easily be made more effective by including in it those who lived in the vicinity of a crime

---

75 *Ibid.*, 13 September 1919.
76 *Ibid.*, 31 January 1920.
77 TNA, CO904/115, IGMR, May 1921.

and had done nothing to prevent it. Denouncing the killing of two constables in August 1919, Father William Mullins, curate in Lahinch, County Clare, said that though his parishioners had no sympathy with the crime, 'yet because it occurred in their midst they incurred the odium and disgrace which attached to the place wherein that fiendish crime had been committed'.[78] And when an RIC sergeant was shot dead in Balbriggan, County Dublin, on 14 April 1920, the parish priest, Eugene Canon Byrne, told his audience that 'he hoped that the scourge of God would not fall on his parish' on account of the crime.[79]

Handbooks of moral theology did offer one category of sins that provided theological substance to this talk of divine wrath. 'Wilful murder' was one of the *peccata in coelum clamantia*, sins that cry to heaven for vengeance.[80] Besides involving a transgression of the moral order, they also entailed 'a violation of the laws of nature' and therefore provoked 'divine wrath in a special manner'.[81] This theme featured often in clerical denunciations. Father John O'Donoghue, administrator of Fermoy, County Cork, commented in September 1919 that the killing of soldiers was 'a terrible crime, which cried to heaven for vengeance'.[82] And Father Florence McCarthy, administrator of Skibbereen pro-cathedral, denounced the killing of a constable in March 1920 in a similar way: 'when men so far forgot the law of God as to stain their hands with the blood of their fellow-man the crime cried to heaven for vengeance. He asked the congregation to appeal to God not to visit the people with his wrath.'[83] Archbishop Gilmartin, condemning the killing of two constables in Tuam in July 1920, said that 'in the present circumstances it was

---

78 *Irish Catholic*, 23 August 1919.
79 *Ibid.*, 1 May 1920.
80 Hieronymus Noldin, *Summa theologiae moralis*, i: *De principiis theologiae moralis* (Innsbruck: Felix Rauch, 1910), pp. 391–2. See Michael Sievernich, *Schuld und Sünde in der Theologie der Gegenwart* (Frankfurt am Main: Knecht, 1982), p. 271, for the history of the *peccata clamantia*.
81 Antony Koch and Arthur Preuss, *A Handbook of Moral Theology*, ii: *Sin and the Means of Grace* (St Louis, MO, and London: Herder, 1919), p. 86.
82 *Irish Catholic*, 20 September 1919.
83 *Ibid.*, 20 March 1920.

not likely the perpetrators would be brought to justice'. However, 'blood haunted, and often in strange ways revealed the murderer', while 'those concerned must answer before the bar of divine justice'.[84]

The notion that the killer's deeds would come back to haunt him even on earth was also a popular theme. Father Michael K. Ryan, curate in Thurles, asserted after the killing of a district inspector that 'the memory of that awful deed would haunt the guilty man all his life, and would rise up before him on his death bed'.[85] Bishop Patrick Finegan of Kilmore told an audience in Cootehill, County Cavan, in the summer of 1920 that 'it was true that God forgave even the murderer on sincere repentance, but if he did he very often made an example of him. If there was no public punishment, the torture of a guilty conscience was sufficient for him.'[86] And the parish priest of Leitrim, Thomas Canon O'Reilly, denounced the killing of a soldier by warning his congregation in January 1921 that 'people who were guilty of murder had their blood spilt, and he knew of instances where they died in asylums or other places which brought disgrace on themselves and their families'.[87]

Reparation

Irish Catholics were well acquainted with the necessity of averting the vengeance of God through spiritual acts of reparation. This was an important devotional notion: those who committed a sin had to ask God for forgiveness by going to confession, and then had to make reparation to expiate the guilt they had incurred. It was not just a personal affair, and sins could cause collective guilt that required collective atonement. As Bishop Kelly asserted in a sermon in Skibbereen in spring 1919, recent 'deeds done in Ireland' were 'a blot on their country; almighty God must be insulted at these wicked things, and it was their business to try to avert the vengeance of God'.[88] Consequently bishops from time to time ordered the performance of public acts of reparation to atone

84 *Ibid.*, 31 July 1920.
85 *Ibid.*, 5 July 1919.
86 *Ibid.*, 19 June 1920.
87 *Ibid.*, 5 February 1921.
88 *Ibid.*, 19 April 1919.

for IRA killings. Thus Bishop O'Dea of Galway, in a letter sent in February 1920 to Father R. McHugh, parish priest of Castlegar, ominously referred to the biblical story of the punishment of the people of Israel after they had worshipped the golden calf:

> The recent murder in your parish is a shocking insult to God, which calls for public atonement from your people. When the Jews long ago offered a similar insult to God by their worship of the golden calf, their leader stood in the gate of the camp and said – 'If any man be on the Lord's side let him join with me'. A multitude joined him, and going through the camp from gate to gate, they punished the guilty by putting 23,000 of them to death. Let the atonement be the joint offering by priests and people of all the masses in the parish on tomorrow, for the purpose of appeasing God's anger, followed immediately, or in the course of the day, by the public performance of the stations of the cross.[89]

O'Dea's reference demonstrates, apart perhaps from irritation at the local clergy's inability to restrain extreme elements, a belief that individual deeds affected the moral status of the community. Around the same time Father Bernard McKenna, curate in Kilbrittain, County Cork, referred to similar instructions issued by Bishop Cohalan after a policeman had been killed in the parish:

> It was a crime which demanded reparation. The bishop had directed that even where the people had no responsibility for the crime, reparation should be held, to beg God's pardon, and to pray for the soul of the victim. Therefore, in accordance with His Lordship's direction, he had decided to say the litany of the Blessed Virgin at the conclusion of mass during Lent, to be devoutly answered by the whole congregation.[90]

The IRA's habit of attacking constables on their way to or from church naturally aroused the particular indignation not only of the British authorities, but also of the clergy.[91] If blood was shed

---

89 *Ibid.*, 13 March 1920. The biblical reference is to Exodus 32:25-9. Exodus mentions 'only' 3,000 victims. O'Dea's 23,000 was probably taken from 1 Corinthians 10:8, which is perhaps a reference to the golden calf episode. Incidentally, the killing that O'Dea referred to was probably not an instance of political violence.
90 *Irish Catholic*, 28 February 1920.
91 For an example see *ibid.*, 27 March 1920. For the British authorities' indignation, see Armagh Diocesan Archives (hereafter ADA), Michael

in a church building, canon law required a liturgical 'reconciliation' or rededication of the edifice, providing an opportunity for public reparation.[92] On a Sunday morning in July 1920, Sergeant William Mulherin of the RIC made his way to eight o'clock mass in St Patrick's church in Bandon, County Cork.[93] As he entered the porch, two armed men jumped out from behind the church doors and fired shots at him. The parish priest, Jeremiah Canon Cohalan, came out of the sacristy to administer extreme unction and Mulherin died about ten minutes later. Cohalan announced to the congregation that the building had to be reconciled before mass could begin and proceeded to perform the required ritual. When mass was finally celebrated at ten o'clock, the canon condemned the killing in his sermon and observed that it had always been the case throughout the 'ages of Catholic history' that church buildings were places of sanctuary where even criminals found protection. His brother, the bishop of Cork, denounced the crime in a public letter some days later and imposed the canonical censure of interdict on the guilty parties, which, among other things, deprived them of the right to receive the sacraments.[94]

The last months of 1920: a new departure

Paul Bew has observed that many moderate nationalists, 'initially inclined to condemn republican violence, fell silent when confronted with British reprisals'.[95] This was also true for the clergy. As has been seen, the last quarter of 1920 saw a significant drop in the frequency of clerical denunciations of republican violence, just as the violence itself became more widespread. Tomás Ó Fiaich has suggested that this was due to the fact that the clergy's moral assessment of the 'open-air ambushes' that became common in this period was more 'circumspect' than that of the barrack attacks of 1920.[96] In fact there is no evidence that priests made this

---

Logue papers, ARCH9/5/1, Greenwood to Logue, 30 September 1920.
92 *CIC*, canon 1172, par. 1.
93 *Irish Catholic*, 31 July 1920.
94 *Ibid.*
95 Bew, 'Nationalism', p. 741. See also Augusteijn, *Defiance*, p. 271.
96 Ó Fiaich, 'Clergy', p. 484.

distinction, and there are many examples of the tropes established after Soloheadbeg being used even in 1921.[97] The clergy's new approach was actually due to the fact that the escalating violence caused a change in the British campaign. As IRA attacks intensified, the crown forces – newly supplemented by Black and Tans and Auxiliaries – became more aggressive and engaged in increasingly violent reprisals. This altered the nature of the conflict, giving bishops and priests a convenient alternative focus of attention. Moreover, priests increasingly discovered that they were themselves no longer immune from interference by the crown forces. By consequence the focus of clerical pronouncements shifted from the immorality of republican violence to the immorality of the British campaign.[98] A joint pastoral letter issued by the hierarchy on 19 October 1920 set a new tone by focusing almost exclusively on the horrors of British rule and merely counselling 'self-restraint' to its own people.[99]

It was significant that the public clerical response to two dramatic highpoints of the War of Independence in November 1920 was muted. On the morning of 'Bloody Sunday', 21 November, Michael Collins's 'squad' of IRA members killed eleven British intelligence officers and two Auxiliaries in Dublin, while fourteen civilians were killed by way of reprisal by crown forces at a Gaelic football match in Croke Park in the afternoon. A week later, on Sunday 28 November, the IRA's West Cork brigade carried out a large-scale ambush on Auxiliaries at Kilmichael, County Cork, killing seventeen officers. Bloody Sunday occurred on the day after the remains of a priest were found in County Galway. A Galway city curate called Father Michael Griffin had gone missing from his house on 14 November, and was found dead in a bog on the night of Saturday 20 November.[100] From the time of his disappearance it was widely assumed that he had been taken by members of the crown forces. For clerical commentators in the week following these violent events, the Bloody Sunday killings were entirely

---

97 For just a few examples see *Irish Independent*, 1 February 1921; *Irish Catholic*, 26 March 1921, 9 April 1921 and 25 June 1921.
98 Marie Coleman has observed this phenomenon in County Longford: Coleman, *Longford*, p. 157.
99 *ICD 1921*, pp. 556–61.
100 *Freeman's Journal*, 22 November 1920.

overshadowed by Griffin's murder, the first priestly fatality of the war. This was true even for much lay commentary.[101] The *Irish Independent* started on Monday 22 November by deploring the Dublin killings, but then opined that 'the death of the Rev. M. Griffin, C.C. is the most appalling. Not in Ireland alone, but throughout the length and breadth of the civilised world, this crime will be reprobated.'[102] As will be seen later, Bishop O'Dea stated publicly that 'this murder makes a new departure in the campaign, indicating, it would appear, the beginning of an attack on the church and religion'.[103]

The clerical mood was changing. Priests maintained their earlier objections to republican violence, but their public statements were increasingly directed at the crown forces. In his Advent pastoral, published on Sunday 28 November, Cardinal Logue strongly condemned the 'squad' killings of Bloody Sunday morning – 'no object would excuse them; no motive could justify them; no heart ... would tolerate their cruelty' – but then said that 'if a balance were struck between the deeds of the morning and those of the evening, I believe it should be given against the forces of the crown'.[104] The Kilmichael ambush took place on the same day and received similarly understated clerical commentary. Michael Canon Higgins, parish priest of Macroom, made a silent statement by following the funeral cortege of the dead Auxiliaries to the outskirts of the town as the remains began their voyage to London.[105] And Bishop Cohalan complained that the ambush had 'involved the murder of 15 Englishmen, the death of three of the ambushing party, several deaths since, and it has not brought us nearer the republic'.[106] Otherwise, few priests chose to single out the ambush for special public condemnation.

Cohalan had only recently earned the sympathy of republicans by visiting Terence MacSwiney in prison during his hunger-strike. MacSwiney was the Sinn Féin mayor of Cork and was arrested on charges of sedition in August 1920. Shortly afterwards he began a hunger-strike to protest against his internment. Cohalan's visit had

101 Cf. Leeson, *Black and Tans*, pp. 52 and 62.
102 *Irish Independent*, 22 November 1920.
103 *Irish Catholic*, 4 December 1920.
104 *ICD 1921*, p. 545.
105 *Irish Independent*, 3 December 1920.
106 *Cork Examiner*, 16 December 1920.

been interpreted as an important sign of clerical support for the republican cause. However, during the month and a half leading up to his complaint about the Kilmichael ambush, the city and county of Cork had been the scene of numerous hard-hitting IRA actions and reprisals by crown forces, and this changed the bishop's attitude. Canon law provided bishops with a number of ecclesiastical penalties that could lend force to the rhetoric of condemnation. The most serious of these was excommunication, which was defined in the 1917 *Code* as 'a censure by which a person is excluded from the communion of the faithful' and which deprived her or him of the right to assist at the church's public worship, to receive the sacraments or to receive a Christian burial.[107] Cohalan imposed it in December 1920 upon anyone 'who, within this diocese of Cork, shall organise or take part in ambushes or kidnapping, or shall otherwise be guilty of murder or attempted murder'.[108] Strictly speaking the decree applied to all persons who engaged in such activities, and it was presumably also intended to give Catholic members of the crown forces food for thought.[109] But it was clear to all that the IRA was the main target of Cohalan's measure, and his vigorous critique of republican ideology in subsequent pastoral letters confirms that he himself also saw it in this way.[110]

Cohalan was the only bishop to issue a decree of excommunication during the War of Independence. His diocese and cathedral town had seen much heavier fighting than elsewhere in the country.[111] Cohalan's decree came a day after the killing of a soldier at Dillon's Cross on 11 December, which had caused Auxiliaries to carry out the 'burning of Cork'. Faced with these extreme circumstances, Cohalan decided to employ extreme meas-

---

107 *CIC*, canons 2257 and 2259–60.
108 Cork and Ross Diocesan Archives, Cork (hereafter CDA), Daniel Cohalan papers, box vi, pastoral letter, 12 December 1920.
109 Catholic members of the 'old RIC' were very numerous, but there were also Catholic Black and Tans: Leeson, *Black and Tans*, p. 73. Some members of the crown forces even converted to Catholicism during their Irish tour of duty: in October 1920 Archbishop Harty of Cashel received seven – newly engaged? – British soldiers into the church: *Irish Catholic*, 29 October 1920.
110 CDA, Cohalan papers, box vi, pastoral letter, 19 December 1920.
111 See Miller, *Church, State*, p. 457.

ures. His own personality doubtless also played its part. He was more of a dogmatist than a diplomat, and the practical ramifications of his actions were less important to him than the necessity to speak his mind. However, the fact that Cohalan's decree was greeted by silence on the part of his colleagues is more significant than the decree itself. For the other bishops, even for conservatives like Gilmartin and Morrisroe, it seemed both more just and more expedient to concentrate on the sins of the government: more just, because according to them the crown forces had by this time become the aggressor; and more expedient, because the Dublin Castle government was fast losing legitimacy and the church needed to look towards establishing desirable relations with the men who constituted the country's future regime.[112] It is telling that the two other Cork bishops, Kelly of Ross and Browne of Cloyne, also refrained from following Cohalan's example, even though their dioceses had been equally hard-hit by violence. Kelly was actually a much more likely source of such a decree than Cohalan, because whereas the latter had previously been regarded as a cautious supporter of Sinn Féin, Kelly had a strong public record of hostility towards republicanism. But even the bishop of Ross decided against adding his voice to Cohalan's. The Cork decree was thus the exception that proved the rule. Clerical condemnation of republican violence waned at the end of 1920.

112 *Ibid.*, pp. 483–4.

3

Interfering where they shouldn't: interaction with republicans

When Dean Daniel O'Connor, parish priest of Carrickmacross, County Monaghan, preached a sermon in August 1919 condemning the killing of policemen and defending the character of the constabulary, one member of the congregation stood up and walked out, while another interrupted him and started an argument.[1] This incident demonstrates that pulpit condemnations were part of a conversation with the flock rather than authoritative monologues. Priests did not operate in isolation from lay Catholics and could expect a response from their audience. The previous chapter has focused on the incidence and contents of clerical denunciations. This chapter examines the ensuing interaction with republicans. Often the response took the form of verbal criticism, either in the church itself or elsewhere. The interaction included theological arguments about the legitimacy or otherwise of IRA killings. Moreover, priests did not always stop at words, and some intervened actively to prevent the carrying out of IRA operations. By way of response, Volunteers sometimes resorted to intimidation of clerics. This chapter looks first at instances of clerical obstruction of the IRA and its consequences, and then at republican criticism of clerical condemnation. Subsequently, it analyses the different theological arguments about the moral status of the guerrilla war and their implications. Finally, it looks at another important question concerning the clergy's response: it asks whether clergy furthered or countered the allegedly sectarian nature of the guerrilla campaign.

1 TNA, CO904/109, IGMR, August 1919, p. 755.

Intervention by priests to call off IRA actions

Joost Augusteijn has observed that there were reports from all over the country of priests who intervened to stop IRA actions.² The Bureau of Military History's witness statements and other sources amply confirm this. Most of these interventions were motivated by the desire to keep the parish quiet and to avoid reprisals. When a battalion of the IRA's Kilkenny brigade planned an attack on Callan barracks in February 1921, the parish priest came to visit one of the officers, asking: 'What's this ... I hear [you] intend to do tomorrow night?' When the officer refused to disclose any information, the priest continued to give him 'a lot of advice, saying things were bad enough without making them worse, that the military and police would wreck the town if anything happened and so on'.³ And in a case recounted by a number of the Bureau's witnesses, Father Patrick Brennan, curate in Castleisland, County Kerry, intervened one night to stop a planned ambush on a military picket in the town. About half an hour before the picket was due to appear, when the men were already in their positions, Brennan came on the scene and demanded that the action be called off.⁴ He argued that the battalion commandant had not authorised it and he threatened to go to the barracks to inform the picket.⁵ Brennan was by no means out of sympathy with the republican cause. One local IRA man stated that he was well known for his support for Sinn Féin and that in fact 'it was embarrassing for Volunteers to listen to him attack the English forces from the altar'.⁶ On one occasion Brennan had even said during a sermon that 'shooting was too good for the Tans and military' who carried out reprisals.⁷ This horror of reprisals, rather than animosity towards the IRA, was the reason for Brennan's demarche. According to one IRA veteran, the

---

2 Augusteijn, *Defiance*, p. 307.
3 MA, BMH, WS1642, Edward Halley, p. 12.
4 MA, BMH, WS882, Thomas McEllistrim, pp. 19–20. See also T. Ryle Dwyer, *Tans, Terror and Troubles. Kerry's Real Fighting Story 1913–23* (Cork and Dublin: Mercier Press, 2001), p. 226.
5 MA, BMH, WS1110, Peter Browne, p. 35; and WS882, Thomas McEllistrim, p. 20.
6 MA, BMH, WS1110, Peter Browne, p. 35.
7 *Ibid.*

Ballymacelligott Volunteers had informed him of the impending Castleisland ambush so that he would be able to take precautions for the reprisals.[8]

Priests more skilled in the art of diplomacy had no need of reverting to threats, but instead came up with tactical objections, real or imaginary. When a local IRA company was lying in wait for a Black and Tan lorry to drive past its ambush position near Kilfinane, County Limerick, in December 1920, the local priest, Father Robert Ambrose, made an appearance in a pony and trap.[9] He warned the commandant that the enemy knew of the ambush and advised the column to disperse.[10] It is possible that Ambrose was telling the truth – it is even possible that he himself had told the crown forces – but it is more likely that he was using a ploy to stop the ambush and its consequences. IRA leaders were aware of this possibility. The commandant of an IRA company in Donegal decided to ignore warnings from the local parish priest on one occasion, believing – erroneously, as it happened – that it was 'a ruse' by the priest 'to get us to move out of his parish'.[11] A similar example has been recorded by W. H. Kautt concerning an incident in Coachford, County Cork, in January 1921.[12]

The success rate of such priestly interventions varied, depending on the personalities and determination of the priest and commandant in question. In the Callan case just mentioned, the IRA man who was accosted refused to be swayed by the priest's words: 'needless to remark, I gave him no information'.[13] Similarly, the *Irish Catholic* reported in August 1920 that Father Joseph Houlihan, curate in Kinnitty, King's County, had unsuccessfully called on the local IRA branch to desist from their preparations to

---

8 *Ibid.* Cf. MA, BMH, WS1181, John O'Connor, p. 14.
9 MA, BMH, WS1435, Daniel O'Shaughnessy, p. 59.
10 O'Shaughnessy says Ambrose told them they were too close to a safe resting place: *ibid.* But see MA, BMH, WS992, Denis Noonan, p. 13, and WS1069, William Regan, p. 6. See also WS1151, Patrick Luddy, p. 16.
11 MA, BMH, WS1516, P. H. Doherty, p. 13.
12 W. H. Kautt, *Ambushes and Armour. The Irish Rebellion, 1919–1921* (Dublin and Portland, OR: Irish Academic Press, 2010), p. 126. See also Hopkinson, *War*, pp. 110–11.
13 MA, BMH, WS1642, Edward Halley, p. 12.

destroy the local police barracks.[14] But often enough such attempts were successful. Despite mutterings from men in the column – 'he interfered where he shouldn't' – Father Brennan managed to persuade the IRA commandant in Castleisland to call off his ambush.[15] Father Ambrose's intervention was also successful.[16] And Michael Henry, a battalion commandant of the IRA in the North Mayo brigade, recounted as a matter of course that the parish priest of Belmullet, John Canon Hegarty, 'compelled' him to open a bridge that would have trapped RIC men and soldiers in the town as they were raiding a republican court.[17] This choice of words is significant, and there is no doubt that strong clerical characters were able to affect the decisions of IRA units. Dick Walsh, another IRA leader in Mayo, stated that he even knew that 'local priests were able to influence GHQ to stop planned operations' after the national command started to centralise activities from mid-1920 onwards.[18] Another veteran recalled that Volunteers in Bohola, County Mayo, were 'plainly being restrained from activity' by the local curate, Father Michael O'Hara, even to the extent of souring relations between them and more active brethren elsewhere in the county.[19] Similarly, veteran Pat Fallon told Ernie O'Malley that the 'fair grip' which Martin Canon Healy of Kilmaine, County Mayo, exercised over his parishioners had turned the area against the movement.[20]

Much of this depended on the personal prestige of the priest in question. Senior priests who had strong local positions of authority could hope to thwart IRA activity successfully. It is easy to see how the parish priest of New Ross, County Wexford, managed this in December 1920. According to a newspaper report, Walter Canon Rossiter went in among a group of men who had reportedly

---

14 *Irish Catholic*, 21 August 1920. For another example see MA, BMH, WS436, James McKeon, p. 6.
15 Brennan: MA, BMH, WS882, Thomas McEllistrim, p. 20; mutterings: MA, BMH, WS1110, Peter Browne, p. 35.
16 MA, BMH, WS1435, Daniel O'Shaughnessy, p. 59.
17 MA, BMH, WS1732, Michael Henry, p. 7.
18 MA, BMH, WS400, Dick Walsh, p. 66.
19 MA, BMH, WS1588, Seán Ruane, p. 24.
20 University College Dublin Archives, Dublin (hereafter UCDA), Ernie O'Malley papers, P17b/109, Pat Fallon, and Augusteijn, *Defiance*, p. 307.

assembled in the district for a planned ambush, and told them that 'he knew everyone present, and that if they did not disperse he would punish every one of them. They immediately cleared off.'[21] But the determination of the IRA men involved was a crucial factor too. William O'Hora, a veteran officer in the North Mayo brigade, recalled that Monsignor Patrick McAlpine, parish priest of Clifden, had once forbidden the local Volunteers to hold a dance in the town hall. The Volunteers decided to hold the dance anyway for the sake of defying McAlpine's authority. They held up the caretaker of the town hall one Saturday night and 'had just the form of a dance lasting thirty minutes'. The next day a member of the hall committee advised O'Hora to leave the town for a few days, as Monsignor McAlpine, who 'always carried a big, heavy stick', had been looking for him. O'Hora told the man that 'if the P.P. came to me and commenced to abuse me, as threatened, I would finish the matter'.[22] For this IRA man, his newfound position of authority came at the expense of the local priest's. McAlpine never called.

Such psychological contests were common. In 1919, they mostly focused on recruitment for the IRA on Sunday mornings near the church. William O'Hora had had another brush with clerical authority in 1919, when the parish priest of Attymas, County Mayo, ordered him and some fellow Volunteers off the church grounds as they were trying to recruit young men for the IRA.[23] The seizure of arms in 1919 also provided fertile ground for battles of wills, as Volunteers went round confiscating arms from private properties, including rural presbyteries. A Kerry IRA veteran recalled that they asked the local parish priest in Sneem for his shotgun at the end of 1919. The priest denied having one, but the IRA company raided his house and found a gun, which they took. 'The priest made no complaint in public about the raid but he was unfriendly afterwards.'[24] And the commandant of a battalion of the North Roscommon brigade mentioned that he raided the house of a local curate in 1919 while the latter was saying mass. The takings were very satisfactory, as the men found a revolver, a shotgun, ammunition and a

21 *Irish Independent*, 20 December 1920.
22 MA, BMH, WS1554, William O'Hora, p. 6.
23 *Ibid.*, p. 4.
24 MA, BMH, WS961, Michael Teehan, p. 2. For the same incident see MA, BMH, WS958, Denis O'Sullivan, p. 3.

bayonet. The reason why the Volunteers did not ask first, as their colleagues in Sneem and elsewhere had done, was that the curate in question was known to be 'hostile to the Volunteers'.[25]

Other symbolic stand-offs happened in the context of funerals. In Ennistymon, County Clare, the parish priest, Father Andrew Nestor, refused to allow the remains of one fallen Volunteer into his church in 1920.[26] There was little the IRA could do about this, and the body had to be taken to the chapel of the local workhouse instead. On another occasion, fund-raising by the IRA also became a bone of contention. In his report for June 1921, the RIC inspector general wrote that in some parts of County Tyrone, Catholic priests had denounced collections that had recently been held for the IRA because the collectors supposedly lacked the required authority from Sinn Féin.[27]

IRA intimidation of priests

In areas where the IRA had become strong, continued clerical opposition not infrequently resulted in intimidation of priests.[28] When Father Daniel Coughlan, parish priest of Aughrim, County Galway, refused to appoint a Sinn Féiner as teacher in the local school in February 1919, local republicans declared a boycott of the school. Shortly afterwards shots were fired into the house of a local man who had defied the boycott.[29] And when Father Patrick Tuite, parish priest of Delvin, County Westmeath, refused to give permission to Sinn Féin leader Father Michael O'Flanagan to use the parish hall in July 1919, a shot was fired at the door of his presbytery at night. According to the RIC inspector general, it was believed locally that Tuite, who was 'opposed to Sinn Fein', had not only refused permission to hold the meeting, but had also caused it to be proclaimed by the police.[30] These measures did not apply only to hostile priests. Father John Hurley, curate in Bantry,

25 MA, BMH, WS954, Sean Leavy, p. 6.
26 MA, BMH, WS1044, Patrick Devitt, p. 11.
27 TNA, CO904/115, IGMR, June 1921, p. 694.
28 For more examples see Augusteijn, *Defiance*, p. 305.
29 TNA, CO904/108, IGMR, February 1919, p. 247.
30 TNA, CO904/109, IGMR, 12 July 1919. For the refusal see also *Irish Catholic*, 3 May 1919.

County Cork, was banned by the IRA from attending an open-air festival or *aeridheacht* in his parish after he foiled the attempted arrest of a local bank manager by the IRA in early 1921. When two members of the IRA went to arrest the bank manager, they found him in a 'bathing-box' or beach cabin together with Hurley. When the two Volunteers made their purpose known, the bank manager 'appealed to F[ather] Hurley for sanctuary', and Hurley obliged. The Volunteers then left and nothing further was apparently done until the local IRA company organised a fund-raising *aeridheacht* together with the Bantry Sinn Féin and Gaelic League branches. When the IRA let it be known that Hurley was not welcome at the event, the Sinn Féiners and Gaelic Leaguers withdrew their support, because Hurley was president of the local branches of both organisations.[31]

Others were targeted for condemning the IRA from the pulpit. Father Gleeson of Lorrha received several 'abusive and threatening letters' after his condemnation of the Brady killing in September 1919.[32] When James Canon Cregan, parish priest of Abbeyfeale, County Limerick, said publicly that the British authorities should 'deal mercilessly with the rebels responsible for the murder' of a constable, he received a message from the local IRA brigade commandant 'warning him of the consequences of his talk from the altar'.[33] Father John Godley, parish priest of Adrigole, County Cork, had his motorcar stolen and destroyed after a pulpit condemnation of the IRA.[34] And when the parish priest of Timoleague, County Cork, denounced the IRA in March 1920, he was 'warned that the Volunteers would not stand for any more of his sermons'. But the brunt of the local Volunteers' anger fell on a local man who had sent a report of the sermon to

---

31 UCDA, Richard Mulcahy papers, P7/A/24, Hayes to Mulcahy, 15 September 1921.
32 TNA, CO904/110, IGMR, September 1919, p. 8.
33 MA, BMH, WS1272, James Collins, p. 39.
34 Godley: *Irish Independent*, 26 November and 2 December 1920. Godley was known for being anti-republican: Kerry Diocesan Archives, Killarney (hereafter KyDA), Charles O'Sullivan papers, 'Parish correspondence', Adrigole, Dunne to O'Sullivan, 4 May 1922.

the press. This man was arrested, court-martialled and ordered to leave the area.[35]

The discrepancy between the treatment meted out to the priest and the man who made his sermons public shows that IRA intimidation of antagonistic priests knew clear boundaries. Volunteers were not always agreed on the right way to treat recalcitrant clerics, but more radical voices were suppressed. During the war the West Mayo brigade intercepted a letter from Father John Flatley, parish priest of Aughagower, to Dublin Castle, denouncing his curate's seditious activities. The brigade adjutant, Thomas Hevey, argued that Flatley should be shot as a spy, as would have happened if Flatley had been a layman, but he was overruled.[36] A similar case occurred in Tralee, County Kerry, in April 1921, when a Dominican priest called Father Hyacinth Collins was caught informing the RIC of the fact that he had heard a lady worshipper at the Dominican church endorsing the recent killing of an Auxiliary officer by the IRA. The woman's house was subsequently burned by Black and Tans. Tadhg Kennedy, the intelligence officer of the North Kerry brigade, reported the matter to the priest's namesake Michael Collins, who sent Kennedy to meet the provincial of the Irish Dominicans.[37] The provincial received Kennedy in the company of an older Dominican called Father R. M. Headley, who was described to Kennedy as having been a Fenian in his younger days.[38]

> Father Headley, when I was finished, asked me what I would do if [Collins] weren't a priest. I told him and he said: 'You are a brave man. This is no priest of God. Do your duty, boy, and you need have no fear of the future'. He said words to that effect several times and

---

35 MA, BMH, WS1250, John O'Driscoll, p. 3.
36 MA, BMH, WS1668, Thomas Hevey, p. 26.
37 MA, BMH, WS1413, Tadhg Kennedy, pp. 99–102. Collins's name has been erased from the statement, but it is certain that Kennedy's statement refers to Collins. Parts of Kennedy's story also appear in a letter from Art O'Murray to John Hagan and are there attributed to Collins: AICR, Hagan papers, HAG1/1921/298, O'Murray to Hagan, 1 June 1921. For accounts of the events described here, see also Dwyer, *Tans*, pp. 305–6, and Annie Ryan, *Comrades. Inside the War of Independence* (Dublin: Liberties Press, 2007), pp. 93–4.
38 This is confirmed by MA, BMH, WS586, Kathleen O'Donovan, p. 2.

walked out of the room. I don't know whether it was [the provincial] or I was in the greater state of fright, but I think I recovered more quickly. I said I would go back and consult again my superior officers, but he may rest assured that I would submit being put against the wall myself before I would do my 'duty' on a priest, no matter how bad the case was.[39]

Apart from Headley's astonishing intervention, the notable aspect of this conversation is that Kennedy did not consider the shooting of a spy-priest in any way an acceptable course of action. It was never appropriate to deal with clergy in the way lay people were dealt with, 'no matter how bad the case was'. In the event, the provincial moved Collins to another priory.[40] When a flying column belonging to the South Tipperary brigade discovered that another priest had informed the crown forces about their activities, they showed similar indulgence. Following this priest's tip-off, the military descended upon the column in its position and the Volunteers only barely managed to get away. Instead of blaming the priest for the betrayal, however, the members of the column in fact attributed their escape to him. One of the veterans testified later that the priest had spent 'the whole day praying in the church without ceasing', and that his intercession had been the cause of their lucky escape.[41]

The examples of intimidation mentioned above show that priests were not always able to oppose the IRA with impunity. Although Peter Hart's judgement that 'clergymen could give information without suspicion or punishment' is not universally true, it is clear that the clerical state counted for a lot when it came to meting out punishment.[42] Priests were never subjected to the kind of treatment that lay persons received under the same circumstances. The IRA was a respecter of persons.

Exchanges

The more common way for sympathisers with the IRA campaign to express their discontent with clerical denunciation was through

39 MA, BMH, WS1413, Tadhg Kennedy, pp. 101–2.
40 *Ibid.*
41 MA, BMH, WS783, Thomas Ryan, pp. 62–3.
42 Peter Hart, *The I.R.A. and its Enemies. Violence and Community in Cork, 1916–1923* (Oxford: Oxford University Press, 1998), p. 303.

public or private criticism. As has been seen, Bishop Kelly of Ross was a habitual target for comments of this nature in the *Catholic Bulletin*.[43] He was mentioned in October 1920 as an example of the 'slavish statements on our national aspirations that have brought unenviable notoriety on many pulpits ... in Ireland'.[44] A few months earlier, Archbishop Gilmartin had received a letter from the prominent Sinn Féiner and Dáil minister Eoin MacNeill protesting against the fact that he had publicly described the killing of two policemen near Tuam as a 'dastardly murder'. MacNeill argued that civilians were entitled to bear arms in defence of Ireland against the British forces. Since the possession of arms was a stated reason for the crown forces to shoot civilians at sight, he contended that it was lawful for anyone carrying arms to shoot the military first, or indeed the police, who were 'a mere branch of the British military forces'. He called on Gilmartin to 'define the extent of resistance that is morally justifiable' and said that the present situation was 'surely not a case for vagueness'. Until the church declared differently, MacNeill believed he was right in protesting against the epithet of '"murder" even without the qualifying adjective'.[45]

Too much clarity was not appreciated either, however, as Bishop Cohalan discovered when he issued his excommunication decree. In a private letter to John Hagan, the Dáil's Parisian and Roman envoy Seán T. Ó Ceallaigh wrote that the decree was 'a horrible and most disgraceful document for which, I am sure, I personally could never forgive him'. Cohalan's 'unmerited and unjust attack on the republican forces should make particularly all Cork people, thoroughly ashamed of their bishop'. Ó Ceallaigh said he would love to have a chance of telling Cohalan 'straight to his face what a cowardly slave and traitor to Ireland' he was, and also mentioned that Bishop Fogarty had been pained by Cohalan's decree.[46] Terence MacSwiney's sister Mary was of the same opinion, and told all the

43 *Catholic Bulletin*, 9:5 (May 1919), pp. 217–19, at p. 218.
44 *Catholic Bulletin*, 10:10 (October 1920), p. 586. For another example of criticism of Kelly, see *Catholic Bulletin*, 11:1 (January 1921), pp. 15–16.
45 Tuam Diocesan Archives, Tuam (hereafter TDA), Thomas Gilmartin papers, B4/8-ii/8, MacNeill to Gilmartin, 22 July 1920.
46 AICR, Hagan papers, HAG1/1920/485, Ó Ceallaigh to Hagan, 23 December 1920.

bishops in December 1920 that Cohalan lacked the 'right power' to excommunicate conscientious Catholics who fought for the republic.[47] She also referred to the recently canonised Joan of Arc to show that those condemned by the bishops in their own day might well be vindicated in the future.

Priests also came under fire in their parishes. The walk-out at mass in Carrickmacross has already been mentioned above. A similar incident took place in a parish in King's County in March 1921. The RIC county inspector claimed that a parish priest's entire congregation walked out of the church one Sunday after he exhorted them to abstain from crime.[48] Priests were also reported to their bishops for being hostile to the IRA. In December 1921, Bishop Charles O'Sullivan of Kerry received a letter from an anonymous person from Causeway near Tralee, who complained that the priests of the local parish had visited the premises of a woman boycotted by the IRA for having been a spy for the crown forces during the War of Independence. O'Sullivan's correspondent protested that Father J. Cahill, the curate, had called those supporting the boycott 'scoundrels'. He wondered whether Cahill's hostility was due to the fact that his 'brother was reduced in the ranks of the IRA'.[49]

Far from indicating a rift between the clergy and republicans, these complaints to bishops reflect the extent to which a rift was avoided, as channels of communication remained open. Moreover, republican priests publicly criticised their more conservative colleagues, thus undermining the image of unanimous ecclesiastical opposition. As has been seen, the killing of an RIC sergeant in Lorrha in September 1919 elicited an emotional condemnation from the local parish priest, Father John Gleeson. Among other things, Gleeson said that

> It is stated – I do not know if it is true – that fifteen men are appointed in each district to shoot the police. I find it extremely

47 UCDA, Mary MacSwiney papers, P48a/192, MacSwiney to bishops, 30 December 1920.
48 TNA, CO904/114, IGMR, March 1921, p.729.
49 KyDA, O'Sullivan papers, 'Parish correspondence', Causeway, anon. to O'Sullivan, 28 December 1921; see also UCDA, Mulcahy papers, P7/A/21, Clifford to Cahill, 9 July 1921, Cahill to Clifford, 10 July 1921, and Clifford to Cahill, 11 July 1921.

difficult to believe that statement, but if there is truth in that statement, the cause which advocates such methods is a doomed cause.[50]

Gleeson's challenge to the legitimacy of physical force, his suggestion that it was orchestrated by a secret organisation and his damning of the cause offended more republican-minded colleagues. In a letter published in the *Irish Independent*, the parish priest of Tober, King's County, took Gleeson to task for his 'insinuations, ... which reflect gravely and unjustifiably ... on Irish character'. Father John Magee did not object to Gleeson's condemnation of the crime, but branded his assumption that the sergeant had been killed by Irishmen 'not only strange, but un-Christian and unpatriotic'. According to Magee, the Irish people were well aware of the church's teachings about the immorality of murder, and Gleeson's implication that some held a different view was 'but a backhanded method of striving to blacken our people'. Magee suggested that Gleeson's mention of the appointment of fifteen men per district to kill police was most likely a rumour that emanated from the Castle. He said the tone of Gleeson's remarks was indicative of the 'remnant of the slave-spirit still present amongst us'. Magee asked whether Gleeson had been motivated by cowardice in choosing to denounce the killing of an officer of the crown rather than that of Irishmen 'coldly murdered by the agents of foreign government'.[51] Gleeson's comments also drew the ire of his own curates. Fathers D. Crowe and B. McMahon wrote to the *Irish Independent* in early October to distance themselves from their parish priest's statement. They explained that they had investigated the truth of the allegation that men had been appointed to murder policemen. After 'mature and earnest investigation', the details of which they unfortunately did not divulge, they came to the conclusion that there was no foundation for such an allegation as far as the parish of Lorrha was concerned.[52] These public protests from priests against their colleagues' condemnations were important as they gave courage to troubled republicans.

It was a matter of some tactical significance for IRA companies to know whether the local clergy were friendly or hostile. One

50 *Irish Catholic*, 13 September 1919.
51 *Irish Independent*, 11 September 1919.
52 *Ibid.*, 10 October 1919.

IRA veteran of the Ballina company in County Mayo, Stephen Donnelly, recalled that in the summer of 1920 'the local clergy had not come out in the open and we did not know how we stood with them'. In order to find out, the company decided that one member would go to confession and state that he had been involved in a recent ambush, to see what the priest would say. Donnelly volunteered and went to confession one Saturday night in the cathedral in Ballina. Father William Greaney, the administrator, told Donnelly that he personally sympathised with the IRA, but that the bishop had made involvement in ambushes a reserved sin, meaning that it could be absolved only by the bishop himself or by a priest specifically delegated for that purpose. As it happened, Bishop James Naughton of Killala was also hearing confessions in the cathedral at the time, and Donnelly was invited to go and see him across the aisle. Naughton told Donnelly that the IRA was a secret society and that he was a murderer, and demanded that he sever his connections with the movement. Donnelly argued with the bishop for nearly two hours. Worn out by these lengthy exchanges, Naughton eventually absolved Donnelly, giving proof to the Ballina company that they could expect forgiveness rather than support.[53] This distinction was an important one. Absolution not only implied but explicitly affirmed that a sin had been committed, as it was conditional upon the penitent's own acknowledgement of his sinfulness. The willingness of hostile clerics to absolve from involvement in IRA violence theoretically reinforced rather than weakened their message of condemnation, because absolution required the penitent's submission. In practice, however, the fact that forgiveness was always available in the sacrament of penance inevitably lessened the urgency of clerical pulpit denunciations. Even though the church did not give moral sanction in advance, it always offered reconciliation afterwards. That was all that some active Volunteers needed.

Just war: theological arguments against the IRA campaign

Despite widespread clerical condemnation of the Soloheadbeg killings in January 1919, by that time retrospective clerical assessment of the Easter rising had become generally quite positive. This

53 MA, BMH, WS1548, Stephen Donnelly, pp. 13–14.

was obviously not very consistent, and conservative critics did not hesitate to point this out to their republican colleagues. Canon O'Donnell of Rathkeale discussed the issue at length in his letter to Rector O'Riordan in Rome in January 1919:

> My contention is that the Easter week rebellion was morally wrong – that consequently it is wrong to approve of it, to praise those who took part in it, especially its instigators [and] leaders ... or to do or say anything that would naturally be interpreted *by your audience* ... as approval of same.[54]

Defenders of the Easter rising's legacy pointed to the American revolution, which, though violent, had brought about much good and was no longer considered by anyone to have been morally wrong. O'Donnell argued, however, that 'if the American revolt was justifiable, it was not its success that made it so, and if the E[aster w[eek] affair was morally wrong this is not because of its failure'. He did not deny that good might come from movements whose beginnings were bad, such as the American revolution, the actions of the Manchester martyrs and even 'the shooting of two policemen near Tipperary recently'. But in line with Catholic moral thinking, O'Donnell contended that the consequences of actions did not determine their moral status. He concluded by observing that 'the spirit of Easter week is still there', and the Sinn Féiners' 'heart is set on a rising'. The people had

> been taught a lesson, by word [and] example, during Easter week, and has that lesson been since 'un-taught' to them? What difference can those poor fellows see between shooting policemen and soldiers in and around Dublin during Easter week, and shooting policemen around Tipperary another week?[55]

The theological arguments advanced by clerics who condemned the Soloheadbeg shootings and subsequent IRA operations hinged on the assertion that the conditions for just war had not been met. Catholic just war theory conceived of war as existing between two sovereign states, defined as nations that constituted public and

---

54 AICR, O'Riordan papers, 19/190/14, O'Donnell to O'Riordan, 30 January 1919. Italics in the original.
55 *Ibid.*

political bodies through their sovereign governments.[56] A state could wage just war against another state only in its own defence, to protect its life, its possessions or its honour.[57] But the state's sovereign power, which alone had the right to declare war, could do so legitimately only if the evils caused by the war were proportionate to the benefits it was likely to yield.[58] Traditional Catholic theology accepted that there were certain forms of offensive war that could be legitimate, such as the reduction to obedience of rebel subjects, or the obtaining of rights conceded by international law but unjustly withheld. Despite appearances, such wars were actually defensive, because they protected the state in question from injustice perpetrated against it by others. Once a *ius ad bellum*, a 'right to war', had been established, the fighting had to proceed according to the principles of the *ius in bello*, the 'law of war'. As wars were military conflicts between *states*, armies could legitimately attack only each other, and it was not permitted to attack citizens of the enemy who were not actively involved in the hostilities.[59]

As Andrew McGrath has shown, theological supporters of the legitimacy of the IRA campaign appealed not to the theory of just war, but to the legitimacy of revolt against tyranny.[60] But critics of the IRA justified their condemnation by reference to the theory of just war, and therefore it demands some attention here. Although these critics clearly felt that they were on firmer ground with this theory than their opponents, there was still ample scope for diverging interpretations. It all depended on how the principles described were applied to the specific situation. One of the contentious issues

---

56 *Ibid.* T. Ortolan, 'Guerre', in A. Vacant, E. Mangenot and É. Amann (eds), *Dictionnaire de théologie catholique contenant l'exposé des doctrines de la théologie catholique, leurs preuves et leur histoire*, vi:2 (Paris: Letouzey et Ané, 1947), pp. 1899–962, at p. 1900. See also Corkery, 'Cohalan', p. 117, and John A. Gallagher, *Time Past, Time Future. An Historical Study of Catholic Moral Theology* (New York and Mahwah, NJ: Paulist Press, 1990), p. 102. I am grateful to Professor Frans Vosman for this reference.
57 Ortolan, 'Guerre', p. 1908.
58 *Ibid.*, p. 1909.
59 *Ibid.*, p. 1929.
60 Andrew McGrath, 'The Anglo-Irish War (1919–1921). Just war or unjust rebellion?', *Irish Theological Quarterly*, 77:1 (2012), pp. 67–82, at p. 68. I am grateful to John Heffernan for this reference.

was whether Ireland was a sovereign state or a subordinate part of another sovereign state; if the former, then its government could legitimately wage war against an unjust foreign aggressor; if the latter, then the government of the larger state had a moral right to suppress the ongoing rebellion. A second issue was whether the violence used by the IRA was proportionate to the ills it sought to remedy, and closely linked to this was the question of whether the simple fact that somebody was a constable was sufficient reason to regard him as a legitimate target for violence.

The most formidable clerical critique of the view that Ireland was a separate state at war with England came in the autumn of 1919, when Father Walter McDonald, professor of theology at Maynooth, published *Some Ethical Questions of Peace and War*. This book was a response to ten 'recent statements made by representative Irish Catholics' asserting the independence of Ireland.[61] McDonald responded specifically to two articles on the 1918 conscription crisis written by two other priests, one a professor of theology and the other a professor of philosophy at Maynooth.[62] McDonald's book was divided into two parts, the first of which, 'Questions of peace', dealt with the issue as to whether Ireland was indeed 'a united and fully independent nation' and whether British rule in Ireland was legitimate or not. The second, 'Questions of war' among other things also discussed the legitimate form of 'pressure that may be applied to secure local self-government' for Ireland.[63]

Though McDonald did not specifically address the IRA campaign that had haphazardly started in January 1919, he cast doubt on many articles of the separatist creed. Thus he argued that Ireland had never been a single, united nation before the Anglo-Norman conquest of the twelfth century. He also contended that the leaders

---

61 McDonald, *Questions*, pp. 3–9.
62 Peter Coffey, 'The conscription menace in Ireland and some issues raised by it', *Irish Ecclesiastical Record*, 11 (1918), pp. 484–98, and Peter Finlay, 'Irish Catholics and conscription', *Irish Independent*, 14 May 1918. See Murphy, *Bulletin*, pp. 259–62 for a discussion of similar debates conducted in the pages of the *Irish Ecclesiastical Record* and the *Irish Theological Quarterly*.
63 'Questions of peace': McDonald, *Questions*, pp. 1–88; 'fully independent nation': *ibid.*, p. 10; 'Questions of war': *ibid.*, pp 89–140; 'legitimate pressure': *ibid.*, p. 106.

of the Irish people had acquiesced in colonial constitutional arrangements and that this acquiescence had established their legitimacy. Having denied that a claim of full Irish independence held any credibility, McDonald went on to defend the implementation of home rule in Ireland:

> Local governments should rule by consent of the majority of those whom they govern; even though these should differ, in politics and otherwise, from the majority of some larger place or kingdom in which the district in question is contained.[64]

This principle, of course, applied also to unionists in Ulster, and McDonald consequently argued in favour of a separate measure of home rule within Ireland for the north-east. Referring to the Easter rising, he then asserted that the use of physical force had been unethical, because it had been used to obtain the illegitimate aim of full independence rather than home rule. Moreover, it treacherously came at a time of great danger for the United Kingdom:

> I cannot see my way to approve of any such active or passive resistance to a government recognised as legitimate as would leave this exposed to be crushed by a powerful foreign enemy with whom it was engaged in a life-and-death struggle at the time. I would press it to grant any measure of home rule which I regarded as due, but not for more than was due; nor even for what was due would I allow any pressure that might seriously endanger the whole commonwealth.[65]

McDonald's book amounted to treason in the eyes of many republicans, and even senior churchmen without sympathy for republican violence viewed its publication as an embarrassment. Monsignor Terence O'Donnell, a vicar general of Archbishop Walsh's, wrote to Walsh after attending a meeting that 'there was a good deal of talk about the book in Maynoot[h] yesterday, and I fear it is likely to create a regular furore'.[66]

While few bishops and priests shared McDonald's enthusiasm for the union or for partition, many agreed with him in rejecting the view that republican violence was legitimate warfare. Another stalwart clerical conservative, Dean Innocent Ryan of Cashel,

---

64 *Ibid.*, p. 68.
65 *Ibid.*, p. 109. Home rule for Ulster: *ibid.*, pp. 69–70.
66 DDA, Walsh papers, 386/6, O'Donnell to Walsh, 21 October 1919.

had in early 1920 condemned the killing of RIC members on the basis of the *ius in bello* principle that non-belligerents must be left untouched. Ryan observed at a meeting of the local temperance society that 'someone or other had said, in justification or palliation of those loathsome deeds, "We are at war with England, and can, therefore, shoot down the upholders of the English law".' He rejected this claim and said that 'if people are justified in killing the props of English rule in Ireland, England's soldiers in our midst would be justified in shooting us'.[67] Bishop Kelly repeated the same argument some months later: 'it took two nations to make war, and if England be at war with Ireland the representatives of England were perfectly justified in shooting down the Irish'. He concluded with the dire observation that 'they depended at the present moment on England, and, if England wanted to conquer them, there was not a man or woman listening to him that would not starve, so that they were entirely in her hands'.[68]

Cardinal Logue addressed the same issue in August 1920 when he commented on a fatal IRA attack on a police patrol in Dundalk. He wrote:

> Am I to be told that this is an act of war? That it is lawful to shoot at sight anyone wearing a policeman's uniform and honestly discharging a policeman's duty? I prefer to call it by its true name – a cool, deliberate, wilful murder, pure and simple.[69]

The most publicised controversy over the just war argument came in December 1920. As has been seen, on 12 December Bishop Cohalan of Cork issued a decree excommunicating all those involved in acts of violence. Two days later, the lord mayor of Cork, Domhnall Ó Ceallachain, and J. J. Walsh, Sinn Féin TD for Cork city, sent a letter to all members of the hierarchy to protest against the decree.[70] Ó Ceallachain and Walsh contended that there was underlying the bishop's action 'a false supposition concerning this nation, which we cannot allow to go unchallenged'. They argued that the bishop's action

---

67 *Irish Catholic*, 7 February 1920.
68 *Ibid.*, 19 June 1920.
69 *Ibid.*, 4 September 1920.
70 DDA, Walsh papers, 380/5, Ó Ceallachain and Walsh, 'Communication to all members of hierarchy', 14 December 1920.

assumes that Ireland is not a nation, a complete political community, with all the rights, powers and functions consequent thereon. He assumes that there is no such thing as an Irish government and an Irish army, that the English invaders have a moral right in this country. Furthermore, he implies that we, as an organised nation, have no right of self-defence, no right after an order of murder, arson and robbery, to strike back the criminals who are attacking us.[71]

Cohalan responded vigorously. In a pastoral letter issued five days later, on the fourth Sunday of Advent, he published the decree a second time. He commented that

> some would like at the present moment ... to divert attention ... from the consequences of the false teachings of persons who should know better, that Ireland is at the moment a sovereign independent state, and that consequently Irishmen have authority to kill English forces and to burn English property in Ireland.[72]

The consequences which Cohalan had in mind were reprisals, such as those inflicted upon his city in recent days: 'Patrick Street is an ugly, and to these teachers, disquieting, consequence of their false and immoral teaching.' Cohalan asked 'why should the corporation ... murmur if punishment is decreed for attempt at murder?'[73]

Cohalan addressed the issue of the moral status of the IRA campaign and of the legitimacy of the Dáil administration at greater length in his next pastoral letter. Pádraig Corkery has shown that Cohalan's argument in the letter accompanying the decree focused mainly on the criterion of proportionality, while his Lenten pastoral of February 1921 stressed the lack of a competent authority in Ireland to declare war on Britain.[74] The February letter stated:

> If Ireland is a sovereign state she has the right to use physical force, but if Ireland is not a sovereign state the physical force policy is unlawful. ... The question is: was the proclamation of an Irish republic by the Sinn Fein members of parliament after the last general election sufficient to constitute Ireland a republic according to our church teaching.

71 *Ibid.*
72 CDA, Cohalan papers, box vi, pastoral letter, 19 December 1920.
73 *Ibid.*
74 Corkery, 'Cohalan', pp. 117–19.

I answer: it was not.... However we may desire the position of absolute independence for our country we cannot hold that the proclamation of Dail Eireann constituted Ireland validly a sovereign state.[75]

The practical importance of these somewhat abstruse theological arguments is demonstrated by the attempts made by republican leaders to 'regularise' the guerrilla war. After Éamon de Valera returned from the United States in December 1920, one of his endeavours was to persuade the Dáil to pass a motion acknowledging the existence of a state of war and taking responsibility for IRA actions.[76] It is also evident from an encounter between the commandant of the IRA's West Connemara brigade and Archbishop Gilmartin in spring 1921. Gilmartin had come to Leenane, County Galway, to administer confirmation to the children of the parish. He asked for the brigade commandant, Peter McDonnell, to meet him in the presbytery later that day. At the meeting, a theological debate ensued between the archbishop and the Volunteer. Gilmartin argued that it was 'a very serious thing' to go out shooting police and military without an official declaration of war. And even if there were a legitimate authority to declare war, the conditions for just war would still not have been met, because there was no realistic chance of success. McDonnell replied that Ireland was in fact at war with England, and that Irishmen who fought the crown forces could morally do so on the basis of their right to self-defence. As regards the reasonable chance of success, McDonnell contended that Belgium's right to defend itself against the overwhelming power of Germany was generally admitted, even though it had had no chance of defeating its adversary. The two men parted amicably, with the archbishop giving McDonnell his blessing.[77] The encounter shows that theological arguments were part of the account which IRA members gave of themselves and their actions.

---

75 *Freeman's Journal*, 7 February 1921.
76 'Acceptance of state of war', *Dáil Éireann Debates*, vol. 1, 11 March 1921 (Parliamentary Debates, historical-debates.oireachtas.ie/D/DT/D.F.C.192103110061.html, accessed 12 August 2010). See Arthur Mitchell, *Revolutionary Government in Ireland. Dáil Éireann 1919–22* (Dublin: Gill and Macmillan, 1995), p. 266.
77 MA, BMH, WS 1612, Peter McDonnell, pp. 29–30.

Sectarianism

Arguably the most emotive historical debate about the War of Independence concerns the allegedly sectarian nature of the conflict. It was sparked off by the late Peter Hart, who argued that the IRA campaign was partly directed at the Protestant religious minority. Although it is undisputed that much of the violence between Protestants and Catholics in Ulster was sectarian in nature, Hart's claim that sectarianism was also 'embedded' in the 'vocabulary and syntax' of the IRA campaign in the south was new.[78] Hart did not argue that this campaign constituted ethnic cleansing and acknowledged both the existence of anti-Catholic violence perpetrated by crown forces and the mitigating effect of the official non-sectarian stance adopted by republican organisations.[79] Nonetheless, his assertion that there was at least an element of sectarianism involved provoked fierce debate.

Given the centrality of confessional identity to this debate, it is surprising that few of the contributors have mentioned the role of priests. The question of whether or not the Catholic clergy put a sectarian gloss on the conflict is germane to the discussion and must be considered here. Tomás Ó Fiaich asserted that clergy in the twenty-six counties were unwavering in their condemnation of the attacks on Protestants which took place in 1920 in the aftermath of anti-Catholic violence in Ulster.[80] Other historians have pointed out, however, that southern bishops and priests did not always do much to prevent the emergence of an anti-Protestant animus. Thus Dermot Keogh has quoted the statement of a Mayo Presbyterian at the time of the truce who told of a local priest who had preached against Protestants and had said that Catholics should treat Protestants as St Patrick had treated the snakes.[81] Such rumours are of course difficult to substantiate. But Archbishop Harty referred in his 1920 Lenten pastoral to the government, which had 'trampled on the will

---

78 Peter Hart, *The I.R.A. at War 1916–1923* (Oxford: Oxford University Press, 2003), p. 240.
79 Hart, *War*, pp. 245–6, and Hart, 'Definition', pp. 24–7 and 29.
80 Ó Fiaich, 'Clergy', p. 490.
81 Keogh, *Vatican*, p. 78.

of the people, and [had] upheld the ascendancy of a pampered minority'.[82]

When attempting to interpret these comments, it is necessary to consider the wider context. Ever since the Counter-Reformation, anti-Protestantism had been part of the very 'DNA' of Catholicism, and this not only in Ireland, but across the globe. The rivalry with Protestantism pervaded Catholic culture and theology. Protestants featured as persecutors and aggressors in standard Catholic perceptions of the past, and vice versa. In Ireland, as elsewhere in countries where ruler and ruled professed different religions, this denominational antagonism inevitably also carried strong political overtones, with confessions functioning as 'communities of identity' rather than purely as rival systems of doctrine.[83] It was the duty of bishops and priests to guard the boundaries of both community and doctrine, and therefore it was incumbent on them to remind Catholics from time to time that the heretics must be converted or, failing that, confounded. But it would be a misinterpretation to construe every uncomplimentary remark made by priests about the rival denomination as an incitement to violence. The criterion for determining whether clerics put a sectarian gloss on the conflict must be formulated more precisely. The issue at stake is whether or not bishops and priests regarded and supported the IRA campaign as a struggle to rid the country of Protestants as well as of the crown forces.

In view of the prevalence of clerical condemnation of the IRA campaign discussed in the previous chapter, it is an unlikely hypothesis that many priests actually viewed matters in this light. There are in fact very few indications that clerics perceived the IRA campaign as a struggle against Protestants, and even fewer that they supported it as such. Bishop Kelly revealed an anxiety about this issue when he said after the killing of a constable in Skibbereen in July 1920 that 'if people could not live in peace with almighty God and their neighbours of different religions and races they are no longer Catholics'.[84] Conversely, perhaps a number of priests in King's County were motivated by religious animosity in April 1921 when they reportedly supported the boycott

---

82 *ICD 1921*, p. 507.
83 R. V. Comerford, *Ireland* (London: Hodder Arnold, 2003), p. 119.
84 *Irish Catholic*, 31 July 1920.

of Protestant families in part of the county.[85] Other instances of priestly encouragement of sectarianism have not come to light in the research for this book. The most striking feature of clerical commentary in this regard is the fact that even priests who strongly condemned IRA violence rarely raised the charge of sectarianism. According to the newspapers, Father Florence McCarthy, administrator of Skibbereen pro-cathedral, 'strongly condemned' the killing of a Protestant who had had 'some relations with the crown authorities' in February 1921, but without alleging that the killing had been inspired by sectarian motives.[86] And in County Leitrim, a priest who was asked for advice by a Protestant accused of being an informer called for restraint on the part of the IRA without mentioning sectarianism. Having told the man somewhat pointlessly that 'his conscience must be his guide', the priest said at mass the following Sunday that the leaders of Sinn Féin and the IRA must not do anything 'without giving it very serious consideration first'. If this message was indeed intended to discourage retribution, it was not very effective, and the accused man was shot dead.[87] Given that priests like McCarthy and others were willing to condemn IRA violence, the most obvious explanation for their silence on the issue of sectarianism is that they did not believe that killings of Protestant 'informers' amounted to 'ethnically targeted violence'.[88]

This argument is strengthened by the fact that when Protestant churches or clergymen were attacked, Catholic priests condemned such incidents as violations of sacred places and persons rather than as acts of sectarianism directed specifically at Protestants. This approach implied the existence of a shared respectability that united citizens of both religions against 'vandals', precluding the possibility of making common cause with the attackers on denominational grounds. Thus when the Protestant church in Glenville, County Cork, was broken into in December 1919, the parish priest presided over a meeting of Catholics which passed a resolution condemning the crime.[89] And when a Protestant church in Navan,

85 TNA, CO904/115, IGMR, April 1921, p. 10.
86 *Irish Independent*, 21 February 1921.
87 MA, BMH, WS1263, Charles Pinkman, p. 13.
88 Hanley, 'Terror', p. 12.
89 *Irish Catholic*, 13 December 1919.

County Meath, suffered the same fate, with various parts of the inventory being vandalised in May 1920, a local priest, Father W. Gleeson, referred to the incident at a mission in his parish the next day. He condemned the deed strongly and, on his own behalf and on behalf of the Catholics of Navan, tendered his sympathy with the rector and his congregation.[90]

Catholic priests also condemned the killing in June 1921 of a Protestant clergyman in Bawnboy, County Cavan. In the early hours of 12 June, a group of armed men called at the house of the octogenarian dean of Leighlin, James Finlay. According to a statement made by the chief secretary, Sir Hamar Greenwood, in the House of Commons, the group told the residents to leave. When Dean Finlay's wife returned to the scene some hours later, she found the house completely burned down and her husband dead on the lawn, felled by what appeared to have been a gunshot to the back of the head.[91] On the subsequent Sunday at mass, Father Terence Brady, parish priest of Templeport, County Cavan, denounced the killing, saying that 'where violence was committed, he would condemn it'. He knew that crimes were committed by both sides, but there were circumstances to this case which could not be overlooked: 'the victim ... was an old man, kind and charitable to his Catholic neighbours, and the gravity of the crime made it heinous'.[92] Brady and Father Patrick O'Reilly, parish priest of Swanlinbar, were present at Finlay's burial and wrote a public letter together with Father John McGovern, parish priest of Curlough. The three priests expressed their horror and indignation at the murder and said that they 'imagined [Finlay's] age, his venerable appearance, his kindly relations with everyone in the locality, and, above all, his profession would have saved him from such a sad fate'. They also disassociated their parishioners from the killing, adding that 'such was the respect in which Dean Finlay was held that there is not a single neighbour of his

---

90 *Ibid.*, 8 May 1920.
91 Sir Hamar Greenwood, 16 June 1921, Hansard, series 5 (Commons), cxliii, col. 572. Padraic O'Farrell suggests that there are reasons to believe the killing was an accident: Padraic O'Farrell, *Who's Who in the Irish War of Independence and Civil War 1916–1923* (Dublin: Lilliput Press, 1997), p. 33.
92 *Irish Independent*, 22 June 1921.

who does not view the crime with the same horror as we'.[93] The reference to Finlay's profession is significant, as it shows that the three priests felt a bond with him on the basis of their shared clerical status. It was convenient for Catholic priests to defend the inviolability of clerics and church buildings of whatever denomination. By taking this approach, however, they simultaneously ruled out the sectarian view that the Catholic cause was somehow served by such attacks.

Coverage of sectarian violence in Ulster occasionally caused clerics in the south to warn Catholics to treat Protestants respectfully: an indication that they thought their parishioners were susceptible to sectarian emotions, as well as evidence that they discouraged these. The fact that these warnings often came in the backhanded form of comparisons with the harsh treatment of Catholics in Ulster does not change this, even if it may not have given much comfort to southern Protestants. Thus Archbishop Gilmartin congratulated his congregation in Tuam cathedral in July 1920 on the 'magnificent patience and restraint they had shown' and said that he hoped that, despite the 'fatal and raging bigotry' manifested by the Orangemen in the north, 'no Catholic would dream of insulting a non-Catholic neighbour'. He added that 'religious bigotry would eventually bring about its own defeat and disgrace'.[94] Sometimes priests addressed southern unionists directly. In August 1920, Father Richard Cohalan, parish priest of Bray, County Wicklow, appealed to unionists to remember the contrast between the treatment of Catholic workmen by their Protestant employers in Belfast and the support given to Protestant merchants in Bray by Catholic patrons. 'He appealed to them to give expression to the generous and tolerant support they receive from the Catholics of the district, and also to throw in their lot with the unionists of the other parts of southern Ireland.'[95] Priests also supported the general boycott of goods from Belfast instituted by the Dáil in the same month in response to attacks on Catholics in Lisburn, County Antrim.[96] On a more magnanimous note, James Canon Halpin, parish priest of Tulla, County Clare, told

---

93 *Irish Catholic*, 25 June 1921. *ICD 1921* has McGovern as 'McGauran', p. 172.
94 *Irish Catholic*, 31 July 1921.
95 *Ibid.*, 21 August 1920.
96 TNA, CO904/114, IGMR, February 1921, p. 380.

his parishioners in October 1920 that 'they must be tolerant and broad-minded to those who differed from them, in spite of the example of another part of Ireland'.[97]

Violence in Ulster was not limited to the guerrilla struggle but also involved widespread rioting between the two communities. Catholic clerics often took a conciliatory approach. In April 1920 Cardinal Logue expressed his horror at the fact that Sinn Féin colours had been painted on a pillar at the entrance to the Church of Ireland cathedral in Armagh. He condemned the 'flagrant outrage' and deplored the fact that not even religious edifices had been spared the vandalism of 'reckless characters, to whom nothing is sacred'. He prided himself on the fact that he had always 'by precept and example [tried] to encourage and maintain peace, charity, goodwill and neighbourly feeling ... among the people of every denomination'. Logue's message was unambiguous: 'we have misery enough without the added curse of sectarian strife'.[98] And Father James O'Boyle, parish priest of Ballymoney, County Antrim, told a group of parishioners in November 1920 that his relations with his non-Catholic neighbours had always been cordial and that 'he could never forget their generosity'. He praised the local Orange lodge because its band had always stopped playing when parading past his church while devotions were in progress.[99]

Despite these irenic examples, the upsurge of sectarianism in Ulster also affected the clergy, although there is little reason to regard priests as agitators. Unflattering comments about Protestants in general and Orangemen in particular in the house chronicles of Clonard Redemptorist monastery in Belfast are probably typical for the clerical mood in 1920 and 1921. When recording a mission given by Clonard priests in Aldergrove, County Antrim, the chronicler wrote that 'this portion of the parish [of Glenavy] is still more Protestant than Glenavy itself, but thanks be to God, the Catholics are getting the upper hand; farms formerly held by Protestants are being bought up by Catholics to a large extent'.[100] And his account in July 1921 of the sectarian rioting that engulfed the flashpoint

97 *Irish Catholic*, 9 October 1920.
98 *Ibid.*, 17 April 1920.
99 *Ibid.*, 6 November 1920.
100 Clonard Redemptorist Monastery Domestic Archive, Belfast (hereafter CMA), book A, 'Missionary works 1896–1924', p. 403.

area where Clonard was situated contained numerous references to 'Orange murder gangs' and 'scoundrels'.[101] But these records were private documents not accessible to members of the public. Besides, one Clonard Redemptorist had recently been killed, possibly by Orangemen, and this did not inspire ecumenical feelings in the surviving members of community.

Impact of condemnations on republicans

Volunteers who had already become involved in the guerrilla war were rarely dissuaded by clerical denunciation, although their reaction varied from breezy dismissal to the anguished decision to proceed despite a guilty conscience.[102] In his 1936 book *On Another Man's Wound*, Ernie O'Malley recounted a conversation he had with Liam Lynch about Cohalan's excommunication decree. Lynch was the commandant of the IRA's North Cork brigade and had discussed plans with O'Malley to include the Mid Cork brigade in a new southern division. North Cork brigade territory consisted mainly of areas in the diocese of Cloyne, but Mid Cork brigade territory lay mostly in the diocese of Cork.[103] O'Malley jested that Lynch would be excommunicated when he took Mid Cork into the division. Lynch laughed and replied that 'old Cohalan had dinner with [General Strickland] I suppose, before he took the pen in his fist, but nobody minds him now'.[104]

Tom Barry's 1949 memoir *Guerrilla Days in Ireland* contained no such flippancy. 'Let nobody minimise the gravity of such a decree in a Catholic country', he wrote, adding that his own reaction was one of anger. 'For days I brooded over the decree, knowing full well how deeply religious the IRA were.' This remark suggests that

101 CMA, 'Domestic Chronicle 1896–1930', pp. 318–19.
102 Augusteijn, *Defiance*, p. 308: 'Most Volunteers were … unaffected by the condemnation of their actions by certain sections of the church.' Most of the statements Augusteijn quotes appear to refer to the Civil War.
103 For the territorial descriptions of the Cork IRA brigades see Hart, *Enemies*, p. 53.
104 Ernie O'Malley, *On Another Man's Wound* (2nd edn; Dublin: Mercier Press, 2002), p. 340. General Sir Peter Strickland was the military commander of the British army in Cork.

Barry was more concerned about his comrades' response than about the moral implications for himself. He claimed that these concerns were unfounded, as all 'active service men' in his brigade persisted in the fight as well as in the practice of their religion, aided by priests who continued to administer the sacraments.[105] A month later, Barry and some other leading IRA members went on an inspection tour of various companies in the brigade, to examine, among other things, the effects of Cohalan's decree. The men were given the opportunity to step from the ranks at parade and leave 'if they had any religious scruples about carrying on'.[106] None did so, but it would be wrong to conclude that the decree was ignored completely. One veteran member of the West Cork brigade remembered that there 'was a change in the officers of Schull company' after Cohalan's decree, as two lieutenants had resigned.[107]

The issue was not so urgent for the IRA outside Cork, on the one hand because the excommunication decree did not apply there, and on the other because the fighting was often less intense. Sinéad Joy has observed that 'most IRA veterans [in Kerry] hotly deny that they ever allowed themselves to be intimidated by the local clergy'.[108] And in his 1924 memoir *My Fight for Irish Freedom*, the Tipperary IRA man Dan Breen quoted a local priest who had condemned IRA violence. 'Such were the things said about us', he commented, 'but we kept on our course.'[109] Similarly, Sean O'Neill, adjutant in the Tuam battalion, recalled that clerical condemnation had caused him trouble, although it made him think about giving up his religion rather than his fighting, but eventually he overcame his misgivings. He described sitting in Mountbellew church listening to 'a serious and solemn condemnation of the organisation of which I was a member', feeling that everyone 'was pointing at me and saying, "There he is, that fellow with the long mop of hair who works in Kenny's!"' Such denunciations from the pulpit were

---

105 Tom Barry, *Guerrilla Days in Ireland* (reprint; Dublin: Anvil Books, 1989), p. 57.
106 *Ibid.*, p. 67. See also Kautt, *Ambushes*, p. 113.
107 MA, BMH, WS1519, Charlie Cotter.
108 Sinéad Joy, *The IRA in Kerry 1916–1921* (Cork: Collins Press, 2005), p. 74.
109 Dan Breen, *My Fight for Irish Freedom* (revised edn; Dublin: Anvil Books, 1989), p. 40.

'almost too much for me and at times I felt like leaving the church'. As has been seen, the IRA was worried about press coverage of clerical condemnations. O'Neill's primary concern was not so much that these might affect the Volunteers, but that they 'tended to weaken the morale of some of our supporters'. Press reports about priests denouncing republican violence could easily make the 'simple countryman' wonder 'who is right and who is wrong'.[110]

For those Volunteers who had not become guerrilla fighters and for potential recruits, clerical opposition may well have been a factor in dissuading them from becoming active or from joining. Young men certainly consulted priests about the morality of joining. The parish priest of Waterside, Derry, wrote in September 1920 to Archbishop Walsh asking him what the moral status was of the IRA in the eyes of the church, because 'certain individuals' had asked him if they could join the organisation with a safe conscience.[111] Presumably these individuals attached some weight to the answers they received. And Michael Sheerin, officer of the Derry IRA and member of a flying column in Donegal, recalled that one of the main problems his brigade faced in Derry was the 'serious opposition to our military activities from the Catholic church'. He estimated that only three Derry priests 'showed any interest in the republican movement', and the clergy had 'severely censored' him and his men after they had attacked RIC men while a novena for peace was being held in the cathedral.[112] The fact that Sheerin regarded this as a problem shows that clerical opposition could hamper the IRA, even if it could not suppress the organisation.

---

110 MA, BMH, WS1219, Sean O'Neill, p. 67.
111 DDA, Walsh papers, 380/2, MacFeely to Walsh, 28 September 1920.
112 MA, BMH, WS803, Michael Sheerin, p. 10.

II
Republican priests

4

Sinn Féin priests: support for Sinn Féin, the Dáil and local IRA units

As Part I of this book has shown, a section of the clergy retained its support for the Irish Parliamentary Party even after the major political transformation that followed the Easter rising. But many priests did what the majority of the lay population did, and changed their allegiance to Sinn Féin. Ó Fiaich has plausibly argued that this change was most striking among a new generation of priests trained at Maynooth in the years during which the Gaelic revival was promoted there by such influential and controversial figures as Professors Eugene O'Growney and Michael O'Hickey.[1] These republican priests came in many guises, and the most common type was the 'Sinn Féin priest', not the 'IRA priest'. For most the transformation did not entail a shift to a revolutionary outlook. Instead, it meant changing their political point of view from the demand for home rule to the philosophy of Sinn Féin. This philosophy, enunciated by Arthur Griffith and essentially retained after the overhaul of the party in October 1917, consisted of abstention from Westminster and the immediate establishment of the apparatus of an independent Irish state. This non-violent, if not therefore constitutional, objective of Sinn Féin was the aspect of the 'new politics' that was most acceptable to the clergy, and many priests moved quickly to gain a stake in it.[2]

For many of them, investing in the building-up of the republican political movement became a way of exercising control over young men who otherwise might espouse 'wild' notions of fighting the British forces. Many clerics contrasted the work of Sinn Féin favourably with the activities of the IRA. When the IRA carried

1 Ó Fiaich, 'Clergy', p. 480.
2 'New politics': Fitzpatrick, *Politics*, p. 105.

out a failed attempt to assassinate the lord lieutenant in December 1919, Archbishop Walsh of Dublin wrote a public letter asking whether there was anyone

> capable of deluding himself into the belief that such a method of seeking redress ... is likely to help on the efforts of the righteous men who are working earnestly with the single purpose of re-establishing in our country the reign of liberty and justice?[3]

And Bishop Edward Mulhern of Dromore told Father John Hagan in March 1920 that 'at last ... it must come home even to those unwilling to believe that to be an Irish patriot one need not indulge in outrage'.[4] As some Volunteers became radicalised and turned into guerrilla fighters during the course of 1920, a number of priests who had strong connections with them also became radicalised. But more often than not, IRA units remained inactive, especially outside Dublin and Munster, and the patterns of clerical involvement that had been established in 1919 continued. This chapter looks at the support for the political aspect of the republican movement and for those sections of the IRA that did not become active in the guerrilla struggle.

Supporting the party

The conscription crisis of 1918 had been an important moment in the rapprochement between the clergy and Sinn Féin. From that moment on, republicans fully realised the value of priestly support. During the campaign for the December 1918 elections, party members made a point of canvassing the clerical vote. The superior of the Jesuit community at Milltown Park, Dublin, Father Martin Maher, wrote to his provincial in December 1918 that 'canvassers have been here [and] have shown lists indicating the views of various members of the community'. The canvassers had asked that those priests who had left Milltown but were still on the register should be recalled to vote and offered that travel expenses would be paid by Sinn Féin. They also stated that 'the members of the other

---

3 DDA, Walsh papers, 386, Circular letter to the parish priests of the archdiocese of Dublin, newspaper cutting.
4 AICR, Hagan papers, HAG1/1920/241, Mulhern to Hagan, 22 March 1920.

orders in the division – Carmelites, C.S.Sp. [Holy Ghost Fathers], C.Ss.R. [Redemptorists] –, were to vote [and] presumably in favour of S[inn] F[éin]'.[5]

Police interest in clerical support for Sinn Féin had been in evidence from shortly after the 1916 rising, and it continued during the War of Independence.[6] In his monthly report for January 1919, the RIC inspector general wrote that a curate in County Galway, 'a mischievous Sinn Feiner, was recently transferred at two days notice by the bishop who directed the local clergy to warn their parishioners against joining secret societies'.[7] There were many more police reports about Sinn Féin priests. Collections for Sinn Féin were held at church doors in early 1919, and leaflets with republican messages were handed out at churches on Sundays. As Chapter 1 has suggested, such actions did not take place without at least the tacit approval of the parish clergy, and they can therefore serve as evidence of clerical support for the party. A police report from March 1919 shows that posters in Arklow, County Wicklow, announced that a collection would be made outside the Catholic church on a stated date 'to promote the independence of Ireland and that a S[inn] Fein meeting would be held' later on the same day. Three tables were set up at the church railings for the collection.[8] Similarly, leaflets explaining how 'the English murderer' went about his business were handed out outside Rathfarnham church, Dublin, after 11.30 mass on a Sunday in March 1919.[9]

In early 1919 there was still much left of the funds that had been collected in the previous year to finance the anti-conscription campaign. Parish priests were the local trustees. Very soon Sinn Féin and the local parish became competing contenders for the redirection of this money.[10] The RIC inspector general reported in June 1919 that the church was winning this struggle for possession of the fund, which consisted of about £250,000.[11] According to him as much as

5 IJA, Milltown Park papers, FM/MILL/75, Maher to Nolan, 8 December 1918.
6 Aan de Wiel, *Church*, p. 99.
7 TNA, CO904/108, IGMR, January 1919, p. 17.
8 TNA, WO35/65/1, Police report by C. D. Murphy, 23 March 1919.
9 TNA, WO35/104.
10 Mitchell, *Government*, pp. 57–65.
11 TNA, CO904/109, IGMR, May 1919, p. 11.

£164,000 of this money had been returned to the subscribers, 'or applied with their consent to ecclesiastical charities'. He contended that no more than £17,000 had been handed over to Sinn Féin, and this only because Sinn Féin representatives had been present when the money was being returned to the subscribers.[12] It is indeed clear that much of the money went to the church. Thus Bishop Cohalan appealed to the Catholics of his diocese to divert their subscriptions to a fund for the erection of a new cathedral, arguing that subscribers would somehow help to 'perpetuate the memory of the national opposition to conscription' by doing so.[13]

But this was not a universal practice. Father Matthew Ryan, parish priest of Knockavilla, County Tipperary, wrote to Father Michael O'Flanagan in March 1919 that 'my parishioners and I regard Dáil Éireann as the legitimate custodian and disburser of national funds'. He therefore sent a cheque for the remainder of the anti-conscription funds collected in his parish.[14] And Bishop Thomas O'Doherty of Clonfert refused to let his priests ask that parishioners should redirect their subscriptions to the church. Father Bernard Bowes, parish priest of Tynagh and Killeen, County Galway, explained to O'Doherty in December 1919 that a priest in his parish had told the congregation that they could ask for their money back, but that if they did not, it would be used to improve the curate's residence in Tynagh or the church in Killeen. O'Doherty overruled the priest and 'ordered the money to be distributed'.[15] Once distributed, these funds could still end up being given to Sinn Féin. Many republican priests were active in persuading parishioners to take this course of action. Father James Bergin, parish priest of Phillipstown, County Carlow, said in March 1919 that he would be handing over the £9 that he got back from the anti-conscription fund to the 'self-determination fund' set up by the Dáil, 'and he hoped all in the parish would do the same'.[16]

In April 1919 the Dáil announced the sale of bonds in order to

12 *Ibid.*, p. 12.
13 *The Irish Catholic Directory and Almanac for 1920 with Complete Directory in English* (Dublin: James Duffy, 1920), p. 498.
14 *Irish Independent*, 5 March 1919.
15 Clonfert Diocesan Archives, Loughrea (hereafter CtDA), Thomas O'Doherty papers, xii.c.23, Bowes to O'Doherty, 12 December 1919.
16 *Irish Independent*, 26 March 1919.

obtain further revenue, and priests and bishops were among the investors. Thus Father Thomas Wall, curate in Drumcollogher, County Limerick, and a stalwart republican, purchased bonds to the tune of £20 in October 1919.[17] Father John Madden, curate in Ballinasloe, County Galway, arranged to have a public meeting in support of the loan on the last day of the town's October horse fair in 1919. The RIC county inspector reported that 'the meeting was proclaimed [and] Father Madden was warned accordingly, but he disregarded the warning and attempted to hold it', prompting the police to disperse the crowds with a baton charge.[18]

As Father Madden had realised, the loan campaign was an excellent opportunity to publicise support for the republican cause, and several bishops also made public subscriptions. In November 1919, Archbishop Walsh wrote a letter to the archbishop of Boston in which he announced his contribution, and Archbishop Harty followed suit in January 1920.[19] Religious communities also contributed. At a house consultation in Clonard monastery, Belfast, in December 1919, 'it was decided to give £10. to the Irish national loan'.[20] And Father William O'Kennedy, president of St Flannan's College, Ennis, County Clare, did more than contribute: he acted as the collector for Dáil loan monies in the East Clare constituency. A member of staff in the college recalled later that 'it was in moments of anxiety that thousands and thousands of pounds were checked, counted and consigned to hiding places before the ultimate transfer to Michael Collins'.[21] O'Kennedy was no exception. Kevin O'Shiel, a Dáil official, claimed that in North Fermanagh, the loan 'would have fallen far short of the figure it reached had the younger clergy not taken the active part they did in collecting it'.[22]

---

17 MA, BMH, contemporary document (hereafter CD), 323/5/1, Thomas Wall, Receipt, 26 October 1919.
18 TNA, CO904/110, IGMR, October 1919, p. 384.
19 Walsh: MA, BMH, WS538, Michael Browne, pp. 3–4; Harty: *Irish Catholic*, 31 January 1920.
20 CMA, box G, 'House administration I', 'House consultation 1916–1950', 19 December 1919.
21 Aodh Ó Haichir, *A Rebel Churchman. Very Rev. Canon William O'Kennedy, B.D., St. Flannan's, Ennis* (Tralee: The Kerryman, 1962), p. 4.
22 MA, BMH, WS1770, Kevin O'Shiel, p. 866.

As the Ballinasloe incident illustrates, republican meetings were often banned by the British authorities. Deciding to attend such meetings anyway was a way for priests to show public support for the republican movement. Local clergy presided over many illegal *aeridheachta*.[23] These meetings were ostensibly cultural events, but had a strongly political character. Priests also attended Sinn Féin gatherings that had been banned. In April 1919, the Sinn Féin hall in Caltra, County Galway, was closed under Defence of the Realm Act regulations. Two months later the name of the local curate, Father Malachy Brennan, topped a police list of twelve people who had entered the building in breach of the order.[24] A fortnight later, Brennan and seven others were again found on the premises, only to be apprehended in the same place again a month later. This time Brennan was in the presence of Father Martin Kielty, his parish priest, and Father Michael O'Flanagan.[25] It is no surprise to find the county inspector of Galway East Riding breathing a sigh of relief in November 1920 when Brennan had been moved to a parish outside the county.[26]

After the party was proscribed in the whole country in November 1919 and as violence flared up, all Sinn Féin activists, including Sinn Féin priests, increasingly faced the risk of arrest and prosecution. When a military patrol arrived at the Sinn Féin hall in Crogan, County Roscommon, one afternoon in October 1920, it found a group of people leaving the building and a number of others still inside, including two local curates, Fathers James Roddy of Breedogue and J. Glynn of Drumlion. Father Glynn declared that they had merely come to the meeting to hear what was going on, and to prevent the people getting out of hand, but they were arrested anyway. Roddy and Glynn were convicted of having been present at a proscribed meeting, although they were released without sentence.[27] And when Arthur Griffith and Eoin MacNeill were arrested in November 1920, the prominent Jesuit Father William Delaney complained that the arrests 'make me somewhat

23 For one example see *Irish Independent*, 10 June 1919.
24 TNA, WO35/98.
25 *Ibid.*
26 TNA, CO904/113, IGMR, October 1920, pp. 12 and 167.
27 TNA, WO35/131.

anxious about one of our fathers who made himself auspicious in championing MacNeill'.[28]

As support for the proscribed institutions became more dangerous, clerical endorsement of Sinn Féin became accordingly more meaningful. Republican priests were exposing themselves to danger by supporting the party, and this sometimes made them more amenable to further radicalisation. Sinn Féin leaders and members of the Dáil administration frequently availed themselves of the clandestine hospitality of the clergy. Éamon de Valera was famously given shelter in the gate lodge at the archbishop's house in Drumcondra in February 1919.[29] And Michael Collins and William Cosgrave stayed in the Oblate reformatory school in Glencree, County Wicklow, and in Terenure College, Dublin.[30] Similarly, Father Patrick Doyle, rector of Knockbeg College, County Carlow, recorded frequent visits by the Dáil minister Kevin O'Higgins.[31]

Members of the party

Priests not only supported Sinn Féin activities; they also became members and officials of the party. The most famous of these was doubtless the Elphin priest Father Michael O'Flanagan, appointed vice-president in 1917. O'Flanagan had been a curate in Crossna, County Roscommon, until his flouting of canonical statutes concerning attendance at political meetings caused him to be suspended from his priestly faculties in July 1918. After having spent some time in Dublin, he was reconciled with his bishop in the summer of 1919 and returned to parish work in Roscommon town, although he continued his activities for Sinn Féin.[32] He was regarded as a moderate in the Sinn Féin leadership. His endeavours during the War of Independence most notably included an

---

28 DDA, Walsh papers, 380/3, Delaney to Walsh, 27 November 1920.
29 MA, BMH, CD131/3/4, Michael Curran.
30 Cosgrave: MA, BMH, WS889, James Kavanagh, p. 133; Collins: Fergus A. D'Arcy, *Terenure College 1860–2010. A History* (Dublin: Terenure College, 2009), p. 140.
31 MA, BMH, WS807, Patrick Doyle, pp. 15–20.
32 Denis Carroll, *They have Fooled you Again. Michael O'Flanagan (1876–1942). Priest, Republican, Social Critic* (Blackrock: Columba Press, 1993), pp. 104–6.

ill-advised overture to the British government in December 1920 and January 1921, which lost him much credit with his colleagues in the party.[33] O'Flanagan was not the only priest to take up senior office in Sinn Féin. Father Patrick Gaynor, Killaloe diocesan schools examiner, was a member of both the national executive council and the standing committee. He was also the chairman of the North Tipperary constituency executive, although he resigned from this position when he was appointed curate in Mullagh, County Clare, in March 1920.[34]

Many priests became active in leading positions in the party at county and parish levels. Michael Laffan has observed that in 1917 most local Sinn Féin clubs in County Clare were presided over by priests.[35] He has also drawn attention to a list of constituency executives composed by the party leadership in January and February 1920, giving an overview of party officials at constituency level.[36] Twenty-four out of eighty-seven constituency executives were presided over by priests, twenty of whom were curates and four parish priests or administrators. Twenty-one other priests – again mostly curates – served as vice-presidents, treasurers and delegates to the national executive. Laffan has noted that priests were proportionally overrepresented in the higher echelons of the party hierarchy: 'if the clergy held any positions in the party, they tended disproportionately to assume the most senior and honorific posts'.[37] Clerical presence in Sinn Féin constituency executives was especially strong in Counties Galway and Clare, with six priests serving on the Galway executives and five on the Clare executives. Otherwise, there were priests on executives in all Ulster and Connacht counties, but only in a few Munster and Leinster counties.

On an even smaller scale, priests were chairmen of Sinn Féin

---

33 Murray, *Oracles*, pp. 156–60.
34 Eamonn Gaynor (ed.), *Memoirs of a Tipperary Family. The Gaynors of Tyone 1887–2000* (Dublin: Geography Publications, n.d.), p. 11. The date of his transfer appears in National Library of Ireland, Dublin (hereafter NLI), MS 5649, List of Sinn Féin officers.
35 Michael Laffan, *The Resurrection of Ireland. The Sinn Féin Party, 1916–1923* (Cambridge: Cambridge University Press, 1999), p. 199.
36 NLI, MS 5649, List of Sinn Féin officers. See Laffan, *Resurrection*, p. 199.
37 Laffan, *Resurrection*, p. 199.

clubs at parish level. Thus Father Doyle, later rector of Knockbeg College, was president of the Naas Sinn Féin club while he was a curate there, and Father Terence Caulfield, curate in Belcoo, County Fermanagh, was described by the *Irish Independent* in September 1919 as a Sinn Féin leader, meaning that he chaired the local party club.[38] Laffan has argued that this involvement 'often represented little more than yet another example of the deference shown to the clergy by a pious people'.[39] As the 'obvious [leaders] of the community', priests were often naturally invited to take up the leadership of the local Sinn Féin club. It also shows that clerical support for republicanism was a matter of securing power in the new political order.

Republican courts

An important part of the Sinn Féin policy of setting up an alternative government in Ireland was the introduction of republican courts. Although arbitration courts had featured on the agenda of the newly established Dáil ministry of home affairs in 1919, they were eventually not imposed from Dublin but established from below.[40] Writing about County Meath, Raé Kearns has observed a distinction between courts run by the Dáil and courts run by the IRA, with priests serving on the former but not the latter.[41] As will be seen, priests who joined IRA companies also occasionally served on IRA courts-martial, but it was more common for priests to serve as judges in Dáil courts. Thus two priests were arrested by the military in Claremorris, County Mayo, in October 1920 during the sitting of a republican court. The Cong curate Father Michael Carney and the Williamstown curate Father J. Burke were among the justices arrested, while litigants, lawyers and solicitors were also

---

38 Doyle: NLI, Patrick Doyle papers, MS 13,561/5; Caulfield: *Irish Independent*, 13 September 1919.
39 Laffan, *Resurrection*, pp. 198–9.
40 Mary Kotsonouris, 'The courts of Dáil Éireann', in Brian Farrell (ed.), *The Creation of the Dáil. A Volume of Essays from the Thomas Davis Lectures* (Dublin: Blackwater Press, 1994), pp. 91–106, at p. 92.
41 Raé Kearns, 'Republican justice in Meath 1919–1922', *Ríocht na Midhe. Records of Meath Archaeological and Historical Society*, 9:2 (1996), pp. 154–63, at p. 163.

apprehended.[42] And when Father Malachy Brennan of Ballinasloe was transferred to another parish outside the county in the same month, the county inspector reported that he had been president of Ballinasloe Sinn Féin court.[43] According to an *Irish Independent* report of October 1920, when a 'lorry-load of men' – presumably Black and Tans or Auxiliaries – visited the village of Duagh, County Kerry, they accosted Father Florence Harrington, the local curate, and asked whether he was the president of the local republican court.[44] Harrington replied in the affirmative, and was told that it would be 'serious' for him if he did not give up the position.[45]

As with leadership positions in local Sinn Féin clubs, the choice of a priest to serve as judge reflected both the social position of clergy and the desire of priests to gain a foothold in the institutions of the 'new order'. Some confusion emerged in the summer of 1920 about whether ecclesiastical legislation prevented priests from serving on arbitration courts. The *Irish Independent* reported in July that Bishop William Codd of Ferns had 'prohibited the clergy of his diocese from taking part in the people's arbitration courts'.[46] The next day it carried a rectification: 'no special prohibition of any kind, said His Lordship, was needed or issued'.[47] The question resurfaced in Galway in August. Archdeacon Patrick Kilkenny, parish priest of Claremorris, was asked to attend a convention for the purpose of establishing Sinn Féin courts, but refused on the grounds that 'recent ecclesiastical legislation' barred him from doing so.[48] Some industrious journalist decided to ask Kilkenny's bishop, Gilmartin, whether this was true. The *Irish Catholic* published the archbishop's response a week later: '[Gilmartin] ... said

---

42 *Irish Independent*, 12 October 1920. For other examples, see MA, BMH, WS1213, Timothy O'Shea, p. 4.
43 TNA, CO904/113, IGMR, October 1920, pp. 12 and 167. Brennan was also the chairman of Sinn Féin in East Galway: see Timothy G. McMahon (ed.), *Pádraig Ó Fathaigh's War of Independence. Recollections of a Galway Gaelic Leaguer* (Cork: Cork University Press, 2000), p. 16.
44 *Irish Independent*, 21 October 1920. See also *Catholic Bulletin*, 10:11 (November 1920), pp. 650–1.
45 See also Leeson, *Black and Tans*, p. 164.
46 *Irish Independent*, 20 July 1920.
47 *Ibid.*, 21 July 1920.
48 *Irish Catholic*, 7 August 1920.

he had issued no regulation whatsoever forbidding priests to take part in arbitration courts. He had left it to the discretion of each priest to do what he thought was best in each case.'[49] Kilkenny was probably reluctant to become involved for political reasons – or out of fear – and therefore pleaded canonical impediments. Another priest, Father Thomas Larkin, curate in Tynagh, County Galway, was willing to lend his car to bring two defendants to a court, but only on condition that the Volunteers would first pretend to hold him up on the road and 'commandeer' the vehicle. Larkin was willing to help, but not to be seen to be helping.[50]

The issue of ecclesiastical permission was addressed by Ireland's main clerical publication, the *Irish Ecclesiastical Record*, in its canonical questions and answers section in 1921. According to the canon law expert Professor Jeremiah Kinane of Maynooth, the new *Code of Canon Law* prohibited priests from assuming the office of judge in a civil court without an 'indult' or special permit from the Holy See. Skilled in the art of casuistry, however, he added that it was 'the *office* of judge in the civil courts that is banned', and not the acting as judge 'by special appointment in individual cases'. Moreover, Kinane argued that 'an arbitrator is not a judge, nor does he exercise jurisdiction in the strict sense'.[51] The relevant canon therefore did not prohibit the participation of priests in arbitration courts. Both hierarchy and canonists made sure not to place any obstacles in the way of priests willing to join the arbitration courts.

David Fitzpatrick has very plausibly argued that the account which Father Patrick Gaynor has left of the functioning of the republican court in West Clare shows that neither priests nor other Sinn Féin officials 'showed great respect for the Dáil courts as constituted, though all shared a robust faith in the efficacy of *force majeure*'.[52] Gaynor's own assessment was that he had to intervene on a number of occasions because the court's judgements were not always just.[53] He mentioned one particular case where he believed that the impartiality of the judges was in doubt. When

---

49 *Ibid.*, 14 August 1920.
50 MA, BMH, WS1062, Laurence Garvey, p. 13.
51 J. Kinane, 'May clerics be judges in the civil courts?', *Irish Ecclesiastical Record*, 18 (1921), p. 522. Italics in the original.
52 Fitzpatrick, *Politics*, p. 150.
53 NLI, Patrick Gaynor papers, MS 19,826, 'Sinn Fein days', p. 466.

a disappointed litigant appealed to him, he dismissed the court for incompetence. A new court was elected, but Gaynor decided that the case would instead be tried by a convention composed of IRA officers and members of the Sinn Féin executive, as well as the judges of the newly elected court.[54] So far from proving that Gaynor's efforts were to 'preserve the integrity of the courts', as Carmel Clancy has contended, the entire affair shows how little the protagonists of the republican administration in this part of the country respected judicial independence.[55] It also demonstrates how large the priest could loom over proceedings as a figure of local authority. This last point is also evident from the fact that trials in Kilfinane, County Limerick, were held on a number of occasions in the parochial house and the church sacristy under the presidency of the local parish priest, Father John Lee.[56] Moreover, it is confirmed by a story from a court in Dublin in 1921, which deferred giving judgement in a case 'pending consultation with a clerical authority' about the 'moral side of the question'.[57]

Priests supported the courts not just by sitting as judges, but also by appearing as litigants. No less a cleric than Bishop Cohalan announced to the faithful of his diocese in August 1920 that

> the arbitration courts of Sinn Fein have almost entirely supplanted the other courts in the country, and people of all creeds and classes have recourse to them for the settlement of disputes. As executor of a will, in the case of a difference of opinion about the value of a small piece of property, I have myself asked that the matter should be left to a Sinn Fein arbitration court.[58]

Cohalan also asserted that 'the capacity for government exhibited by Sinn Fein has won the recognition and admiration of friend and foe'. His words and example are all the more remarkable because of his subsequent argument that a sovereign republic had not yet been established in Ireland. The upsurge in IRA violence and

54 *Ibid.*, pp. 468–9.
55 Carmel Clancy, 'The experiences of a Sinn Féin priest. Father Pat Gaynor and self-government in Clare 1919–1921', *The Other Clare. Annual Journal of the Shannon Archaeological and Historical Society*, 31 (2007), pp. 51–8, at p. 54.
56 MA, BMH, WS1435, Daniel O'Shaughnessy, p. 6.
57 MA, BMH, WS821, Frank Henderson, pp. 66–7.
58 *Irish Catholic*, 14 August 1920.

British reprisals in Cork after August 1920 had the effect of making him more sceptical even of the republican movement's non-violent aspects.

In view of the examples just mentioned of clerical influence on republican courts, it is interesting to note that priests appearing before these courts did not always win their cases. In June 1920 a layman called Daniel Donovan from Whitechurch, County Cork, brought a slander case against a local curate, Father Philip Sheehan, before the king's bench in Dublin. After the jury failed to deliver a verdict and the trial was rescheduled, Donovan decided to bring the case before a republican court in Cork instead. Father Sheehan had accused Donovan of having burgled his house and refused to apologise for the accusation, upon which Donovan sued him for slander. A complication arose when Donovan threatened to withdraw the case again and bring it back to Dublin if the Cork court would not hurry up. Eventually the court found in Donovan's favour, awarding him damages and ordering Sheehan to pay the costs of arbitration. At this stage Sheehan had lost much of the sympathy of his parish priest, Michael Canon Barrett. Barrett appealed to Donovan not to withdraw the case from the republican court as 'the whole parish was in an agony, the case was dragging on so long'.[59] Clerical support for Sinn Féin was never more eloquent than when a priest was seen to be losing a case in a republican court.

Local IRA units

A striking aspect of the period was the seemingly unproblematic integration into parish life of local non-column IRA units, and the cordial relations which existed between them and the clergy. Thus Archbishop Michael Kelly of Sydney told a crowd in New Ross in July 1920 that 'you have Volunteers. A body of them formed a guard of honour for me to-day. I am proud of them.'[60] These commendations continued to issue forth when levels of violence increased from the summer of 1920 onwards, even from those who were among the IRA campaign's most persistent critics. Thus Archbishop Harty replied to an address by Volunteers at Murroe, County Limerick, in October 1920 by saying that the 'Volunteers

59 *Irish Independent*, 12 and 19 June 1920.
60 *Irish Catholic*, 24 July 1920.

were the backbone of the country and the mainstay of law and order.'[61] And Archbishop Gilmartin praised the 'Irish boys', who were a 'magnificent body of men', as late as May 1921.[62] These words of praise stand in apparent contrast to the policy of denouncing republican violence which the bishops maintained throughout the war. In fact, however, they reflect the reality that not all IRA members were engaged in the same activities. Much of the guerrilla warfare that took place from the autumn of 1920 onwards was the work of 'flying columns' or 'active service units' rather than local companies. These columns were special units of IRA men on the run who had become radicalised and were engaged full time in pursuing the guerrilla campaign.[63] They consisted of members of local IRA companies who had become fugitives through their involvement in attacks on the RIC, and who had joined forces with each other. Not all of these columns were equally active, nor were all of the remaining local IRA companies entirely inactive, but the columns were responsible for most of the fighting.

The episcopal plaudits were intended more for what the Clare IRA man Michael Brennan called the 'flag-waggers' than for the fighters among the Volunteers.[64] Support for flag-wagging rather than fighting was, in fact, an important aspect of the clergy's response to the development of guerrilla warfare. Often these companies had been founded by priests, and this continued while the War of Independence was in full swing. Thus Father William Rattigan, curate in Kilkerrin, County Galway, was instrumental in founding the Kilkerrin company in April 1920.[65] Only a minority of priests kept in touch with the radicalised Volunteers who made up the flying columns, and on the whole the integration of local IRA companies into parish life was a way of strengthening control over the young men in the parish and preventing their radicalisation.

Such IRA units performed all kinds of public order functions at parish events. When Patrick Canon Hayes, parish priest of Ballylongford, County Kerry, was transferred to the parish of Berehaven in December 1919, he was given a memorable send-off

61 *Ibid.*, 9 October 1920.
62 *Ibid.*, 7 May 1921.
63 Fitzpatrick, *Politics*, pp. 180–91, and Augusteijn, *Defiance*, pp. 124–86.
64 Fitzpatrick, *Politics*, p. 191.
65 MA, BMH, WS1425, Patrick Treacy, p. 3.

by his former parishioners, when 'Volunteers and a band accompanied [him] through the town, which was decorated with flags and bunting'.⁶⁶ Hayes's involvement with the IRA did not mean that he supported the use of violence, and when two soldiers were killed by the IRA in his new parish in May 1921, he explained at mass that 'the taking of human life, except in war or the circumstances of war, was murder'.⁶⁷ Another example of Volunteers engaging in parish events came from Aughadoon, County Cork. Volunteers regulated the traffic generated by the large attendance at a mass celebrated at a mass rock near the village one Sunday in July 1920.⁶⁸ Similarly, Volunteers held order when the Augustinian church in Galway organised a bazaar to clear off a debt during race week in August 1920.⁶⁹

This public order function filled the vacuum left by the retreating RIC. Father Peter Meskel, curate in Ballinameela, County Waterford, asked Volunteers in October 1920 to help clear local pubs at night as the constabulary was no longer making an appearance on the streets after dark.⁷⁰ The manner in which this switch from the RIC to the IRA took place is evident from an incident in Warrenpoint, County Down, in late 1920. Father William McGinn, a local curate, had been the subject of a number of attempts at molestation by members of the Protestant reserve police force, the Ulster Special Constabulary or 'B Specials', on his regular bicycle trips to a chapel in Burren. The RIC was unwilling or unable to take effective measures to protect him, and even a friendly sergeant had said that 'owing to the state of the country' he could do little to help him. Having had no satisfactory response from the RIC, McGinn went to the Volunteers and got an armed party to protect him instead.⁷¹

Pragmatism was an important motivating factor here, and things could just as easily swing back in the other direction. On

66 *Irish Independent*, 2 December 1919.
67 *Ibid.*, 16 May 1921. Hayes had been more belligerent in 1918: Brian O'Grady, 'Old I.R.A. days in Ballylongford', *The Shannonside Annual*, 4 (1959), pp. 33–7, at p. 37. See also Joy, *IRA*, p. 76.
68 *Irish Independent*, 1 July 1920.
69 *Ibid.*, 3 August 1920.
70 MA, BMH, WS758, Tom Kelleher, p. 5.
71 MA, BMH, WS853, Peadar de Barra, p. 10.

one occasion in 1920, Father John McKinley, parish priest of St Malachy's, Belfast, sought the protection of the IRA for his church, which had been threatened with arson. The armed Volunteers maintained a guard for a couple of nights and even opened fire on the mob on a number of occasions. An IRA veteran recalled that McKinley turned up at two o'clock one morning and told the guard 'to clear at once, as he had arranged with the British military to guard the church for him'. The IRA members had to leave the hall they were in immediately, even though there was a curfew in force which made it dangerous for them to disperse.[72] McKinley's requests for support were evidently motivated by practical rather than political considerations.

Volunteers who had taken over police functions from the RIC soon began to adopt patterns of cooperation with the clergy very similar to those that had existed when RIC constables were still around. After the IRA killed an RIC district inspector in Templemore, County Tipperary, on 16 August 1920, Black and Tans wreaked havoc on the town in reprisal. Shortly afterwards, a local young man called Jimmy Walsh claimed to have seen an apparition of the Blessed Virgin Mary, and before long crowds of pilgrims descended on the town. Initially, Walsh managed to gain the support of IRA members by claiming that the Virgin had 'indicated her approval of guerrilla tactics' and had even called for an intensification of the IRA campaign. The Mid Tipperary brigade became involved in handling the traffic congestion caused by the arrival of pilgrims. Soon enough, however, the commandant, James Leahy, began to feel that the generous tips which his men were receiving were having a negative effect on discipline. When Dean Innocent Ryan began to encourage pilgrims to visit his house in Cashel to venerate a statue which had bled after Walsh had kissed it, Leahy decided to put a stop to the business. He was received rather coldly at the archbishop's house in Thurles, but ended up persuading the archbishop's staff to send the dean on 'a few weeks holidays', while priests were instructed to warn their congregations against going to Templemore.[73]

Among the common occasions for Volunteer public order functions were funerals, even those of local dignitaries without

72 MA, BMH, WS395, Thomas Fitzpatrick, pp. 2–3.
73 MA, BMH, WS1454, James Leahy, pp. 41–4.

direct links to the republican cause. At the burial of Maurice Canon O'Callaghan, late parish priest of Cloyne, County Cork, in September 1920, 'members of the Cloyne corps' of the IRA 'carried the coffin through the streets of the town, and walked in procession after the remains'.[74] This took place in the presence of Bishop Robert Browne of Cloyne and Bishop William Cotter of Portsmouth, who was a native of Cloyne town. More significant, of course, were the funerals of IRA victims of British violence. In the later stages of the conflict these were sometimes conducted in secret on account of the risk of British interference and to avoid episcopal detection. This was especially true in the diocese of Cork, where Cohalan's excommunication decree deprived IRA members of the right to a Christian burial.[75] However, these funerals were often held quite openly in the usual manner. Some priests, such as the parish priest in Ennistymon in 1920 whose example has been mentioned above, refused to allow them in their churches. This priest was no doubt motivated by the desire to avoid a political manifestation. For more sympathetic priests, this could be the very reason to welcome them. The *Irish Independent* described the cortege of a man shot dead by Auxiliaries in Bantry, County Cork, in June 1920 as follows: 'First came the parish clergy, followed by 500 Cumann na mBan, and [a] Volunteers' guard of honour. Next marched 1,000 Volunteers, then the chief mourners.' At the cemetery three volleys were fired over the grave and the parish priest, Martin Canon Murphy, recited the rosary in Irish.[76]

After the atmosphere became more tense in the autumn and winter of 1920, such funerals often became potentially hazardous stand-offs between the IRA and the British forces. The presence of Volunteers and republican paraphernalia inevitably provoked intervention. In many cases, the clergy were called on to de-escalate mounting tensions. At the funeral of a victim of British violence in Kilmallock, County Limerick, in September 1920, the crowds were stopped at the church gates and only clergy and relatives of the deceased were allowed through. When soldiers attempted to seize the flag draped over the coffin, a Volunteer 'quickly took possession

---

74 *Irish Catholic*, 11 September 1920.
75 CDA, Cohalan papers, box vi, Pastoral letter, 12 December 1920.
76 *Irish Independent*, 28 June 1920. For other examples see *ibid.*, 19 April 1920, 29 April 1920 and 1 July 1920.

of the tricolour, and when the coffin had been placed in the church the flag was again placed on it'. Military then entered the church and demanded that one of the priests hand over the flag.[77] On another occasion, IRA members drawn up in military formation received the remains of another victim at a church in Mallow, County Cork, despite the presence of fully equipped and mounted British soldiers. Although the parish priest had been told by the army that attendance at the funeral would be limited to relatives and close friends, a party of Volunteers in uniform managed to fire parting volleys over the grave.[78]

On other occasions officiating priests were served with notices by the military concerning the regulation of the Volunteers and the attending crowds. During the obsequies of a hunger-strike victim in Cork in October 1920, six Volunteers acted as guards of honour at the catafalque in the church. While the parish priest, Patrick Canon O'Leary, was pronouncing the absolution, armed soldiers entered the church and handed him a notice saying that the funeral procession was to be limited to 100, and that no one was to march in military formation. While the soldiers were conversing with O'Leary, the IRA guards slipped away and disappeared, their place being taken by six others. After the ceremony had concluded, Canon O'Leary instructed the congregation to comply with the orders given. One of the curates and the Volunteers then regulated traffic while the people left the church. According to the newspaper report, the large presence of British military and their threats to fire if the order was not obeyed filled many in the crowd with consternation, but 'priests patrolled the route, and their presence did much to calm the people'. Despite the British army presence, Volunteers carried the coffin from the church to the cemetery.[79] The role of priests as local leaders and negotiators thus permitted a limited degree of open display by the Volunteers.

Joining the IRA

Giving any kind of support to Volunteers during the War of Independence inevitably involved countenancing a degree of

77 *Irish Independent*, 27 September 1920.
78 *Ibid.*, 19 October 1920.
79 *Ibid.*, 20 October 1920.

ambiguity with regard to the use of violence. This comes to light very clearly in the case of the Mullagh priest Father Gaynor and his fellow curate Father Michael McKenna. McKenna joined the IRA and became commandant of the local battalion, having been chosen for this post partly because he had been an army chaplain during the First World War.[80] Although McKenna's battalion never actually crossed swords with the crown forces, it did engage in a certain amount of violence, mainly directed at contumacious Volunteers and recalcitrant civilians.[81] In late 1919 or early 1920, McKenna was informed that a cattle-drive was taking place in the neighbouring village of Quilty. The priest went there to put a stop to it and found himself facing a mob on his own. Before long someone from the crowd had thrown a stone at the curate, hitting him in the face. 'Next evening, the Volunteer battalion marched on Quilty and put the fear of death in Michael Casey, the local patriot who had organised the cattle-drive for his own ends.'[82] In another instance, McKenna had an ex-constable called Patrick Connors arrested for terrorising his own uncle, with whom he had a dispute about land. McKenna had Connors tried by court-martial before the battalion staff. During the trial, which took place in the dining room of the curates' house, 'Connors was so impudent that F[ather] McKenna struck him a hard blow in the face.' On Gaynor's advice – which was sought even though he had no part in the court-martial – the sentence was that Connors should be brought to Mutton Island, off the West Clare coast. He was held there in solitary confinement for a month.[83]

Although Gaynor emphasised in his memoir that he was not a member of the IRA, in practice he had a large say in the affairs of the local company, deriving his legal sanction from the fact that he held the position of acting chief of police.[84] As such Gaynor ensured that 'the writ of the Irish government ran merrily in our area of jurisdiction'. When Connors returned from Mutton Island, he refused to abide by terms laid down by McKenna's court. It fell

80 NLI, Gaynor papers, MS 19,826, 'Sinn Fein days', p. 464.
81 *Ibid.*, p. 479.
82 *Ibid.*, p. 464. See also MA, BMH, WS1253, Joseph Daly, pp. 3–4.
83 NLI, Gaynor papers, MS 19,826, 'Sinn Fein days', pp. 470–1. See also Fitzpatrick, *Politics*, p. 150 for this incident.
84 NLI, Gaynor papers, MS 19,826, 'Sinn Fein days', p. 473.

to Gaynor as chief of police to enforce these and evict Connors from his uncle's farm. He wrote later that 'Connors stood in peril of his life, for in no circumstances would I have allowed a miscreant, within our area of jurisdiction, to defy the authority of the Irish government.'[85] Gaynor asked three Volunteers to accompany him, telling them that he took

> legal and moral responsibility: that they were in a position similar to that of organised armed forces in any country and were free, if necessary, to open fire on Connors without any qualm of conscience.[86]

When the party arrived at the farm, Connors fled and the case was settled without force.

Gaynor's retrospective comments on the incident highlight the extent to which his roles as chief of police, Sinn Féin leader and curate were blurred. Although he acted as chief of police in carrying out the orders of a republican court, he attributed his success in enforcing the eviction at least in part to the respect which Connors owed him as a priest: 'Being clever, he did not dare to use his revolver against a priest and against Volunteers on duty.'[87] Gaynor claimed that he would have given the order to use lethal force against Connors if necessary, but was relieved that it had not come to that because it 'would have put an end to my career as a priest on the mission. Even if I were not executed by the British forces I should have had to retire to a monastery.' His conscience would have been unperturbed, however, because he had safeguarded

> the moral position from the viewpoint of the natural law by invoking the authority of all the organised forces which upheld Irish government in West Clare. But there is no safeguard for a priest who takes human life even within the moral law: he is ruined beyond redemption at least in this world.[88]

Elsewhere in the same account, Gaynor discussed his views on the use of violence by the IRA. Commenting on an attack on the RIC in Kilmihil in April 1920, Gaynor said that 'it seems to me – though I thought our appeal to the gun a tactical mistake – that the

85 *Ibid.*, p. 475.
86 *Ibid.*, pp. 475–6.
87 *Ibid.*, p. 477.
88 *Ibid.*, pp. 476–7.

Volunteers acted within their rights as soldiers of the Irish army'.[89] He repeated this view that violence was legitimate but inopportune when discussing the merits of Frank Magrath, the IRA's North Tipperary brigade commandant. According to Gaynor, Magrath

> did not favour the active policy which had [in 1920] been sanctioned by the supreme command in Dublin. I do not criticise him on that score. I did not approve of open war, myself, though I never said a word against the policy; but then I was not a Volunteer and was not free, as a priest, to urge young men into battle when I would not have shared their risks. ... But Mr Magrath should not have clung to his position of honour in the Volunteers if he felt obliged, either by sincere convictions or for personal reasons, to obstruct the policy of his superiors in the organisation.[90]

There is some ambiguity in this passage, as it is unclear whether Gaynor understood 'open war' as including the ambushes characteristic of the IRA's guerrilla campaign. Significantly, Gaynor also made a point of keeping his disapproval of 'open war' concealed: he never said a word against the policy. Moreover, this supposed disapproval is at odds with his comment that the Kilmihil RIC attacks in April 1920 were legitimate.

Gaynor's case shows that priests who became involved in local IRA units always ventured onto a slippery slope. For some priests there was no moral quandary here; they played a role in the process of radicalisation itself. A curate in Callan, Father Patrick Delahunty, had a connection with the IRA very similar to Gaynor's. Although he held no official rank in the Kilkenny brigade 7th battalion, he could nonetheless 'be described as a battalion officer'.[91] Thus Delahunty was 'familiar with and was consulted about Volunteer activities' and attended battalion council meetings. But much more than Gaynor, who insisted on portraying himself as a non-combatant, Delahunty became involved in assisting the guerrilla campaign. He was credited by veterans with providing his battalion with arms and explosives.[92] The next chapter will examine this category of priests more closely.

---

89 *Ibid.*, p. 583.
90 *Ibid.*, p. 455.
91 MA, BMH, WS1642, Edward Halley, p. 4.
92 *Ibid.*, pp. 5 and 7.

Seditious statements

The situation in Ireland provided republican priests with ample opportunity to show their contempt for the British authorities and to make seditious statements. Priests had been making such utterances ever since the rise of advanced republicanism after the Easter rising.[93] In August 1919, the RIC county inspector for Cork noted that a Father O'Shea had behaved in a 'most extraordinary manner' in Blarney Castle. O'Shea, a native of Dungarvan, County Waterford, but living in the United States, had been observed waving a Sinn Féin flag from the castle, singing the Soldier's Song and shouting, 'Up the republic!' When police officers were sent up to remove him, he resisted, perhaps encouraged by the crowd, which showed signs of hostility towards the police.[94]

The first priest to be arrested during the War of Independence was charged with sedition. Captain Thomas O'Donnell, a chaplain in the Australian imperial forces, was accused in October 1919 of having used language disloyal to the king. The prosecutor at his court-martial in London alleged that O'Donnell had argued loudly in a hotel in Killarney that 'the king and the royal family are no use to this or any other country'. Having denied the charges, he was acquitted.[95] Several other priests took the opportunity of court appearances to demonstrate their contempt for British rule in Ireland. Thus Father Edward O'Reilly, a curate in Carrick-on-Shannon, County Leitrim, refused to attend a hearing and was consequently fined £10 for contempt of court in March 1919. O'Reilly had returned the subpoena citing conscientious objections. He subsequently spoilt the effect of his defiance somewhat by explaining that his refusal was 'because of the sacredness of the oath administered, the priestly character, to save his soul, ill-health and other reasons'.[96] And Father Malachy Brennan of Ballinasloe refused to take off his hat in a court in Galway in November 1919 when attending a case against parishioners for unlawful assembly. During his ejection from the courtroom, Brennan explained that 'he

---

93 See for instance TNA, WO35/97 and WO35/99.
94 TNA, CO904/109, IGMR, August 1919, p. 931.
95 *Irish Independent*, 26 November 1919.
96 *Ibid.*, 10 and 15 March 1919.

had no respect for the court or for any English court'.⁹⁷ Similarly, when Archdeacon John Power, parish priest of Dungarvan, County Waterford, was charged with having presided at an unlawful meeting, he refused to plead before the court in Fermoy in May 1921. He was convicted and fined, but refused to pay, causing the court to issue a distress warrant.⁹⁸

Refusing to recognise the legitimacy of British courts in fact became an eloquent way for priests in the dock to demonstrate their republican views. When Fathers Gaynor and McKenna were court-martialled in Limerick in May 1921, a court official attempted to administer the oath. Gaynor 'protested fiercely against this travesty as an insult to almighty God when [the court's] rules were devised not to give justice but to facilitate injustice'.⁹⁹ The two curates then refused to recognise the authority of the court and made no defence.

A convenient moment for priests to express the highest praise for Volunteers was after their execution by the British. Fourteen Volunteers were officially executed by the authorities during the War of Independence.¹⁰⁰ In November 1920 Daniel Canon Downing, parish priest of St Joseph's, Berkeley Road, Dublin, told a congregation during a mass for the repose of the soul of Kevin Barry: 'I have not found in the lives of the saints anything more beautiful and more edifying than his heroic death and resignation and tender piety in death.'¹⁰¹ For any Volunteer looking for reassurance on the morality of IRA violence, such language was significant. The importance of positive portrayals of republican heroes was borne out by a comment made by a Wexford priest in November 1920 that 'things are looking pretty bad here just now, but then men have become "shinners" during the past fortnight who until then were opponents of the movement'. The priest in question, Father James Sinnott, attributed this happy development to the death of

---

97 *Ibid.*, 18 November 1919.
98 *Irish Catholic*, 14 May 1921, and *Irish Independent*, 5 May 1921. The *Irish Independent* mistakenly gave his name as Ryan. He is listed as Power in *ICD 1920*, p. 268.
99 NLI, Gaynor papers, MS 19,826, 'Kilmihil parish. Its origins and scraps of its history', p. 530.
100 Hopkinson, *War*, p. 202.
101 *Irish Catholic*, 13 November 1920.

Terence MacSwiney and the execution of Kevin Barry, which had 'brought a great change over many ardent supporters of English rule in Ireland'.[102]

There were a thousand other gestures that republican-minded priests could make to show support for Sinn Féin without getting themselves into quite as much trouble as some of the priests did who have just been mentioned. This was especially true early on in the conflict. Newspaper reports of the first session of the Dáil on 21 January 1919 noted with satisfaction that many priests were among those who went into the Mansion House to witness proceedings.[103] A few weeks later, Father Michael Breen, parish priest of Dysart, County Clare, urged a Clare county committee to decline 'to make any arrangement for the conduct of commercial classes for [decommissioned] English soldiers while the English government has under lock and key our members of parliament and other men who are dear to the Irish people'.[104] Even after Sinn Féin and the Dáil had been proscribed, it was still possible to make some gestures without fear of repercussion. In February 1921, the clergy of Omagh, County Tyrone – one of whom was president of the local Sinn Féin constituency executive –, 'asked the R[oman] C[atholic] traders ... to do no business with any Belfast firms or banks until the R[oman] C[atholic] workers in Belfast are unconditionally restored to their former employment'.[105] Clerical support for the Belfast boycott also caused the Omagh St. Vincent de Paul society to transfer its funds from a bank account in the Northern Bank to one in the Bank of Ireland.[106]

Although it was important for priests to gain a foothold in the emerging local institutions of the new political order, such involvement became more hazardous, and therefore politically more meaningful, as the conflict progressed. A number of the examples

---

102 AICR, Hagan papers, HAG1/1920/409, Sinnott to Hagan, 5 November 1920.
103 *Irish Independent*, 22 January 1919. Mitchell says there were 'about fifty priests' in the audience: Mitchell, *Government*, p. 17.
104 *Catholic Bulletin*, 9:3 (March 1919), p. 111.
105 TNA, CO904/114, IGMR, February 1921, p. 380. Father John McKenna, president of Sinn Féin constituency executive: NLI, MS 5649, List of Sinn Féin officers.
106 TNA, CO904/114, IGMR, February 1921, p. 309.

mentioned here have shown that there was a fine line between support for the republican movements' non-violent activities and involvement in guerrilla warfare. Some priests turned out to be quite as amenable to radicalisation as the Volunteers who joined flying columns. The next chapter will examine these IRA priests.

5

Aiding and abetting: priests involved in the IRA campaign

As Volunteers on the run began to form flying columns from the spring of 1920 onwards and as the British government started to deploy Black and Tans and Auxiliaries to aid the hard-pressed RIC, violence escalated in certain parts of the country. For priests in areas where local Volunteers remained impervious to this process of radicalisation, things remained much the same. In these areas, the connections between the clergy and the republican movement described in Chapter 4 continued as before. But in regions where Volunteers became guerrilla fighters, priests were faced with a dilemma. Most distanced themselves from the fighting men and condemned violence: Chapter 2 has demonstrated that until the end of 1920 condemnations began to rise as the levels of violence increased. The present chapter will examine priests who threw their lot in with the radicals and gave support to the IRA campaign.

This immediately raises a conceptual problem, because while it is easy to define what constitutes condemnation of republican violence, it is more difficult to decide which kinds of behaviour amount to support for a guerrilla campaign. This is especially true for a clerical population whose job it was to minister to all Catholics regardless of their deeds. This question runs as a thread through the present chapter, and it will be addressed when each specific form of behaviour is discussed. But it is as well to make a number of distinctions from the beginning. The behaviour that presents the fewest interpretative problems consists of activities that did not involve the exercise of priestly ministry, such as providing shelter for men on the run or storing arms and ammunition for the IRA. Whether carried out by priests or by lay people, doing these things meant giving support to the IRA campaign. As will be seen, priests could initially do these things somewhat more easily than lay people, as their clerical status afforded them a degree of immunity from interference from the crown forces. But that does not change the fact that their actions constituted aiding the IRA campaign.

More difficult to interpret is the spiritual aid which priests gave to active Volunteers. When a priest heard the confession of a man on the run, did that mean that he was endorsing the Volunteer's actions, or was he simply doing what any Catholic priest was required to do under the circumstances? The criterion is whether such spiritual aid had – or could reasonably be expected to have – political significance in the eyes of those who received it. In some cases, the question is easily answered. Priests who described themselves as 'column chaplains', for instance, were making a clear political statement: the IRA was the army of the Irish republic, and they were its chaplains. Although this did not perhaps imply approval of each and every decision made by the IRA, by thus endorsing the organisation's legitimacy, these priests' spiritual ministry amounted to giving support to the IRA campaign. But most priests who gave spiritual aid did so by occasionally hearing confessions of men on the run, by secretly celebrating mass for them, by giving them communion and by officiating at their funerals. This chapter will argue on analysis of specific examples that these actions nonetheless had political significance, and that they were tantamount to support for the IRA because they provided legitimacy and moral reassurance to Volunteers involved in the guerrilla war.

Quantifying clerical support for the IRA campaign

Hopes of quantifying spiritual support for guerrilla fighters flounder on the secrecy which shrouded such contacts, and which came over and above the confidentiality that was usual in pastoral encounters between priests and lay people. A systematic search in the Bureau of Military History's witness statements – as well as research in many other collections – has uncovered only a handful of priests who could be described as 'chaplains to the forces'.[1] Although there may well have been a few more, it is not probable

---

1 The search in the BMH witness statements was carried out through the search engine at www.bureauofmilitaryhistory.ie/index.html (accessed 4 March 2013), using the terms 'priest', 'Father', 'Fr', 'Rev' and 'Canon'.

that large numbers of them have gone unmentioned in the sources. Occasional spiritual assistance, such as hearing confessions of Volunteers or giving them communion, is even more difficult to quantify. There may have been quite a lot of priests who did this, as the secrecy involved will have lowered the threshold for sympathetic but fearful clerics to aid the campaign. Lacking the means to quantify this kind of activity, this chapter must concentrate on offering a qualitative analysis.

It is somewhat easier to quantify the giving of material support by priests, such as providing shelter or storage for arms. Naturally there will have been much overlap between the categories distinguished here: priests who gave material support will probably also have given spiritual support at some stage or other, although the converse may not have been true to the same extent. The figure resulting from the research carried out for this book provides an estimate. A list reproduced in Appendix 2 includes seventy-one priests whose activities have been described in the Bureau's witness statements, police files and a number of other sources.[2] Again, this number must be regarded as a minimum figure, since giving material support to the IRA was illegal and priests who gave it therefore went to considerable lengths to conceal their actions from the public eye. Seventy-one priests made up a mere 1.9 per cent of the total clerical population, and the figure at least points to the small scale of active clerical assistance.

Chapter 2 has shown that senior clerics were overrepresented among those who condemned IRA violence, although some of this at least must be ascribed to bias in newspaper reporting. The figure is more evenly balanced for these seventy-one priests. Of the sixty-one whose canonical status could be established, 61 per cent were junior, and 39 per cent senior clergy.[3] As has been seen, roughly 66 per cent of the Irish clergy consisted of junior priests,

---

2 Three entries are for religious houses and one for a college, and although it is likely that more than one member of those communities assisted, they have each been counted as one.
3 Thirty-seven junior priests and twenty-four senior. 'Junior' includes curates, a hospital chaplain and a teacher in a college; 'senior' includes parish priests, an administrator, a college rector and vice-rector, a prior of a religious house and a religious priest who was a 'definitor' (a member of his provincial's council).

while the remaining 33 per cent were senior clerics. This means that senior clergy were almost proportionally represented among supportive priests, even slightly overrepresented. Senior clerics were just as likely as junior clerics to support the IRA, but since they were in a minority among the clergy in general, supportive priests were most often curates.

A previous chapter has discussed the chronological distribution of published clerical condemnations. It is more difficult to analyse instances of support in a similar manner. Sources – mainly the Bureau's witness statements – are often vague on precise dates. It stands to reason that these instances increased in number as violence became more frequent from the summer of 1920 onwards. As has been seen, condemnations went into decline from the last quarter of 1920 as the British forces stepped up their efforts. However, it is not at all certain that support for the IRA was inversely proportional to condemnations. The fact that priests turned their attention more to the crown forces from the end of 1920 onwards does not necessarily imply that they became any more disposed to endorsing the IRA.

As has been seen, the national figure of priests found to have given material support to the IRA was 1.9 per cent. This figure varied considerably per county. Appendix 3 reveals that County Sligo had the highest proportion with 5.5 per cent, but since the numbers were very small (three priests out of a total clerical population of fifty-five), it is difficult to draw convincing conclusions. The same is true for County Longford at 4.7 per cent (two priests out of a total clerical population of forty-three), although this county had high levels of IRA activity, and, incidentally, also a high percentage of priests who condemned violence. Other violent counties such as Cork and Tipperary were below the national average, with very few supportive priests. If these figures are compared with Hart's data on IRA violence, a weak positive correlation (0.16) emerges, indicating the sporadic and individual nature of clerical material support for the IRA.

These statistics must not obscure the fact that even small networks of supportive priests in a county could have quite an impact on local Volunteers. The eight Galway priests who aided the IRA accounted for less than 4 per cent of the total clerical population of the county. But for the Volunteers around Headford, for instance, it was significant that both the parish priest and the curate of the town could be relied upon to provide shelter and to store arms and ammunition.[4] The two parish priests of the neighbouring parishes of Kilfinane and Glenroe, County Limerick, formed another pocket of known 'friendly' priests, even though supportive clerics only made up 3 per cent of the clergy in County Limerick.[5] Statistical insignificance made these republican priests nonetheless important to the IRA.

'Chaplains to the forces'

The clearest example of spiritual support for the IRA campaign is provided by those priests described as 'brigade chaplains' or 'chaplains to the IRA'. Thus Father John Kelly, curate in Rathoe, County Carlow, was described in the summer of 1920 as a 'chaplain to the IRA', as were Father William Swan, curate in Moynalty, County Meath, and Father Eugene McSweeney, curate in Fairview, Dublin.[6] And the commandant of the Mid Limerick brigade's flying column mentioned that Father Joseph Carroll, curate in Fedamore, County Limerick, had been appointed 'chaplain to the column' or 'battalion chaplain' some time in the autumn of 1920.[7] The most famous of these clerics was the Capuchin priest Father Dominic O'Connor, who styled himself 'brigade chaplain' in his correspondence with the Mid Cork brigade in December 1920.[8] The designations differed, with priests being called brigade, battalion and column chaplains as well as simply 'chaplains to the IRA'. Nonetheless all of these descriptions suggest a more or less permanent link with a specific unit, or with the IRA in a specific area, rather than merely incidental contact.

At the time of the Easter rising, the leadership of the Irish

---

4 MA, BMH, WS1735, P. J. Kelly, p. 12, and *Irish Independent*, 8 October 1920.
5 MA, BMH, WS883, John MacCarthy, p. 61, and WS1435, Daniel O'Shaughnessy, p. 38.
6 Kelly: MA, BMH, WS1441, Nan Nolan, p. 5; Swan: WS1650, Patrick O'Reilly, p. 20: McSweeney: Ó Fiaich, 'Clergy', p. 499.
7 MA, BMH, WS656, Richard O'Connell, p. 14, and WS1279, Sean Clifford, p. 2.
8 NLI, Florence O'Donoghue papers, MS 31,170, Dominic to O'Donoghue, 15 December 1920.

Volunteers tried to secure episcopal appointments for priests as chaplains to Irish Volunteer units. The Clare IRA veteran Sean O'Keeffe mentions rumours that Bishop Fogarty of Killaloe appointed a curate as chaplain to the Irish Volunteers in the whole county.[9] Tomás Ó Fiaich recounts that chaplains were appointed to some battalions during the conscription crisis, but does not say whether these appointments were made by the bishops.[10] In fact it is unlikely that other bishops followed Fogarty's example, and it is positively out of the question that chaplains to flying columns in the later stages of the war held appointments from their local ordinary. Ó Fiaich contends that Dominic, when he had become chaplain of the Mid Cork brigade, himself 'organised a system of battalion chaplains who received their instructions from him'.[11] But most priests' connections with local IRA companies simply arose from the fact that they had taken a special interest in the 'movement' in their parishes. When Volunteers from these companies went on the run and became involved in guerrilla fighting in the course of 1920, these radical priests kept in touch with them. This was also true for the religious involved. Dominic as a Capuchin priest did not work in a parish, but his connection with the Mid Cork brigade stemmed from his office as chaplain to the city's mayor, Terence MacSwiney. Nevertheless it must be borne in mind that since not all flying columns showed the same level of activity, even some 'column chaplains' could find themselves with very little to do.

What activities did chaplains to active IRA columns engage in? Little is known of Dominic's involvement with his IRA brigade before he was arrested in December 1920. He had been absent from Cork since MacSwiney's hunger-strike in October, first accompanying MacSwiney to England and then taking up residence in the Capuchin house in Church Street, Dublin, because of threats he had received.[12] John Borgonovo has called him a 'source of great spiritual and occasional physical assistance' to the Volunteers of

9 MA, BMH, WS1261, Sean O'Keeffe, pp. 5–6.
10 Ó Fiaich, 'Clergy', p. 499.
11 *Ibid.*
12 Capuchin Provincial Archives, Dublin (hereafter CPA), Dominic O'Connor papers, CA/IR/1/5/3/8, Aloysius Travers, 'An account of the arrest, trial and imprisonment of Fr. Dominic O'Connor'.

Cork city.[13] The nature of the spiritual assistance he gave is evident from a letter he sent a day before his arrest in Dublin. The brigade adjutant, Florence O'Donoghue, had written to Dominic to ask whether Bishop Cohalan's excommunication decree would cause difficulties for the brigade. In a truly impressive display of hermeneutical creativity, Dominic's letter reassured him that this was not the case. Cohalan had excommunicated everyone who 'shall organise or take part in ambushes or kidnapping, or shall otherwise be guilty of murder or attempted murder'.[14] Dominic explained that the decree did not in fact apply to anyone involved in any of these activities, so long as they were acting 'with the authority of the state – the republic of Ireland'. If the Volunteers did these things as private persons, they would fall under the excommunication; if they did them as soldiers of the army of the republic, these deeds were 'not only not sinful but ... good and meritorious'. Therefore, he wrote, 'the excommunication does not affect us. There is no need to worry about it.' In fact, he informed O'Donoghue: 'had I been at home I would have urged you to ambush each day'.[15]

Of the Limerick Jesuit priest Father William Hackett it has been said that 'he was not a fighting man: he regarded himself as the chaplain to the IRA and a non-combatant'.[16] But other chaplains took their role to mean that they must join the men in the field, and even Hackett kept a rifle hidden in his room. Borgonovo's comment about Dominic's 'occasional physical assistance' also suggests more than just the provision of theological clarifications. This is confirmed by information about some other IRA chaplains. Father Carroll of Fedamore was said to have taken part in ambushes as a matter of course: he gave 'every encouragement and subsequently accompanied us on ambushes and often heard our confession preparatory to an attack on the enemy'.[17] It is not implied, however,

---

13 John Borgonovo (ed.), *Florence and Josephine O'Donoghue's War of Independence. A Destiny that Shapes our Ends* (Dublin and Portland, OR: Irish Academic Press, 2006), p. 232.
14 CDA, Cohalan papers, box vi, pastoral letter, 12 December 1920.
15 NLI, O'Donoghue papers, MS 31,170, Dominic to O'Donoghue, 15 December 1920.
16 IJA, 'Brief lives' papers, J172/1, J. Dennett, '"'Tis sixty years since". Fr. William Hackett and the Irish Troubles' (1984), p. 15.
17 MA, BMH, WS1279, Sean Clifford, pp. 2, 5.

that any of these chaplains actually fired shots themselves, and one of them, Father Swan, was described simply as 'the comforter of the wives and mothers of those "on the run" and in prison; the confessor and adviser of all IRA men'.[18]

A number of other priests whose status as IRA chaplains is nowhere explicitly mentioned also accompanied the Volunteers on ambushes. It was said of the Capuchin Father Albert Bibby, a close companion of Dominic's, that 'in the thick of the fight, when the bullets were flying, you could imagine him hardly knowing that shots were being fired'.[19] And Dan Breen has recounted that Father Richard McCarthy, curate in Ballyhahill, County Limerick, accompanied a flying column out into the field, although he left before the actual ambush took place.[20] McCarthy's association with the West Limerick brigade was well established at that time, and he reportedly represented it at a meeting of IRA commandants in Dublin in July 1920.[21] According to Breen, McCarthy had been 'bivouacking' with a flying column on the Limerick–Kerry border, but he had to go into hiding after his hat was discovered by crown forces at the scene of the ambush. This caused him to go on the run 'from church and state', according to one Limerick Volunteer, and McCarthy remained an important figure in the Limerick IRA.[22]

Providing occasional spiritual assistance

Spiritual assistance was also forthcoming from priests who were not involved with the IRA to the degree that these semi-official chaplains were. There are countless examples in the Bureau of Military History's witness statements of local priests who heard the confessions of IRA men before they set out for an ambush,

---

18 MA, BMH, WS1650, Patrick O'Reilly, p. 20.
19 Bernard, 'Fathers Albert and Dominic, O.F.M.Cap. The repatriation of their remains', *The Capuchin Annual* (1959), pp. 380–3, at p. 380.
20 Breen, *Fight*, p. 48. The IRA veteran Tadhg Crowley also testified to McCarthy's presence 'near the ambush position' on one occasion: MA, BMH, WS435, Tadhg Crowley, p. 63.
21 Liam Deasy, *Towards Ireland Free. The West Cork Brigade in the War of Independence 1917–1921* (Dublin and Cork: Mercier Press, 1973), p. 132.
22 MA, BMH, WS1435, Daniel O'Shaughnessy, p. 45.

or celebrated mass for them and gave them communion. It could be argued that these priests were just doing what canon law and theology expected of them and that the provision of such services had no political significance. Their activities could be regarded as simply preparing men in danger for their possible death, without amounting to support for the IRA campaign. Certainly this is the way such priests liked to portray things themselves when they were caught by crown forces or when their superiors asked hard questions. In a letter to the Spanish general of his order, Father Albert described his work during the war as follows: 'my mission as a priest was not to any one section or party, it was to "embrace all in one sentiment of charity"'. He claimed that he 'strictly adhered to my principle of absolute impartiality', and in fact there is no reason to doubt that he actually did minister to members of the crown forces too. Albert – who was opposed to the treaty during the Civil War – described his ministry to the anti-treatyite republicans in 1922 and 1923 simply as a matter of preparing 'human souls for their going forth to meet their Heavenly Father'.[23]

Yet providing secret ministrations to IRA men on the run, absolving them in confession and giving them communion at mass were not instances of neutral ministry devoid of political meaning. The context and setting are crucial in determining whether or not spiritual aid had such a political significance. It was one thing for a priest to absolve a Volunteer who came to him in the confessional seeking forgiveness for a murder he had committed, but quite another for a priest to go to a secret place at night to hear the confessions of a flying column preparing for ambush. Priests who did the former were facilitating the reconciliation of a repentant sinner; priests who did the latter were giving legitimacy to the Volunteers' activities. To give 'spiritual consolation' to warriors preparing for battle is to strengthen them for the fight.[24] As such this kind of spiritual aid must be regarded as support for the IRA campaign. The crown forces certainly interpreted it in this way, as did IRA members themselves. Column members knew precisely which priests could and which could not be approached to hear confessions and give communion. Canon law and theology required that

23 CPA, Albert Bibby papers, CA/IR/1/1/2/4/6, Albert Bibby, 'The case of Father Albert, O.S.F.C., Franciscan Capuchin Friary, Dublin'.
24 MA, BMH, WS1425, Patrick Treacy, p. 15.

persons receiving the sacraments should at least have the intention of living lives that accorded with the precepts of morality. A penitent who had the obvious determination to commit murder did not meet this requirement and could not be absolved, much less given communion, even if he was about to put himself in danger of death. Priests who did absolve Volunteers on their way to an ambush and gave them communion were therefore making a statement about the moral implications of the intended action; namely that such killings were not murder.

In order to assess the significance of these spiritual ministrations more precisely, it is necessary to take a number of specific circumstances into account. In normal life, communion was given in public, for example in a church before, during or after mass. In this situation, priests were obliged by canon law to give communion to all baptised Catholics who asked for it, with the exception of the excommunicate and 'public sinners'.[25] People whose sins were not publicly known, even though they may have been known to the priest, had to be admitted, as a refusal would cause 'scandal' by revealing them as sinners to the congregation. In consequence, priests who gave communion to active Volunteers during regular parish masses were not necessarily making a statement about the morality of IRA actions, as their decision could have been motivated by the desire to avoid scandal. Some flying columns attended regular scheduled Sunday masses in the area where they were billeted. Michael Brennan, veteran commandant of the East Clare brigade's flying column, recalled: 'I doubt if we ever missed mass on a Sunday from the time the column was formed.' Brennan wrote that they picked their masses carefully, the criterion being the speed with which the priests on duty were known to say them. 'Once in Bodyke, we attended the parish priest's mass at 11 and he finished at 1.30. After that we avoided Bodyke on Sundays.'[26]

Needless to say, attending scheduled masses was a dangerous business, as it was never certain whether members of the congregation could be trusted. The IRA veteran P. H. Doherty attended mass while on the run one Sunday morning in January 1921 in Culdaff, County Donegal, and went to communion. This 'caused

---

25 *CIC*, canons 853 and 855.
26 MA, BMH, WS1068, Michael Brennan, pp. 88–9.

some comment', and the house he was staying in that night was surrounded by crown forces the same evening. This led the curate, Father James McGlynn, a few days later to denounce the informers from the pulpit, saying that the 'information must have been carried direct from the church' to the RIC.[27] After the crown forces introduced the practice of surrounding churches while services were in progress to search the congregation as it emerged, attending scheduled masses became even more dangerous. In contrast with Brennan and his men in Clare, the South Tipperary IRA veteran Richard Dalton recalled that 'as a precautionary measure whilst on the column we rarely, if ever, went to mass on Sundays'.[28]

An alternative was to make special arrangements with a priest to come and hear confessions and say mass separately just for the column. Here, other criteria apply for gauging the political significance of the priests' actions. The fact that a priest agreed to these private sessions in itself was an endorsement of the column's activities. Moreover, the canonical rule that sinners should be admitted to communion in order to avoid scandal did not apply in the absence of a congregation.[29] When priests did give communion to IRA fugitives during such private masses, they were consequently giving a clear message that the Volunteers' actions were morally acceptable and involved nothing sinful.

Such specially arranged masses and confession times were quite frequent. According to Michael Brennan, confessions were 'a simple matter', as priests 'everywhere were most helpful'. He recounted that a curate in Broadford once heard the men's confessions in a field on the mountainside: 'a large body of heavily armed men stood at one side of a field while a priest sat on a low wall some distance away. One by one the armed men walked over to the priest, removed their hats and knelt down.'[30] Other examples from the Bureau's witness statements include Father James Slattery, curate in Annascaul, County Kerry, who made himself available for men of the 5th battalion, North Kerry brigade on a night before

27 MA, BMH, WS1516, P. H. Doherty, pp. 8–9.
28 Tony Patterson, 'Third Tipperary Brigade, number two flying column, January to June 1921', *Tipperary Historical Journal* (2006), pp. 189–206, at p. 203.
29 *CIC*, canon 855, par. 2.
30 MA, BMH, WS1068, Michael Brennan, pp. 88–9.

an ambush in March 1921 to hear their confessions.[31] A member of a Mid Cork brigade flying column recalled that on one occasion they went at three o'clock in the morning to a church near Ballydesmond, where the local priest – 'a great friend of the boys' – heard their confessions and said mass for them.[32] And when the men of the West Connemara brigade flying column wanted to go to confession and receive communion in April 1921, the commandant arranged for a priest to be ferried across Killary Harbour at night to meet them in a safe house nearby.[33] Similarly, Father James Dwan, curate in Rathcormac, County Tipperary, visited a South Tipperary brigade flying column once in April 1921 while it stayed in a safe house close by. Dwan 'generally visited the column whenever we were near his parish, and occasionally he said mass for us in some farmer's house where we could be present'.[34] The fact that priests participated in these special sessions for men whose business they understood and were known to understand is not devoid of political significance. In these cases, the rites performed amounted to the giving of moral support.

Sometimes there was no time to hear individual confessions before a column took up an ambush position, and then priests gave 'conditional absolution' to the group. About 100 men from the Mid Clare brigade assembled in Kilnamona, County Clare, for an ambush nearby in May 1921. At daybreak Father M. Hamilton, a professor at St Flannan's College, Ennis, came out and gave conditional absolution to the group before it marched to the ambush position.[35] The term 'conditional absolution', which is used often in the Bureau's witness statements, is somewhat misleading. Its official meaning was not that the priest absolved the men from intended sins they were about to commit, such as killing members of the crown forces during an ambush. Such a device did not exist

---

31 MA, BMH, WS951, Robert Knightly, p. 4.
32 MA, BMH, WS1726, Cornelius Cronin, p. 9.
33 MA, BMH, WS1611, Martin Conneely, p. 17. See also WS1612, Peter McDonnell, p. 63, and WS1692, John Feehan, pp. 63–4. A similar incident is recounted in WS1102, James Brennan, pp. 6–7. See also WS1271, Patrick Dunphy, p. 12.
34 MA, BMH, WS1187, Patrick Butler, p. 17.
35 MA, BMH, WS1075, Thomas Shalloo, p. 25. See also WS1326, Andrew O'Donoghue, p. 48.

in the handbooks of theology, nor would it have been consistent with the republican notion that these killings were morally acceptable. In fact the term meant that the priest gave absolution for past sins to people in danger of death without hearing everybody's individual confessions.[36] The absolution was conditional upon each man's personal contrition for the sins he had already committed, and on his resolve to make a normal individual confession as soon as the opportunity presented itself. Thus, officially, it was a matter of preparing the men for death, not of soothing consciences to make them ready to kill others. Consequently, Dominic's letter to Florence O'Donoghue after the Cohalan decree stressed that 'the boys' should not tell priests in confession that they were in the IRA or that they had taken part in an ambush or kidnapping, 'just as there is no necessity for telling a priest in confession that you went to mass on Sunday'.[37] Where there was no sin, there was no need for absolution. In practice, however, the consciences of men involved in ambushes did trouble them, and they inevitably experienced the giving of conditional absolution as a blessing on the work they were about to do.

Moreover, there is evidence that priests who gave spiritual aid to the IRA intended their ministrations to have this meaning. Needless to say, sources for the conversations that went on during confessions are rare. But there are at least two accounts that show how such encounters could unfold. Stephen Donnelly, whose argument with Bishop Naughton of Killala has been recounted in Chapter 3, also mentioned that when he was a member of a flying column in Mayo he once went to confession to a parish priest in a country parish. Donnelly mentioned that he had missed mass on a few occasions because he was on the run. Hearing this, the priest asked

---

36 See A. Beugnet, 'Absolution conditionelle ou sous condition', in A. Vacant, E. Mangenot and É. Amann (eds), *Dictionnaire de théologie catholique contenant l'exposé des doctrines de la théologie catholique, leurs preuves et leur histoire*, i:1 (Paris: Letouzey et Ané, 1930), pp. 252–5, and T. Ortolan, 'Confession. Questions morales et pratiques', in *ibid.*, iii:1 (Paris: Letouzey et Ané, 1938), pp. 942–60, at pp. 956–7. The practice is sometimes called 'general absolution', and this term also appears in the witness statements: MA, BMH, WS1348, Michael Davern, p. 21.
37 NLI, O'Donoghue papers, MS 31,170, Dominic to O'Donoghue, 15 December 1920.

him how many policemen he had shot. Donnelly 'knew [the priest] was our way of thinking' and told him three, to which the priest replied: 'You're no bloody good if that's all you have shot.'[38] And the words that Father Patrick MacHugh, curate in Aughagower, County Mayo, spoke in May 1921 to a man he believed to be a Volunteer have also been recorded. The penitent turned out to be a 'pretend Volunteer', who sent a report of MacHugh's comments to the British authorities.[39] MacHugh told the informant that 'as long as he got the orders he was not responsible' for the deaths of policemen that he would kill during an ambush.[40] Moreover, the morality of these killings depended 'on the intention he had at the moment'. Evidently neither Donnelly nor the informant was in need of moral reassurance himself. But the point is that the priests they spoke to used the confessional to reassure them that killing members of the crown forces was not a sin. This is where their role was the most important: in providing moral reassurance.

IRA commandants became adept at choosing confessors for their men carefully, as it became clear to them that discouragement by a confessor could have a strong impact on their men. When members of the Maam company of the West Connemara brigade went to confession in Leenane one day they were told by the priest 'that he could not give them absolution if they went out on active service'. The result was that the men failed to report for duty.[41] A similar danger had threatened to happen in Lorrha in September 1919 after Father Gleeson had condemned the killing of an RIC sergeant in his parish. Gleeson's attitude caused the men involved in the attack to stop going to confession. After a while, one of the company officers went to a sympathetic curate in a neighbouring parish, Father T. Porter, who told the officer to send the men to him so that he could give them absolution.[42] Similarly, members of the West Connemara brigade in Leenane were told to go to confession to two Redemptorist missioners in the parish, 'who were very sympathetic to the cause'.[43]

38 MA, BMH, WS1548, Stephen Donnelly, pp. 13–14.
39 TDA, Gilmartin papers, B4/8-ii/5, Flatley to Gilmartin, 23 May 1921.
40 TDA, Gilmartin papers, B4/8-ii/5, John Pierce statement, 20 May 1921.
41 MA, BMH, WS1692, John Feehan, pp. 31–2.
42 MA, BMH, WS1323, Martin Needham, p. 8.
43 MA, BMH, WS1731, John King, p. 13.

Some priests took the initiative to offer spiritual reassurance themselves. Thus in May 1920 Father Michael Hayes, curate in Newcastle West, County Limerick, 'had it arranged' for the Volunteers of the Rathkeale company to have their confessions heard before they set out on an attack on Kilmallock RIC barracks.[44] Similarly, in December 1920, Father David Fitzgerald, curate in Abbeyfeale, County Limerick, contacted the local IRA company to tell them he would say mass for them on Christmas day if they could find a suitable house. A place was found, and at half past four on Christmas morning Fitzgerald came and said mass for them. 'After mass, he saw each man individually and gave each his blessing with the sign of the cross on the forehead.'[45] And Father Patrick O'Reilly, curate in Feakle, County Clare, sent word to a battalion of the East Clare brigade at the same time that 'he would like if all the men of the battalion who participated in raids and ambushes would attend … to receive the sacraments of confession and holy communion'.[46]

The previous chapter has observed that funerals of dead IRA men often set the scene for republican manifestations. Although some bishops and priests refused to give republicans a Christian burial, republican funerals were regularly held in the usual manner in broad daylight. Officiating at such ceremonies was not necessarily a sign of support for the IRA campaign, although the words and actions of the celebrant could easily make it so. When two Volunteers were killed during an ambush at Islandeady, County Galway, in May 1921, Black and Tans and soldiers took the bodies of the victims with them and delivered them the next day to the Catholic church. Father Paul McLoughlin, the parish priest, was instructed to have their funeral the following day at one o'clock in the afternoon and to allow nobody but their families to attend. McLoughlin heeded neither of these instructions, commencing the obsequies at noon and allowing the local IRA company to stage an elaborate funeral with flags, wreaths, guards of honour and a large number of mourners. When the crown forces turned up close to one o'clock, the mass was over and the coffins had been interred. Some men on the run, for whose benefit the arrangements had been

44 MA, BMH, WS1225, James Roche, p. 5.
45 MA, BMH, WS1272, James Collins, p. 21.
46 MA, BMH, WS983, Thomas Tuohy, p. 26.

changed, escaped in the general confusion, leaving McLoughlin to face the insults of a furious officer.[47]

Presiding over secret nocturnal burial services of fallen Volunteers was always a gesture of clerical support. Such funerals were not uncommon; Seán MacBride recounted that they were held at Whitefriar Street Carmelite church in Dublin in 1920.[48] Only trustworthy priests were selected for the task. These funerals were prime moments for republican priests to give the troops some encouragement. Father Patrick O'Connell, parish priest of Enniskean, County Cork, heard the confessions of the men who carried out the Kilmichael ambush in November 1920 before they set out, and also subsequently presided at the funerals of those who had been killed. Liam Deasy has given an account of the funeral of the three Volunteers killed during the attack. The remains of the dead men had been hidden in a bog until coffins could be procured. On the night of the funeral, a cortege was formed and it made its way to a local cemetery, where it arrived around eleven o'clock in the evening. At two o'clock in the morning, O'Connell performed the burial service and gave a sermon in which he paid tribute to the dead and their glorious fight for freedom. Deasy commented that 'his consoling words made such an impression that they were soon being repeated all over the district'.[49]

Priests who engaged in these activities put themselves at considerable risk. In December 1920 a member of the IRA's Meath brigade mistook a fellow Volunteer for a Black and Tan and shot him dead.[50] Seán Boylan, the commanding officer, sent for Father Patrick Kelly, curate in Dunboyne, to attend the unfortunate victim. Kelly's role soon became known to the British authorities, because he was asked to bring the news to the deceased's relatives. Kelly found himself in an unenviable predicament, with the authorities

---

47 Patrick Maye, 'A short history of the I.R.A. in Islandeady, 1919–1921', *Cathair na Mart. Journal of the Westport Historical Society*, 15 (1995), pp. 106–9, at pp. 108–9.
48 Seán MacBride, *That Day's Struggle. A Memoir 1904–1951* (Blackrock: Currach Press, 2005), p. 89. For other examples see MA, BMH, WS881, James Kilmartin, p. 12; WS600, Donnchadh O h-Annagain, p. 37; WS1640, James Doyle, p. 21; WS788, Sean Scully, p. 16.
49 Deasy, *Free*, pp. 176–7.
50 MA, BMH, WS1715, Seán Boylan, p. 32.

very curious to know who had called him to the scene, whom he had seen there and what he had been told about the incident. Kelly refused to say anything, claiming that this was 'by reason of my being a priest'.[51] Sir Nevil Macready unsuccessfully solicited Cardinal Logue's assistance in getting Kelly to talk.[52] In the event, Kelly escaped sanctions, but the incident shows that priests who ministered to IRA men in secret did so at some peril to themselves.

Ministering to prisoners of the IRA

The moral reassurance that spiritual assistance provided is starkly evident in cases where priests were asked to minister to 'spies and informers' taken prisoner by the IRA and condemned to death.[53] There are many examples in the Bureau's witness statements.[54] It appears to have been standard procedure to call a priest before the execution took place. Even a condemned spy of no religion was offered the services of a priest in County Roscommon in June 1921. The man accepted and was baptised minutes before being drowned in the river Suck.[55] Joost Augusteijn has argued that the presence of priests at the execution of spies served to relieve IRA officers of moral responsibility.[56] He has given an example of a priest who explicitly sanctioned the killing of a man in IRA custody whose confession he had just heard. It could be objected that this form of ministry must not automatically be classified as support for the IRA campaign, because priests may have felt that the needs of the victim

---

51 ADA, Logue papers, ARCH9/5/4, Macready to Logue, 17 December 1920, 'Evidence of Rev. Patrick Kelly, C.C., Dunboyne'.
52 ADA, Logue papers, ARCH9/5/4, Macready to Logue, 17 December 1920.
53 For IRA treatment of spies and informers, see Thomas Earls Fitzgerald, 'The execution of "spies and informers" in West Cork, 1921', in David Fitzpatrick (ed.), *Terror in Ireland 1916–1923. Trinity History Workshop* (Dublin: Lilliput Press, 2012), pp. 181–93.
54 See for instance MA, BMH, WS479, Michael Murphy, p. 10; WS966, John Walsh, p. 16; WS1187, Patrick Butler, p. 14, and WS1450, John C. Ryan, p. 13. Another example is in TNA, CO904/115, IGMR, April 1921.
55 MA, BMH, WS817, T. Crawley, p. 11, and WS692, James Quigley, pp. 13–14.
56 Augusteijn, *Defiance*, pp. 308–9.

overrode any misgivings they had about participating in something they otherwise found objectionable.

As with Father Albert's protestations of impartiality mentioned above, this was the way in which these priests presented their role themselves when they were caught. In one bizarre incident in Kilmessan, County Meath, in March 1921, the identity of a priest who ministered to prisoners of the IRA was revealed. According to a veteran, an IRA battalion had arrested a gang of robbers in the area and sentenced them to death. A local curate, Father James Gilmore, was summoned to hear their confessions. At the last minute, the men's sentences were commuted to deportation to England. One of the deported men, called Byrne, took his revenge by joining the Black and Tans and returning to Ireland. There he participated in the capture of some of the Volunteers who had been involved in his own arrest. During the trial of one of these, Byrne testified that the defendant had impersonated a priest to hear his confession while in IRA custody. Thus it was that Father Gilmore was called upon to state that he had actually been the priest who had heard Byrne's confession.[57] The case received much attention in the press, and Gilmore explained himself in a letter to the *Irish Independent*: 'I, being the curate of the parish, was summoned to a certain house, where three men were detained in custody. I was told they expressed a desire to see me. I attended the call, as I was bound to do.'[58] Gilmore emphasised that it was simply a matter of exercising his priestly ministry regardless of the political context.

There is also some evidence that priests called to hear prisoners' confessions sometimes tried to persuade their captors to reprieve them. Brian O'Grady, veteran captain of the Ballylongford company, County Kerry, recalled that a local curate, Father Timothy O'Shea, was called out to hear a convicted man's confession in the spring of 1921. Afterwards, O'Shea asked O'Grady if the man's life could be spared.[59] In this case the sentence was carried out despite the priest's attempts, but Father James Moloney, curate in Clonoulty, County Tipperary, had better luck regarding another prisoner. The day before the truce in July 1921, Moloney pleaded with the IRA men who were about to execute a convicted robber:

---

57 MA, BMH, WS1696, Patrick Quinn, p. 3.
58 *Irish Independent*, 12 March 1921.
59 MA, BMH, WS1390, Brian O'Grady, p. 16.

'You will all be free tomorrow at 12 o'clock, and give this poor divil a chance!'[60]

On the whole, however, the priests whose services were mentioned in the witness statements came, heard the victim's confession and left again. There is every appearance that they accepted the legitimacy of proceedings and simply played their part, thus at least tacitly giving moral sanction to the affair. In fact, Volunteers carefully selected priests for this task, not only to avoid danger to themselves, but also to ensure that they would have somebody who would play along with the script. Thus the members of Kinvara company, County Galway, decided not to send for the local priest when they were preparing to execute a spy in the winter of 1920, because he 'might intercede for [the spy] and influence us against our better judgment'.[61] IRA men chose friends to perform this service for them. Thus Father Swan of Moynalty, 'chaplain to the IRA', rendered spiritual aid to two spies executed in the Kells battalion area during the War of Independence.[62] Conversely, there are examples of unsympathetic priests who refused to attend, such as John Canon Doherty, parish priest of Ardara, County Donegal, who 'did not approve of the movement at all'.[63] He refused to accompany the Volunteer who had come to collect him to hear a spy's confession in June 1921. Priests who did come by their very presence gave a sense of legitimacy to proceedings.

Sheltering men on the run

Apart from these forms of spiritual aid, priests also gave material support. The most frequent form of this was giving shelter to fugitives. When IRA activity picked up in early 1920 with more regular attacks on RIC barracks, Volunteers who became known to the police had to go on the run.[64] These men were constantly in need of safe houses, and they began to form flying columns in the spring and summer. Charles Townshend and Joost Augusteijn

60 MA, BMH, WS1348, Michael Davern, p. 56.
61 MA, BMH, WS1173, Michael Hynes, p. 9.
62 MA, BMH, WS1650, Patrick O'Reilly, p. 20.
63 MA, BMH, WS803, Michael Sheerin, p. 25. For another example see WS1226, Michael Russell, p. 8.
64 Augusteijn, *Defiance*, p. 124.

have contended that the fugitive life of these Volunteers, which took them away from the 'restraining influence of the community', was an important factor in the radicalisation of the movement. As the restraints imposed by interaction with relatives, friends and the wider community were removed, such Volunteers became likely to engage in ever more violence. This continued until British countermeasures made flying column activity increasingly ineffective in the course of the spring of 1921.[65] The existence of safe houses was obviously important to the functioning of these columns, and providing shelter was thus a significant contribution to make.

Not every priest who put up a Volunteer for the night was an ideologically motivated supporter of the IRA. James Canon O'Connor, parish priest of Gurteen, County Sligo, gave shelter to the IRA man Patrick Hegarty in the winter of 1919 even though he had condemned Hegarty's activities from the pulpit a short time previously.[66] O'Connor's hospitality was no doubt motivated more by thoughts of Christian charity than by a desire to aid the Volunteers in their efforts, although he also stored a car used by the IRA. Nonetheless, his activities helped to further the cause, and he was thus a material, if not an ideological supporter of the campaign. By contrast, the ideological component was not lacking with Thomas Canon Langan, parish priest of Moate, County Westmeath, who put up an entire column at a farm he owned in the winter of 1920.[67] The same was true of Father John Magee, parish priest of nearby Tober, who housed a column in his stables.[68] Moreover, there were considerable risks involved in sheltering men on the run, even for priests who gave occasional shelter to individual Volunteers. Thus Father John Larkin, curate in Windgap, County Kilkenny, was interrogated by Auxiliaries within twenty-four hours of putting up two Volunteers for Christmas in 1920.[69] The possible repercussions required strong motivation on the part of those who provided shelter.

65 Charles Townshend, 'The Irish Republican Army and the development of guerrilla warfare, 1916–1921', *The English Historical Review*, 94:371 (1979), pp. 318–45, at p. 330, and Augusteijn, *Defiance*, pp. 312–34, 344.
66 MA, BMH, WS1606, Patrick Hegarty, p. 18.
67 MA, BMH, WS1337, David Daly, p. 16.
68 MA, BMH, WS1308, Henry O'Brien, p. 11.
69 MA, BMH, WS1335, James Leahy, p. 16.

IRA veterans praised the intrepidity of their hosts. The Meath Volunteer Seamus Finn stayed with some comrades in the house of Father P. Norris, curate of Kildalkey, and called the priest 'a fearless, patriotic "sagart" who well knew the risk attaching to his hospitality'.[70] And Dan Breen praised Father McCarthy, the Ballyhahill curate, because he 'never counted the cost of "harbouring outlaws"' during the War of Independence.[71] The difficulties involved are clearly illustrated in Father Patrick Gaynor's account of the hospitality that he and his fellow Mullagh curate provided to a Volunteer in 1920. Ignatius O'Neill had been in charge of the Rineen ambush in September 1920, which killed six constables.[72] Gaynor wrote:

> Gaiety was the order of the day – and of the night – during the mad year and a half which I spent with F[ather] McKenna in Mullagh. Sometimes I tried to call a halt, adverting that the Tans might raid the house and find a festive party in the small hours, and, worse still, might capture a frequent guest, Ignatius O'Neill, whom they would have burned to death after the Rineen ambush.[73]

Gaynor suspected that neighbours would eventually disclose O'Neill's whereabouts to the authorities, also putting himself and McKenna at risk. The RIC made a few visits to the house before the curates were eventually arrested. After one of these visits, when the police were fobbed off by the housekeeper, Gaynor tried to convince McKenna that O'Neill was no longer safe. McKenna, however, refused to 'insult a guest', and moreover 'had great belief in his luck though his experiences in laying wagers should have made him distrust the fickle goddess'.[74]

Religious houses were ideal safe houses, because they could accommodate relatively large numbers of guests without arousing suspicion. Thus the Trappist abbey of Mount Melleray, County Waterford, gave food and shelter to men of several IRA brigades as well as their prisoners, and also provided spiritual services. The commandant of the Waterford brigade wrote that the abbey was

---

70 MA, BMH, WS1060, Seamus Finn, p. 20.
71 Breen, *Fight*, pp. 44, 48–9.
72 Hopkinson, *War*, p. 130.
73 NLI, Gaynor papers, MS 19,826, 'Sinn Fein days', p. 494.
74 *Ibid.*, p. 496.

'always a port of call' for his brigade and that the monks heard the men's confessions and gave them food to eat while listening to their stories.[75] Colleges run by religious were also suitable places. Father Patrick Doyle, rector of Knockbeg College, stated that 'many of the prominent men in the movement came regularly to us in Knockbeg', meaning not only Sinn Féin leaders but also IRA men such as Rory O'Connor. According to Doyle, police and military in Carlow referred to the college as 'The Rebels' Paradise'.[76] And there were rumours that the Benedictine priest Dom Francis Sweetman hosted IRA men at his Mount St Benedict school in Gorey, County Wexford.[77]

Priests with guns

It was not unusual for priests in country parishes to own shotguns for their farms. Often farmers' sons themselves, many of them dabbled in agriculture to supplement their parishioners' offerings.[78] Canon Langan's farm in Moate has just been mentioned, and there are other examples of priests and religious communities who held cattle.[79] Priests kept shotguns to keep the fox from the chickens or the birds from the land. But possession of arms could bring them very quickly into contact with guerrilla warfare. In 1919 and 1920, as the Volunteers were trying to arm themselves, presbyteries became interesting targets. The previous chapter has already shown that hostile priests reluctant to hand over their guns to the

---

75 James Mansfield, 'The Decies brigade – 1920', *The Capuchin Annual* (1970), pp. 377–83, at p. 381. See also MA, BMH, WS1667, Paul Merrigan, pp. 12–13.
76 MA, BMH, WS807, Patrick Doyle, p. 17.
77 Dominic Aidan Bellenger, 'An Irish Benedictine adventure. Dom Francis Sweetman (1872–1953) and Mount St Benedict, Gorey', in W. J. Sheils and Diana Wood (eds), *The Churches, Ireland and the Irish. Papers Read at the 1987 Summer Meeting and the 1988 Winter Meeting of the Ecclesiastical History Society* (Oxford and New York: Basil Blackwell, 1989), pp. 401–16, at pp. 410–11.
78 O'Shea, *Priest*, p. 21.
79 See for instance *Irish Independent*, 2 July 1921, Seán Enright, *The Trial of Civilians by Military Courts, Ireland 1921* (Dublin and Portland, OR: Irish Academic Press, 2012), pp. 233–5, and IJA, Tullabeg papers, FM/TULL/289, 30 June 1920.

IRA could expect to have their houses raided. More sympathetic clerics handed over their rifles themselves, such as Father Slattery of Annascaul, or Father James Maguire, parish priest of Louth, who told police calling to confiscate his shotgun in September 1920 that the IRA had anticipated them by thirteen hours.[80] He even had a receipt signed by the commandant of the local IRA company.

When possession of arms was prohibited by the British authorities in the autumn of 1920, presbyteries and religious houses came in for a good deal of attention from the crown forces. Many of the raids revealed that the inhabitants still owned arms and ammunition. Thus a fowling piece and ammunition belonging to Father P. J. Clyne of Boyle, County Roscommon, was confiscated in September 1920, and the same happened to Father Philip Mulligan, parish priest of Curracastle in the same county in the same month.[81] Some priests were court-martialled for this offence. Father George Culhane, parish priest of Cratloe, County Clare, was sentenced to a fine of £5 or a fortnight's imprisonment in default of payment for possession of a sporting rifle and ammunition in November 1920.[82] And Father John McCaughan, a teacher in St Malachy's College, Belfast, was given the same sentence in April 1921 after a raid on the college discovered his miniature rifle, cleaning rod and revolver cleaning brush under a staircase.[83] McCaughan explained that he used the rifle for shooting birds and cats.

Unlike these priests, none of whom appear to have harboured strong political views, republican clerics with connections to the IRA held on to their guns with a view to self-defence. Father Michael O'Flanagan's biographer has mentioned that O'Flanagan carried a gun in October 1920, and Jesuit Father William Hackett wrote that he kept a rifle in the chimney of his room in Crescent College, Limerick.[84] Father Gaynor also admitted to having had

---

80 *Irish Independent*, 7 September 1920. For local competition between the crown forces and the IRA to impound arms in private possession, see Townshend, *Campaign*, p. 62.
81 *Irish Independent*, 23 September 1920.
82 TNA, WO35/123.
83 TNA, WO35/126; sentence: TNA, WO35/135, Register of cases tried (1921 Feb – Apr), p. 250.
84 O'Flanagan: Carroll, *Fooled*, p. 116; Hackett: IJA, 'Brief lives' papers, J172/5, William Hackett, 'Seven years in Limerick', p. 1.

a revolver during the War of Independence.[85] Apart from these personal weapons, which were unused as far as can be ascertained, there is much evidence that presbyteries, religious houses and churches were used for storing arms and ammunition for the IRA. Joost Augusteijn has quoted from a Volunteer's statement to Ernie O'Malley that arms and ammunition had been hidden in statues of the Blessed Virgin and St Joseph in the church of Shough, County Tipperary.[86] And a Wexford veteran recalled that a tomb in Ballindaggin churchyard was filled with gelignite.[87] These feats could hardly have been accomplished without the connivance of the local priest.

Clerical involvement was even clearer in the case of Father Michael Morley, curate in Headford, County Galway. A raid on his house by crown forces in October 1920 revealed the presence of three detonators, nine revolver cartridges, three fuses and one round of .22 ammunition, as well as a full box of sporting cartridges and a sporting gun, for which he had a permit. Morley could not, of course, have had legitimate agricultural need for detonators and fuses, or for the ammunition that did not fit his fowling piece. His republican views were evident from the fact that he denied the court's right to try him and made a speech which the press was not allowed to report. He was sentenced to nine months in prison with hard labour, but the sentence was remitted.[88] It is not in doubt that he was storing these arms for the IRA.[89] Apart from the practical benefits which this form of material support provided for the IRA, it also had an important psychological component. A Mayo IRA veteran described bringing weapons to Kilbride presbytery, which doubled as the local company's arsenal. He added: 'it gave us great confidence to have the priest on our side'.[90]

Religious houses were also ideal hiding places. When the Capuchin priory in Church Street, Dublin, was raided in December

---

85 NLI, Gaynor papers, MS 19,826, 'Sinn Fein days', p. 475.
86 Augusteijn, *Defiance*, p. 309.
87 MA, BMH, WS1298, Patrick Doyle, p. 11.
88 *Irish Independent*, 8, 9, 19 and 20 October 1920. See also MA, BMH, WS424, Geraldine Dillon, p. 11.
89 Other examples in TNA, WO35/129 and WO35/70, and MA, BMH, WS1182, George Kiely, pp. 12–13.
90 MA, BMH, WS1735, P.J. Kelly, p. 13.

1920, revolver ammunition, blank cartridges and one round of 12-gauge bore ammunition were found in the Father Mathew Memorial Hall beside the priory.[91] And when a raid was carried out on the Carmelite priory in Whitefriar Street, Dublin, in the same month, a revolver was found as well as two old guns and a substantial amount of ammunition. These items were hidden in the cellar and the chimney among other places.[92] The Carmelite community later released a statement to the press, saying that it was 'somewhat misleading' to state that the objects were found in the monastery. In fact, they had been found in a 'very old part of the basement of the monastery', to which there was 'comparatively easy access from the street', and which had been in constant use as a workshop and store by many engaged in building work during the previous few years.[93] This explanation did not satisfy the authorities, and the provincial received a letter from army GHQ a few days later asking him to state what steps he proposed to take to ensure that 'monasteries, churches, buildings or grounds under [his] control, are not used to secrete arms, ammunition, equipment or seditious persons or literature'. Without satisfactory assurances that these buildings would be confined to sacred use only, the commander-in-chief announced that he would regard them as on the same footing as 'putative centres of rebel action'.[94] More ammunition was found in Terenure College, Dublin, only a month later.[95] And Father Hamilton of St Flannan's College, Ennis, recounted that a lay professor kept a gun in his rooms, while a steward, who was 'an active member of the IRA', had a rifle stored in the building.[96]

Apart from storing arms, a number of priests on the list in Appendix 2 supported the IRA by helping to procure arms and ammunition. Thus Father James Smyth, curate in Martinstown, County Antrim, was in the habit of 'collecting ammunition and equipment in Belfast from sources he knew'. An IRA member

91 TNA, WO35/81.
92 *Ibid.*
93 *Irish Independent*, 24 December 1920.
94 Carmelite (Calced) Provincial Archives, Dublin, Colonel on the staff of GHQ, Parkgate, to provincial, 3 January 1921. The letter is reproduced in D'Arcy, *Terenure*, pp. 152–3.
95 TNA, WO35/82.
96 Ó Haichir, *Rebel*, pp. 13–15.

joined him on his exploits 'to take responsibility for the stuff in case of a hold-up or search by British forces'.[97] Father Delahunty of Callan also procured gelignite and rifles, while Father Doyle of Knockbeg remembered distributing rifles to Volunteers on the islands in Baltimore harbour.[98] Shortage of weapons and ammunition was a chronic problem for the IRA, and both GHQ and individual units attempted to purchase them abroad.[99] Priests could help with this too, and Father McCarthy of Ballyhahill went to the United States in 1920 to buy Thompson machine guns for the East Limerick brigade.[100] The Irish College in Rome was the scene of an ineffectual attempt by the IRA to procure arms from the Italian government in November 1920. The rector and vice-rector, Fathers John Hagan and Michael Curran, hosted two Irishmen who were ostensibly on a mission to discuss trading prospects in Italy, but who were actually there 'for the direct purpose of buying arms from the Italian ministry of war'. Curran wrote that 'although we were fully aware of the nature of the mission and keenly interested in it, our formal attitude was one of non-interference'.[101] Given the fact that Curran and Hagan provided the two Volunteers with a cover by introducing them to some Italian shipping directors, their attitude was in fact more involved than Curran was prepared to admit. Although clerical intervention cannot be credited for the provision of arms on a large scale – the Italian expedition ended in failure, for example – there was symbolic value in the involvement of priests.

Priests who helped store or procure arms calculated that their clerical status made them immune from government interference. As Chapter 7 will demonstrate, this had become a vain hope by the end of 1920. By that time the crown forces widely suspected priests and their houses were raided frequently. But the Cork hospital chaplain Father Thomas Duggan showed that there were still ways in which a priest could use the cover of his clerical state to help the IRA. Duggan, who described himself as a 'combatant (more or

97 MA, BMH, WS609, Feidhlim MacGuil, pp. 4–5.
98 Delahunty: MA, BMH, WS1642, Edward Halley, pp. 5, 7; Doyle: WS1298, Patrick Doyle, p. 7. For another example see WS1379, Peter Howley, p. 32.
99 Augusteijn, *Defiance*, p. 148.
100 MA, BMH, WS435, Tadhg Crowley, p. 65.
101 MA, BMH, WS687, Michael Curran, pp. 493–4.

less) against the Black and Tans', had been appointed chaplain to the Bon Secours hospital after an unsatisfactory stint as secretary to Bishop Cohalan.[102] The hospital was located beside Cork jail, and Duggan occasionally did duty for the prison chaplain. On one of these occasions he 'was made beast of [burden]' for the republican prisoners who were hatching plans to blow up the prison walls so that they could escape. Duggan carried in a wooden mallet – 'to percuss the warders' – a knuckle-duster with dagger and two slabs of gun cotton.[103] In the event the action was called off. This did not exculpate Duggan according to his priest-biographer: Father Carthach MacCarthy observed quite accurately that Duggan 'was taking advantage of his position of a priest to become directly involved in acts of violence which might have caused deaths and injuries'.[104]

Informing on enemy activity and helping IRA communications

Priests in rural parishes were often in the confidence of all sections of the population, including Volunteers and constables. Both belligerent camps realised that if priests could be persuaded to pass on information about the other party, the clergy could be of invaluable assistance to their intelligence efforts. The list in Appendix 2 includes a number of priests who helped the IRA by informing on the activities of crown forces. Chapter 3 has already mentioned the example of priests warning Volunteers that planned operations were known to the crown forces, and has speculated on their motives. Even if genuine, such warnings did not necessarily imply a commitment to support the IRA campaign; just a desire to avoid bloodshed. But the priests mentioned as IRA informers in the Bureau's witness statements clearly went beyond any duty that Christian charity may have imposed. For instance, Father Thomas Hobbins, curate of Ferrybank, Arklow, had a brother who was a constable in the RIC

---

102 Secretary to Cohalan: Carthach MacCarthy, *Archdeacon Tom Duggan in Peace and in War* (Tallaght: Blackwater Press, 1994), p. 57; quotation: MA, BMH, WS552, Thomas Duggan, p. 5.
103 MA, BMH, WS552, Thomas Duggan, pp. 4–5. See also Barry, *Days*, p. 167.
104 MacCarthy, *Duggan*, p. 64.

in Cork. Throughout 1920, Hobbins passed on his brother's letters to a local Volunteer, who sent them on to GHQ.[105] And Father Philip O'Doherty, parish priest of Carndonagh, County Donegal, reportedly passed on information he got from a friendly RIC constable to the IRA 'with the least possible delay'.[106] There is also the example of a priest who warned the IRA that a woman in Armagh claiming to be Dan Breen's mother was in fact a spy. Father Arthur Toner, curate in Armagh, suspected that Mrs. Breen was not whom she claimed to be. After some intelligence work that involved procuring a sample of handwriting, Toner had enough evidence to conclude that the woman was a spy. He presented his information to the local Volunteers, who 'chased her from the area'.[107]

Finally, a small number of priests are also on record as having aided the IRA by assisting in internal communications. Thus the head of communications of one of the Dublin brigade battalions delivered dispatches from GHQ for the southern and western divisions by hand to two people in County Kildare, among them a priest in Kill. The priest subsequently sent the letters on to contacts further south and west.[108] One of these may well have been a curate in Kilreekil, County Galway. Bishop O'Doherty of Clonfert received a letter from the British military authorities in December 1920 complaining that Father Martin O'Farrell had been found in possession of a letter from which 'it would appear that he is acting as an intermediary for members of the Irish Republican Army'. The letter was signed 'M.' and contained instructions about IRA orders. There was a covering note to O'Farrell asking him to 'give enclosed to the captain of company'.[109] And the Dublin Volunteer Garry

105 MA, BMH, WS1472, Matthew Kavanagh, p. 12. Kavanagh calls the brother a district inspector, but Terence MacSwiney called him simply 'Constable Hobbins': DDA, Walsh papers, 380/4, MacSwiney to Walsh, 8 April 1920.
106 MA, BMH, WS1516, P. H. Doherty, p. 11. Other examples in WS997, James Feely, p. 10; WS424, Geraldine Dillon, p. 2, and WS1417, Martin Ryan, p. 6.
107 MA, BMH, WS612, Patrick Beagan, pp. 3–5. For a slightly different example see WS714, Thomas Hynes, p. 12.
108 MA, BMH, WS327, Patrick Egan, p. 50.
109 CtDA, O'Doherty papers, xii.c.6, Brigadier general to O'Doherty, 9 December 1920. Another example in UCDA, O'Malley papers, P17b/105, Garry Hoolihan.

Hoolihan recounted that he once went to see Father Albert at the Capuchin priory in Church Street, Dublin, as night was falling, and it was necessary to have word of impending British actions sent to other members of the IRA.[110] As a priest, Albert had a permit to be out after curfew hours. He was happy to oblige.

---

110 UCDA, O'Malley papers, P17b/105, Garry Hoolihan. See also Augusteijn, *Defiance*, p. 309.

6

Troublesome priests: responses to clerical support for republicanism

Unlike condemnation of republican violence, support for the IRA took place as far away from the limelight as possible. Nevertheless republican priests had to account for themselves often enough, to their bishop or religious superior for example, or, if they were curates, to their parish priest. This was also true for priests who supported Sinn Féin. The current chapter examines the interaction between these priests and their social surroundings, ecclesiastical and lay. Bishops, religious superiors and parish priests had agendas of their own that determined their responses. It was important to the bishops not to alienate the republican camp, but they also had to respond to the criticisms of scandalised conservatives, while ensuring that lines of communication with the government in Dublin Castle remained open. Moreover, they were concerned for the Irish church's reputation abroad, especially in the Vatican. Religious superiors wanted to avoid internal conflict within their communities, and parish priests often simply wished to keep trouble away from their church doors. How did these ecclesiastical authorities respond to the activities of republican priests? Which forms of support were acceptable to them and which were not? And how did the priests in question defend their actions to their superiors?

Episcopal responses

The image of the priest favoured by the nineteenth-century ideologues of ultramontane Catholicism was of an 'objective bearer of holiness', whose 'one prime function' was 'to help his people to become holy'.[1] The pursuit of a political career did not accord

---

1 Peter Doyle, 'Pastoral perfection. Cardinal Manning and the secular

easily with this exalted image, particularly as it might threaten unity among the ordained ministers of the church. Canon law discouraged priests from assuming overtly political roles without sanction from the relevant church authorities. The *Code of Canon Law* allowed priests to seek election as members of legislative assemblies on condition that they received permission from the appropriate ecclesiastical authorities. They were normally forbidden to accept public office involving the exercise of civil jurisdiction unless they had obtained an indult from the Holy See.[2] But these rules must be understood more as attempts to strengthen episcopal control over the political activism of priests than as a way to limit clerical influence to the strictly ecclesiastical sphere. In the age of mass politics and expanding electorates, too much was at stake for the bishops to be neglectful of the political realm. Significantly, Pope Benedict XV ended his predecessors' long sulk at the theft of the Papal States by revoking the famous ban on Catholic participation in Italian politics in 1919.[3] Priests in fact served as members of parliament in several European countries during the 1910s and 1920s. They did so usually as representatives of Catholic political parties, examples being Monsignors Ludwig Kaas in Germany, Ignaz Seipel in Austria and Willem Nolens in the Netherlands.[4] A similar tradition of priestly parliamentarianism did not emerge in Ireland for the simple reason that ordained priests of all denominations were barred by civil law from sitting in the House of Commons.[5]

---

clergy', in W. J. Sheils and Diana Wood (eds), *The Ministry. Clerical and Lay. Papers read at the 1988 Summer Meeting and the 1989 Winter Meeting of the Ecclesiastical History Society* (Oxford: Basil Blackwell, 1989), pp. 385–96, at pp. 393–4. 'Objective bearer of holiness' is a quotation from G. P. Connolly.

2 *CIC*, canon 139, pars. 2, 4.

3 John F. Pollard, *Benedict XV. The Unknown Pope and the Pursuit of Peace* (London and New York: Continuum, 2005), p. 175.

4 *Ibid.*, p. 172. For Nolens see J. P. Gribling, *Willem Hubert Nolens 1860–1931. Uit het Leven van een Priester-Staatsman* (Assen: Van Gorcum, 1978).

5 Oonagh Gay, 'The *House of Commons (Removal of Clergy Disqualification) Bill*. Bill 34 of 2000–01', House of Commons Library Research Paper 01/11, 26 January 2001, www.parliament.uk/documents/commons/lib/research/rp2001/rp01-011.pdf (accessed 26 August 2010).

This certainly did not mean that priests in Ireland were any less involved in politics, and 'the priest in politics' was in fact a very familiar phenomenon. It is no surprise that the episcopal propagators of ultramontane Catholicism in Ireland were every bit as keen as their foreign brethren on bringing their priests' political activism into the orbit of their control. The decrees of the 1875 and 1900 plenary synods of the Irish church provided the canonical instruments. The 1875 First Synod of Maynooth admonished all priests to avoid arguments and disputes about political matters in public meetings and in magazines and newspapers, 'lest priestly dignity suffer some detriment, or that charity which is the strength of the church be violated, or they become embroiled in strife or conflict with others'.[6] The 1900 Second Synod of Maynooth reaffirmed this article and also stipulated in its 'decree to avoid dissensions among churchmen' that priests were forbidden from assuming any public or civil position without the bishop's written permission.[7] In a different article, the same decree also repeated and confirmed a statute adopted by the bishops at a meeting in 1882 which regulated the attendance of priests at public meetings. The statute prohibited all priests from participating in these without the express permission of the parish priest in whose parish the meeting was held, and forbade curates from attending them even in their own parishes without their parish priest's permission.[8]

Of course it was a matter for debate where religion ended and politics started. None of the statutes mentioned were intended to stop priests from interfering in political affairs to further the cause of the Catholic religion. As Patrick Murray has noted, there were other statutes which explicitly stated as much. The 1853 Provincial Council of Dublin – a meeting of the archbishop of Dublin and his suffragans – gave the familiar exhortation that priests must not

---

6 *Acta et decreta synodi plenariae episcoporum Hiberniae habitae apud Maynutiam, an. MDCCCLXXV* (Dublin: Browne and Nolan, 1877), pp. 95–6, 'Decretum de vita et honestate clericorum', art. 128.

7 *Acta et decreta synodi plenariae episcoporum Hiberniae habitae apud Maynutiam an. MDCCCC* (Dublin: Browne and Nolan, 1906), p. 121: 'Decretum de dissensionibus inter viros ecclesiasticos evitandis', art. 396.

8 *Ibid.*, p. 121, art. 397.

speak about 'merely secular things or political elections ... which may easily encourage disagreement between the pastors and the people, and excite great unrest for souls'. However, in a following decree, the council expressly allowed priests to 'show pious solicitude lest detriment to religion flow from political elections'.[9] Murray has described the forms that such involvement might take: 'canvassing, resolutions of support for candidates, conveying voters to the polls, addressing meetings, ... hiring intimidatory mobs and ... the supply of intoxicating drink to the electors'.[10]

The cause of the Catholic religion was not noticeably at issue during the 'national struggle' that took place in Ireland from Easter 1916 onwards. Of course republicans frequently availed of Catholic religious imagery, and the 'religious motif' was central to their ideology.[11] But the bishops enjoyed a comfortable working relationship with the Castle administration, and at least until 1919 none of the interests which they wished to see protected were much in danger from the British authorities. There was no specifically ecclesiastical incentive to support the revolutionaries. Many bishops therefore felt quite entitled in the years immediately following the Easter rising to take disciplinary action against priests who had made themselves conspicuous for their republican activism. Bishop Bernard Coyne of Elphin used a statute of the Second Synod of Maynooth to suspend Father O'Flanagan in 1918 when he had attended political meetings without the local parish priest's permission.[12] Often these disciplinary measures came at the behest of the British authorities, who still preferred to deal with troublesome priests through their bishops. It had been an important sign of the changing clerical mood that Bishop O'Dwyer of Limerick had refused to grant the government's request to remove two republican priests from

---

9 *Synodus dioecesana Dublinensis, habita in ecclesia Sanctae Crucis, Dublini, die 25 Nov., 1879 una cum statutis concilii provincialis Dublinensis an. 1853, et synodi dioecesanae Dublinensis an. 1831, necnon aliis documentis usui cleri accommodatis* (Dublin: Joseph Dollard, 1879), pp. 56–7. See Murray, *Oracles*, p. 2, and John H. Whyte, 'Political problems, 1850–1860', in Patrick J. Corish (ed.), *A History of Irish Catholicism*, v (Dublin and Melbourne: Gill, 1967), pp. 1–40, at pp. 31–2.
10 Murray, *Oracles*, p. 2. See also Newsinger, 'Sword', p. 611.
11 Newsinger, 'Sword'.
12 Carroll, *Fooled*, pp. 82–3.

ministry in May 1916.¹³ But in fact this case was an exception, and most bishops continued to concede such requests, no doubt spurred on by the thought that General Maxwell might take measures himself if they did not.¹⁴ At the same time as O'Dwyer was challenging Maxwell, Bishop James Browne of Ferns was advising a curate he had moved at the general's recommendation: 'let your motto in future be: ... keep out of politics'.¹⁵

This is not to say that the bishops wanted priests to sever all connections with republicans, and as Sinn Féin's star continued to rise in 1918 it became ever more important to the episcopate to keep in touch both with the party and with the Irish Volunteers. Even conservative bishops were convinced of the wisdom of this policy. In May 1919 Archbishop Harty went to Galbally, County Limerick, to give confirmation. His visit came on the day after the killing by the IRA of two constables at nearby Knocklong, and Harty denounced the crime from the pulpit. At lunch in the presbytery afterwards, the local curate, Father James O'Brien, surprised the archbishop by saying that he had been out all night attending the wounded Volunteers who had taken part in the rescue. According to an IRA veteran who recounted the story, Harty was very interested and in subsequent years always asked O'Brien about his 'Volunteer friends'.¹⁶

Public statements from priests to the effect that IRA killings were not murder were not acceptable, however, even to bishops whose republican views were stronger than Harty's. Not only did they contravene their own policy of condemning violence from whatever side it came; they also gave the Irish clergy a bad press. Such publicity scandalised the faithful in Ireland and abroad, and

---

13 Aan de Wiel, *Church*, p. 105.
14 For examples of episcopal compliance, see Tom Williams, 'Fr. Patrick Walsh – the republican priest', *The Journal of the Taghmon Historical Society*, 4 (2001), pp. 13–22, at p. 13; Galway Diocesan Archives, Galway (hereafter GDA), Thomas O'Dea papers, 40/224, Maxwell to O'Dea, 6 May 1916; TNA, WO35/99, Bushmill to Fitzgerald, 1 November 1917; Killaloe Diocesan Archives, Ennis (hereafter KDA), Michael Fogarty papers, F9A10, Dublin Castle statement, 21 October 1917; MA, BMH, WS325, Eugene Coyle, p. 6.
15 MA, BMH, CD277, Browne to Murphy, 10 May 1916.
16 MA, BMH, WS1451, Edmund Tobin, p. 104.

a constant fear was that it would eventually elicit Vatican interference. Archbishop Walsh's secretary Father Michael Curran gave an interview with the English anti-republican newspaper the *Morning Post* in December 1919. Curran argued that the British government rather than the republican killers bore responsibility for the fatal casualties that sometimes occurred in the course of arms raids. During the conversation he corrected his own use of the word 'murders', saying instead the 'shooters [*sic*] of these soldiers and police'.[17] Walsh could not countenance the implication that Curran believed that there were 'murderers who are not murderers', as the newspaper headline helpfully spelt out. A few days later Curran wrote to Rector John Hagan that 'His Grace of course was very annoyed with me', and that the archbishop had decided in view of the interview that Curran could not remain as his secretary.[18] Curran's subsequent appointment to the vice-rectorship of the Irish College in Rome was hardly a demotion, but the incident shows that the bishops expected discretion in priests' public comments on the IRA campaign.

As Chapter 7 will show, Dublin Castle's attitudes towards priests changed during the course of the War of Independence. By the autumn of 1920 crown forces dealt directly with priests who had made themselves a nuisance to them. At that stage conservative bishops looked back wistfully to the days of O'Dwyer and Browne, when deals with the authorities had still been available. In October 1920 Archbishop Gilmartin had to take the initiative himself to intervene in the case of an arrested priest. Father John Meehan, a curate in Castlebar, County Mayo, and a well-known Sinn Féiner, had been apprehended for possessing shotgun ammunition and seditious documents.[19] While Meehan awaited a decision about his case, Gilmartin wrote to the under-secretary asking for a passport for the priest to go to his brother in the United States.[20] The archbishop blithely asserted that Meehan's intended departure

---

17 *Morning Post*, 9 December 1919. See Miller, *Church, State*, p. 433 and Morrissey, *Walsh*, pp. 326–7 for accounts of the affair.
18 AICR, Hagan papers, HAG1/1919/558, Curran to Hagan, 13 December 1919.
19 TNA, WO35/117; Sinn Féiner: NLI, MS 5649, List of Sinn Féin officers.
20 TNA, WO35/117, Gilmartin to under-secretary, 15 November 1920.

was for 'purely *ecclesiastical* reasons', but he was willing to give the assurance that Meehan would stay in America for at least six months and would not engage in political propaganda there.[21] He got his way and Meehan left within days, the RIC county inspector for Mayo exclaiming joyfully that 'one of the strongest supporters of Sinn Fein has gone'.[22] He added that 'another, Father Carney is preparing to follow him', perhaps an indication that Gilmartin had also encouraged this Sinn Féin curate from Cong to visit American relatives.[23]

It must not be presumed that bishops were always aware of everything their priests were doing, and republican priests were often very keen to keep it that way. Father Patrick Markey, parish priest of Ballinalee, County Longford, was well-connected with local IRA men. When these killed a constable in November 1920, Markey heard the firing and rushed out, finding the killers still on the scene. Afterwards he hesitated to contact the crown forces, fearing that he might be forced to reveal their identity. Everyone else involved either feared the same or was himself a Volunteer, with the result that the dead man's body lay on the road for more than twenty-four hours before it was removed for burial. Despite his best efforts, suspicion soon fell on Markey and the crown forces arrested him. After he was released, he went on the run, taking refuge with Seán MacEoin's column. Soon after these incidents Markey was visiting his curate, when the housekeeper announced the arrival of an enraged Bishop Hoare of Ardagh and Clonmacnoise. Hoare demanded to know why Markey was absent from his house without telling anyone where he was, and also why he had left the body of a Catholic lying on the road for twenty-four hours. Not wishing to explain that he was on the run, or why he had failed to inform the authorities, the unfortunate parish priest made no reply. Hoare 'inquired whether he was dumb, and then informed him that he was suspending him'. The bishop also demanded that Markey and his curate denounce the men responsible for the attack at mass the next Sunday. Markey's refusal to agree to this did not brighten the

---

21 TNA, WO35/117, Gilmartin to Chaplin, 2 December 1920. Italics in the original.
22 TNA, CO94/114, IGMR, January 1921, p. 23.
23 Carney was the treasurer of the South Mayo Sinn Féin constituency executive: NLI, MS 5649, List of Sinn Féin officers.

bishop's mood, and Hoare left, slamming the door behind him.[24] In a similar case a few months later, a concerned Bishop Patrick McKenna of Clogher went to visit a republican priest in prison, Father Eugene Coyle, curate in Clontibret, County Monaghan. Dublin Castle had sent McKenna worrying reports that Coyle and other Clogher priests had attended meetings at which plans for attacks on the crown forces had been made.[25] McKenna told Coyle that he wanted to know the truth. It is unclear whether he got it, but Coyle denied that he was guilty.

Bishops also tried to persuade republican priests to tone down their activities to avoid arrest and prosecution. Thus Bishop Foley of Kildare and Leighlin charged a trusted senior priest in his diocese in December 1920 to talk to Father Thomas Burbage, curate in Geashill, King's County, a strong republican. Another senior priest in the diocese who was consulted told Foley that the bishop's concern should be presented to Burbage 'as a mark [and] proof of very real friendship'. Nonetheless he did not think there was much chance of success, because Burbage 'holds his view with such intensity of conviction that arguments which might tell with others are only thrown away upon him'. Foley's correspondent had asked a friend of Burbage's whether the curate would 'consent to leave himself in the bishop's hands'. The reply had been: 'F[ather] Burbage w[oul]d not part with his rights as a citizen even to secure a mitre.'[26] Foley's endeavours proved fruitless. Burbage had already been shot at from a military lorry once while cycling through his parish in October 1920, and his house had been raided and searched in November. He was arrested only a few weeks after the Foley correspondence, in January 1921.[27]

On the other hand, bishops of a more republican slant sometimes regarded the arrest of priests on sedition charges as a badge of honour. This was true for Bishop Fogarty of Killaloe, who

24 MA, BMH, WS1716, Seán MacEoin, pp. 108–10, 126–8.
25 MA, BMH, WS325, Eugene Coyle, pp. 7–8.
26 Kildare and Leighlin Diocesan Archives, Carlow, Patrick Foley papers, BP17/1920/47, Lalor to Foley, 26 December 1920. Burbage was president of the North Offaly Sinn Féin constituency executive: NLI, MS 5649, List of Sinn Féin officers.
27 *Irish Independent*, 16 October 1920, 10 November 1920, 17 January 1921.

effectively took over from Edward O'Dwyer as the leader of the hierarchy's republican faction after O'Dwyer's death in 1917. When Fathers Gaynor and McKenna were released from prison in 1921, Fogarty promoted them to important curacies some years before their time. He also invited them to his residence in Ennis and complimented them on having done credit to the diocese.[28]

Whatever about their propensity for taking on the British authorities, republican priests mostly tried to avoid conflict with their ecclesiastical superiors. This was a matter of preserving their livelihood, of course, but it also shows that they were political rather than religious revolutionaries. 'Modernism', that dreaded heresy of Pope Pius X's pontificate, was never very popular among radical priests in Ireland. In fact one of the few Irish priests to come into conflict with the Holy Office was the decidedly anti-republican Maynooth professor Walter McDonald. Clerical support for republicanism rarely implied rebellion against the authority of the church. Father Dominic responded angrily to a report in the *Morning Post* in September 1920 that he was in disagreement with Cardinal Logue's condemnation of an IRA attack on a police patrol in Dundalk earlier that month. In a letter also published in Irish newspapers, Dominic declared: 'I heartily subscribe to His Eminence's statement, and likewise deny "that this is an act of war, that it is lawful to shoot at sight anyone wearing a policeman's uniform and honestly discharging the policeman's duties".'[29] This handsome denial was quite at odds with his private advice to Florence O'Donoghue three months later to 'ambush each day'.[30] But even such principled supporters of the IRA campaign as Dominic wished to distance themselves from the suggestion that they were out of line with the hierarchy. Dominic admittedly had a tactical reason for taking this step. He was Terence MacSwiney's chaplain at the time, and it would have taken away from the lord mayor's public image as an innocent victim of British brutality if his chaplain had publicly confirmed that you could legitimately shoot policemen. Nonetheless, ecclesiastical suspensions of republican priests were not frequent. Father O'Flanagan incurred one in 1918 through his flouting of the authority of parish priests.

28 NLI, Gaynor papers, MS 19,826, 'Sinn Fein days', p. 544.
29 *Irish Catholic*, 4 September 1920.
30 NLI, O'Donoghue papers, MS 31,170, Dominic to O'Donoghue, 15 December 1920.

But it was revoked a year later, and Father Markey's suspension at the hands of Bishop Hoare was also apparently of brief duration.

Religious clergy

With a few notable exceptions, most of the priests discussed in the last two chapters were secular priests. Of the forty-five priests who held office in the Sinn Féin party at constituency level in 1920, only one was a religious priest, an Augustinian who was vice-president of the Limerick constituency executive.[31] But this absence of religious priests on the party executives is easily explained by taking account of how these bodies were formed. They were elected by Sinn Féin parish clubs, and the priests among the delegates were likely to have become involved through these local clubs.[32] Since Irish religious had no parishes, they were much less likely than their secular colleagues to assume office in Sinn Féin.[33] In fact, the apparent lack of religious among republican clergy is quite illusory, and the evidence is that they were represented more or less in proportion to their number. At a mere 19 per cent of the total clerical population, religious priests were a minority among the Irish clergy in general.[34] Five (that is, 7 per cent) of the entries on the list of clerical supporters of the IRA campaign in Appendix 2 refer to religious. But this figure is actually higher, as three of these represent entire religious communities: Capuchin and Carmelite priories in Dublin and Mount Melleray Abbey. It is likely that more than just one member per community was involved. The list includes only clerics who provided material support, and many more religious must have provided spiritual assistance. The Waterford IRA veteran James Mansfield, for instance, mentioned the spiritual aid which the men of his brigade received from the Dungarvan Augustinians.[35]

---

31 NLI, MS 5649, List of Sinn Féin officers. See Laffan, *Resurrection*, p. 199.
32 Laffan, *Resurrection*, p. 170.
33 Jean Blanchard, *The Church in Contemporary Ireland* (Dublin and London: Clonmore and Reynolds and Burns and Oates, 1963), p. 39. See also Murphy, 'Priests', p. 235.
34 Based on figures for 1911 (17.9 per cent) and 1926 (19.7 per cent): Newman, 'Priests', p. 6.
35 Mansfield, 'Decies', p. 381.

Religious orders operated outside the normal parish structures, and this traditionally caused rivalry between them and the secular clergy. When religious priests showed their support for republicanism in parishes belonging to conservative diocesan clergy, it is easy to see how this traditional rivalry could take on a political hue. Thus in early 1921 two Redemptorist missioners giving a mission in Cornamona, County Galway, clashed with the parish priest over local IRA activities. Father John O'Grady, the parish priest, was walking along the road with the two Redemptorists when they came to a bridge just as Volunteers were about to blow it up. O'Grady began a tirade against the IRA while the missioners encouraged them. Then O'Grady stood on the bridge and stated that he would stay there until it was blown up under him, one of the Redemptorists replying: 'Good-bye John! See you in Heaven ... maybe!' The IRA commanding officer was left with the task of moving Father O'Grady off the bridge before it was destroyed.[36]

This amusing incident reflected underlying tensions that also came to light around the same time in Gorey, County Wexford, where the Benedictine priest Dom Francis Sweetman ran into difficulty with the local clergy over his political activities. His superiors had already asked him to step down as president of the North Wexford Sinn Féin constituency executive in March 1919.[37] But in February 1921, Sweetman still controlled much of the party in Gorey, and Bishop Codd of Ferns complained that Sweetman had 'been using the Sinn Fein clubs and workmen's clubs to stimulate an agitation'.[38] The parish priest of Gorey also objected to Sweetman's activities. Underlying the diocesan clergy's irritation was the fact that Sweetman had been 'interfering with the local church by taking congregations away from the local parishes'.[39]

The presence in a religious house of a priest who engaged in republican activism did not necessarily imply that the entire community held the same views. The Jesuit Father William Hackett

---

36 MA, BMH, WS1731, John King, pp. 13–14. *ICD 1920* calls O'Grady a curate.
37 President of executive: *Irish Independent*, 29 January 1919; resignation: TNA, CO904/108, IGMR, March 1919, pp. 503–4.
38 AICR, Hagan papers, HAG1/1921/76, Codd to Hagan, 16 February 1921.
39 Bellenger, 'Adventure', p. 412.

gallantly asked masked raiders who visited him in Crescent College in November 1920 not to search the other rooms, because 'you will cause a great shock to some of the old Fathers who are free from blame as far as want of loyalty is concerned. Nor will you find arms or sedition there.'[40] There are also numerous examples of conflicts about politics arising within religious communities. Thus the rector of Crescent College had a notice read at table in April 1920 stating that 'among ourselves, ... each one [should] be careful not to say anything that could offend the susceptibilities of others, who may perhaps have different political views'.[41] And a Jesuit from Gardiner Street in Dublin denounced a fellow priest from the same community to the IRA chief of staff Richard Mulcahy in June 1921 for deleting the names of fallen Volunteers from the altar list of the dead in St Francis Xavier's church.[42]

Conversely, a strongly anti-republican priest in the community could also cause internal conflict. The case of the Dominican Hyacinth Collins of Tralee, County Kerry, has been mentioned already. This priest had tipped off the crown forces about a worshipper at the Dominican church who had said in April 1921 that she endorsed the recent killing of an Auxiliary officer by the IRA. Collins also mentioned the woman during a sermon in the church, referring to 'this lady, a frequent communicant, who had made use of these uncharitable expressions'. Hearing this, the prior, Father Raphael Ayres, described by one IRA veteran as 'a sincere republican and a friend of every Irishman who had taken up arms for the freedom of his country', stepped into the sanctuary and interrupted Collins. After some whispering, Collins addressed the congregation again with the words 'my superior has forbidden me to preach'. He skipped the rest of his sermon and continued with mass.[43]

---

40 IJA, 'Brief lives' papers, J172/5, William Hackett, 'Seven years in Limerick', p. 14.
41 IJA, Crescent College papers, SC/CRES/4/2/2, 14 April 1920. Similar exhortations came from the master general of the Dominican order in 1918 and 1922: Dominican Provincial Archives, Dublin, Letters of provincials, Theissling to Ryan, 23 November 1918, and Ryan to priors, 19 January 1922. Many thanks to Rev. Hugh Fenning, OP, for these references.
42 UCDA, Mulcahy papers, P7/A/19, anon. to Mulcahy, 10 June 1921.
43 MA, BMH, WS1413, Tadhg Kennedy, pp. 99–102.

Just like bishops, religious superiors took steps to transfer troublesome priests out of harm's way. In contrast with Collins's case, this harm was most likely to come from the crown forces. After the raid on Crescent College, Hackett was transferred to Belvedere College in Dublin. This did not discourage him from sedition, as he spent the next two years acting as a courier between IRA and Sinn Féin leaders in Dublin and Wicklow. He was eventually sent to Australia by the provincial in September 1922.[44] In December 1920, the Augustinian provincial moved Father Joseph Hennessy out of Limerick, where he was the prior of his order's house and vice-president of the Sinn Féin constituency executive. There had been a death threat and an anonymous warning that Hennessy should leave the city. When Father Michael Griffin's body was discovered near Galway some days later, the provincial lost his nerve and sent Hennessy out of the country.[45]

Responses from fellow priests

Among secular priests there was no shortage of conflict, either, between those who disagreed about Sinn Féin and the IRA. The case of Father Patrick MacHugh, curate in Aughagower, County Mayo, has already been mentioned in Chapter 5. MacHugh was reported to the police in May 1921 by a penitent of his, an informer who had pretended to be a Volunteer during confession. MacHugh had advised him that there were no moral impediments to killing members of the crown forces.[46] The curate's activities placed a considerable strain on his relations with his parish priest, Father John Flatley, who even resorted to informing Dublin Castle about MacHugh's doings.[47] After the incident with the informer, the local RIC divisional commissioner visited Flatley and 'accused [MacHugh] of using the confessional, to encourage ambushes, [and] justify, by his theologic [sic] decisions, the murder of police'.

---

44 IJA, 'Brief lives' papers, J172/1, Dennett, 'Sixty years', pp. 10, 15, 16.
45 Moved: F. X. Martin, 'Fr. Joseph Hennessy, O.S.A. The patriot', *Limerick Souvenir* (1962), pp. 20–2, at p. 22. I am grateful to Rev. David Kelly, OSA, for this reference. Sinn Féin: NLI, MS 5649, List of Sinn Féin officers.
46 TDA, Gilmartin papers, B4/8-ii/5, Flatley to Gilmartin, 23 May 1921.
47 MA, BMH, WS1668, Thomas Hevey, p. 26.

Flatley then wrote to Archbishop Gilmartin to complain that he had heard MacHugh a year and a half before 'approve [and] approve determinedly, [and] with passion, the murder of policemen'. After that, Flatley had barred his curate from entering his house. Subsequent exchanges had seen MacHugh declaring 'for the shooting of all tyrants, [and] all landlords [and] all landgrabbers were tyrants [and] should be shot'. Flatley had told him that he must not flout the principles of the institution whose bread he was content to eat. In a show of rebellion against ecclesiastical authority relatively rare for republican priests, MacHugh had answered: 'I am not eating the bread of the church ... I am eating the bread of the people, [and] I am faithful to their principles.'[48]

When his spiritual ministrations to the IRA became known to the RIC, MacHugh understandably feared for his life.[49] He went to ask Flatley for a 'certificate, that he never advocated the murder of police' and that he had 'never had anything to do with politics'. Flatley refused to supply this, and he asked Gilmartin to 'remove Fr. Mac Hugh to some other, [and] a distant parish'. Flatley did write to the divisional commissioner to ask for a guarantee that MacHugh would not be harmed. When this had been obtained, Flatley noted that MacHugh changed into a 'rampant loyalist'; it was a pity, the parish priest wryly observed, that 'the Orangemen had not him in Belfast for the polling day'.[50] MacHugh's conversion is confirmed by the IRA veteran Thomas Hevey, who recounted that when the IRA carried out an ambush at Carrowkennedy some days after the station mass-incident, MacHugh had condemned it as murder.[51] The whole affair ended with a reconciliation between the two priests, and Flatley withdrew his request to have MacHugh changed to another parish.[52]

The Aughagower case was no doubt an extreme example. Father Gaynor of Mullagh recalled that his own parish priest, Father John Glynn, 'preferred milder curates, but ... was very kind to us and let us go our own way without a word of censure'.[53] Glynn had initially

48 TDA, Gilmartin papers, B4/8-ii/5, Flatley to Gilmartin, 23 May 1921.
49 TDA, Gilmartin papers, B4/8-ii/5, MacHugh to Gilmartin, 23 May 1921.
50 TDA, Gilmartin papers, B4/8-ii/5, Flatley to Gilmartin, 27 May 1921.
51 UCDA, O'Malley papers, P17b/120, Thomas Hevey.
52 TDA, Gilmartin papers, B4/8-ii/5, Flatley to Gilmartin, 27 May 1921.
53 NLI, Gaynor papers, MS 19,826, 'Sinn Fein days', p. 464.

been a supporter of Sinn Féin, but according to Gaynor he took no part in the movement.[54] In fact, he was on friendly terms with the RIC, the local sergeant telling him on one occasion that he had 'a pile of reports a foot high' against Glynn's curate, all of them submitted by parishioners.[55] Glynn also had family ties with a local loyalist at the centre of a kidnapping case in April 1920. The son of a local justice of the peace – a relative of Glynn's – was held by the IRA as a ransom to ensure that the crown forces would stop raiding houses in the locality.[56] Gaynor acted as intermediary between the Volunteers and the boy's parents, but all the while Glynn continued to visit his relatives and conveyed messages from them to his curate.[57] After Gaynor was arrested on account of his role in this case, Glynn just as easily drove to the barracks to threaten papal protests if Gaynor were not released immediately.[58] It was obviously possible for priests in the same parish to have connections on opposite sides of the divide without any adverse effect on their relations.

As has been seen in the case of the Curran interview in December 1919, much depended on the level of exposure to publicity. Many conservative priests were willing to overlook support for Sinn Féin and even for the IRA, but once a case came to the attention of the press, different criteria applied. A Plymouth-based newspaper called the *Morning News* reported in July 1920 that a Limerick priest had announced from the altar that he would grant 100 days' indulgence to anyone who would shoot another policeman.[59] The story was derived from a circular produced by the Southern Irish Loyalists' Defence Fund, of which a Catholic, the earl of Denbigh, was the treasurer. The report had caused much adverse publicity internationally and even the pope had apparently made enquiries about the case, which sparked outrage in the Irish nationalist press.[60] Father Stephen Connolly, administrator of Limerick cathedral, engaged a solicitor, who threatened the *Morning News*

54 *Ibid*. See also Fitzpatrick, *Politics*, p. 118.
55 NLI, Gaynor papers, MS 19,826, 'Sinn Fein days', pp. 479–80.
56 *Ibid*., pp. 506–7.
57 *Ibid*., p. 507.
58 *Ibid*., p. 517.
59 *Irish Independent*, 7 and 8 July 1920.
60 AICR, Hagan papers, HAG1/1921/41, Hagan to anon. archbishop [draft], c. January 1921.

with legal proceedings if it did not retract. The newspaper bowed to pressure and apologised, as did Lord Denbigh, who also resigned the treasurership of the Defence Fund.[61]

The importance of publicity was also apparent in a case in February 1921, when a Wexford parish priest complained to Bishop O'Sullivan of Kerry about controversial statements which a curate in the Kerry diocese had allegedly made. The Wexford priest sent O'Sullivan extracts from the American publicist Owen Wister's 1920 book *A Straight Deal, or The Ancient Grudge*. It contained a selection of utterances that Irish priests had used to mobilise their flocks against conscription in 1918. One of these was purportedly from Father Gerald Dennehy, curate in Eyeries, County Cork, who had told a congregation at mass one Sunday that they could kill at sight any Catholic policeman who was assisting in applying the draft to Ireland. 'God will bless you and it will be the most acceptable sacrifice you can offer.' The Wexford priest suggested that Dennehy should assert the falsity of these statements by taking legal action against Wister's publishers.[62] The outcome of this intervention is unclear, but the fact that it was made shows how important the clergy's international reputation was felt to be.

Responses from lay Catholics

Losing this reputation could have some very practical ramifications. The bishops' fear of unfavourable Vatican intervention has already been mentioned. But there were also consequences closer to home. The Black and Tans and Auxiliaries who arrived over the summer of 1920 widely believed that Irish priests were setting the people up against them. When the parish priest of Ballina, County Tipperary, got into an argument with an Auxiliary cadet in June 1921 about repairing a trench cut in a local road, the Auxiliary told him that if

---

61 *Irish Independent*, 7 and 8 July 1920.
62 KyDA, O'Sullivan papers, 'Parish correspondence', Eyeries, Kehoe to O'Sullivan, 24 February 1921. The quotations are from Owen Wister, *A Straight Deal, or The Ancient Grudge* (New York: Macmillan, 1920), pp. 262–3. Hart, *Enemies*, p. 61 quotes this statement in a slightly different version, as does Travers, 'Priest', p. 174, who also mentions a number of similar statements attributed to other priests: *ibid.*, pp. 173–4.

he 'would use his influence in the right way these outrages would cease'.[63] Despite frequent ecclesiastical condemnation of IRA violence, conservative Catholics in Ireland and many others abroad shared this belief that the Irish clergy were 'soft' on republican outrage. Numerous letters from scandalised lay people in Irish diocesan archives testify to this. In July 1919 Detective Sergeant Patrick Smyth of the Dublin Metropolitan Police was shot in Drumcondra by Michael Collins's IRA intelligence unit. He died in September. Four days later a second detective, Constable Daniel Hoey, was shot dead in the city centre of Dublin. On 1 October, the Catholic layman James Fitzgerald wrote a letter to Archbishop Walsh of Dublin complaining that he had

> not heard a word in condemnation of these crimes uttered by any priest in any Catholic church in Dublin. I respectfully point out to you as the spiritual guardian of the Catholics of this city that it is the duty of the clergy to condemn murder and to uphold the commandments of God.[64]

Fitzgerald asserted that

> until our priests take their courage in their hands and openly condemn these revolting crimes the murders will continue and good Irishmen's lives destroyed. If there was one priest in each diocese to speak out like Father Gleeson of Lorrha the murder campaign would soon stop.[65]

Similarly, Walsh received a letter in December 1919 from the prominent Catholic lawyer A. M. Sullivan, who protested that 'the known murderers in this country ... are all notably pious'. According to Sullivan, this was due to the fact that 'no instruction to fortify your flock has been given from any pulpit during the three years in which the agents of the secret societies have represented murder as a sort of religious function'.[66] Sullivan himself had been the recipient of threatening letters because of his work as a prosecutor for the crown, and in fact he was soon to be the target of an

---

63 *Irish Independent*, 2 July 1921. See also Enright, *Trial*, pp. 233–5.
64 DDA, Walsh papers, 386/8, Fitzgerald to Walsh, 1 October 1919.
65 *Ibid.*
66 DDA, Walsh papers, 386/8, Sullivan to Walsh, 22 December 1919.

unsuccessful assassination attempt near Tralee.⁶⁷ Walsh's failure to instruct his flock against 'murder propaganda' had resulted in the situation that 'now a Catholic who will not be silent about an article of his faith is exposed to assassination'. Sullivan continued:

> By instituting a course of moral instruction, in the schools, from the pulpit and from the altar Your Grace may rescue hundreds of our boys and may save many lives if not mine ... The silence of the pulpit is [diligently] misrepresented as the approval of the church. I desire most solemnly to warn Your Grace of this public scandal and to call upon you to end it.⁶⁸

Irish Catholics living in Britain and its dominions also wrote to complain that the Irish clergy's attitude was giving them a bad name. An anonymous Irishman from Glasgow accused Walsh in December 1919 of being a 'partaker with the murderers' and complained that 'Irishmen in Glasgow are looked down upon as never before.'⁶⁹ And Bishop Fogarty was told in January 1920 by a Canadian Catholic called Keogh that the diocese of Killaloe 'has been and is notorious as the most crime laden district in Ireland', a situation made worse by Fogarty's 'brazenly defending such appalling conditions'. The writer hoped that 'the day is not far distant when [the Irish people] shall ... be freed from the dominance of prelates of your stamp who, in the name of religion, seek to gloss over and justify that which is wicked and evil in the sight of God and man'.⁷⁰ Keogh's letter suggests that he had been the subject of abuse on account of his Irish Catholic background. An Englishman wrote to Walsh in March 1921 that 'when you use the word "barbarous" you should apply it to the Catholic cut-throats who started murdering, and those who support them, clergy included'.⁷¹

In December 1920, Sir James O'Connor, the lord justice of appeal, wrote a long letter to Cardinal Logue protesting against priests who had condoned the use of violence against servants of the crown. O'Connor complained that a prominent Jesuit theologian had said in a conversation that the killing of police and military was

---

67 *Irish Catholic*, 17 January 1920.
68 DDA, Walsh papers, 386/8, Sullivan to Walsh, 22 December 1919.
69 DDA, Walsh papers, 386/8, anon. to Walsh, 9 December 1919.
70 KDA, Fogarty papers, F3A21, Keogh to Fogarty, 20 January 1920.
71 DDA, Walsh papers, 380/4, Blaker to Walsh, 2 March 1921.

'a debatable matter' and that another Jesuit had defended the legitimacy of such killings to a colleague. He had also heard from reliable sources that a Maynooth professor and many Redemptorists were of the same view. All of this had a disastrous influence, O'Connor contended, because it disturbed the consciences of many 'sincere and earnest Catholics' and gave a 'false conscience' to many young Irishmen.[72] Logue replied that he had brought the issue to the attention of the bishops and that all of them had assured him that they had placed it before their priests at 'the usual theological conferences'.[73] He also complained that bishops were always the last persons to hear of their priests' imprudent expressions and asserted that they held no jurisdiction over religious. Logue's reply was a polite fobbing off, and it demonstrates the hierarchy's desire to keep on friendly terms with all sections of Catholic society while making no political commitments.

Overthrowing tyranny: theological arguments in support of the IRA campaign

As has been seen in Chapter 3, the theological argument advanced by clerical opponents of the IRA campaign was that it did not meet the criteria for just war and therefore lacked moral legitimacy. Supporters, however, often focused on the issue of legitimate resistance against tyranny. This tenet of political morality had a long and eventful history. In the eleventh century, when the investiture struggle between pope and emperor was in full swing, theological arguments that curbed the power of secular rulers were much favoured by the papacy. All power came from God, but it came to emperors and kings through the medium of the people, and legitimacy depended upon whether or not a ruler governed his people equitably. If a ruler ruled justly, he was legitimate; if he oppressed his people, he was a tyrant, and his people might legitimately rebel against him. In the early modern period a new emphasis on the divine right of kings caused a new class of tyrant to be envisaged beside the oppressor: the usurper. The usurper was a tyrant not

---

72 NLI, MS 21,697, O'Connor to Logue, 21 December 1920. See Miller, *Church, State*, p. 466.
73 NLI, MS 21,697, Logue to O'Connor, 23 January 1921.

because he oppressed his people, but because he overthrew the nation's divinely ordained ruler by revolution or invasion.[74]

Remarkably in view of their subsequent criticism of IRA violence, the first public references to this theory came from two archbishops in their February 1920 Lenten pastorals. Archbishop Gilmartin of Tuam contended that 'if a people think they are mis-governed, they have a right and a duty to seek for a change of government'.[75] And Archbishop Harty of Cashel asserted that the British government in Ireland was 'neither based on the consent of the nation, nor working for the good of the community as a whole', while excelling in 'acts of repression and coercion'.[76] Admittedly Gilmartin did warn that in seeking change, the people must 'keep within the moral law as expressed in the Ten Commandments', while Harty condemned 'crime'. These statements went half-way, apparently establishing the tyrannical nature of the British regime on grounds of oppression, but denying the conclusion that working to overthrow it by means of proportionate violence was morally acceptable. Around the same time, Father Denis Flynn, parish priest of Kells, County Meath, told a congregation at mass that while they were 'perfectly justified in demanding a change of government ... murder, whether of a rich man or poor man, policeman or civilian, was murder'.[77] While these clerics wished to criticise the British government, they had no intention of inciting to republican violence.

In the October 1920 issue of the *Irish Theological Quarterly*, Professor Alfred O'Rahilly of Cork published an article entitled 'Some theology about tyranny', taking up where the archbishops had left off and spelling out the consequences of their view of the British government's legitimacy.[78] O'Rahilly was then a layman, the registrar of University College, Cork, professor of mathemati-

---

74 A. Bride, 'Tyran et tyrannie', in A. Vacant, E. Mangenot and É. Amann (eds), *Dictionnaire de théologie catholique contenant l'exposé des doctrines de la théologie catholique, leurs preuves et leur histoire*, xv:2 (Paris: Letouzey et Ané, 1950), pp. 1948–88, at pp. 1956–7.
75 *ICD 1921*, pp. 506–7.
76 *Ibid.*
77 *Irish Catholic*, 24 January 1920.
78 Alfred O'Rahilly, 'Some theology about tyranny', *Irish Theological Quarterly*, 15 (1920), pp. 301–20. See, for the O'Rahilly and Fitzpatrick articles, Miller, *Church, State*, pp. 463–5.

cal physics and one of the leaders of republican thought at that institution.[79] He was also a member of Cork borough council. The fact that his appointment was in a scientific department did not prevent him from discoursing frequently on theological subjects, Bishop Cohalan once scornfully referring to him as Cork corporation's 'lay theologian'.[80] In his 1920 article O'Rahilly argued from St Thomas Aquinas and the early modern theologian Francisco Suárez that, since power came to rulers from God through the people, the latter had 'an inalienable radical sovereignty' and had the right to revolt against an oppressive and usurping government.[81] This right to revolt was based on the 'natural right to self-defence inherent in every community as in every individual'.[82] O'Rahilly acknowledged that a number of criteria – reminiscent of the *ius ad bellum* criteria mentioned before – had to be met before such a revolt were legitimate. Thus he believed that there must be 'a reasonable probability of success', though he took the convenient view that as 'there are degrees in oppression and in resistance thereto', there are also degrees in success. Intimidation of the oppressor or even the spiritual and moral victory of a military defeat might thus count as success.[83] When these conditions had been met, it was important that the people exercised their sovereign right to repudiate the government.[84] Thereafter it was necessary to have a war that was 'as formal and explicit as possible' even though it might be 'necessarily somewhat informal and irregular'.[85] This meant that 'each individual is free to commit acts of war on the unjust invader of his country'. According to O'Rahilly, this was the opinion of Aquinas, Suárez and 'practically the entire school'. The consequence was that 'regular' warfare, guided as it was by the principles of the *ius in bello*, could be legitimately dispensed with, and that

---

79 John A. Murphy, 'O'Rahilly, Alfred', in James McGuire *et al.* (eds.), *Dictionary of Irish Biography from the Earliest Times to the Year 2002* (Cambridge and Dublin: Cambridge University Press, 2009), vii, pp. 825–6.
80 CDA, Cohalan papers, box vi, pastoral letter, 19 December 1920. O'Rahilly was ordained a priest in 1955.
81 O'Rahilly, 'Theology', pp. 301–2.
82 *Ibid.*, pp. 306–7.
83 *Ibid.*, pp. 311–12.
84 *Ibid.*, p. 313.
85 *Ibid.*, p. 312.

'irregular methods' were morally acceptable until the nation had the means to organise a proper army.[86]

Without referring specifically to the situation obtaining in Ireland at the time, O'Rahilly's article nonetheless provided a clear justification for the IRA campaign. The debate that inevitably followed concerned the question as to whether the people did indeed have the right O'Rahilly ascribed to them. In the January 1921 issue, Professor John Fitzpatrick of Clonliffe College denied O'Rahilly's claim that Suárez had taught that sovereignty was vested in the people and that a popular mandate empowering the civil authorities could be revoked by them.[87] Suárez may have believed that power came to rulers through the people, but once the people had delegated power to the ruler, they could not reclaim this power at will.[88] Fitzpatrick also insisted that the theory advocated by O'Rahilly had been condemned in Pope Leo XIII's 1881 encyclical *Diuturnum illud*. This was a compelling point. The revolutionary upheavals of the late eighteenth century and the nineteenth century had caused Catholic teaching on this issue to develop considerably since Suárez's times.[89] Curbing the power of secular rulers was very far indeed from the minds of Popes Gregory XVI and Pius IX, with their own rule over the Papal States under continual threat from a revolutionary population. Instead, their main preoccupation was to defend the legitimacy of rulers and expound the evil of rebellion. Gregory and Pius had already condemned the principles of revolt against legitimate rulers, but Leo XIII was the first to give a systematic account of this stricter view in *Diuturnum illud* and, a few years later, in *Immortale Dei*. He contended that power came directly from God to the rulers without the consent of the people. If the people appointed their rulers themselves through election – as they did in modern democracies – the electorate's role was to designate the person in whom God vested power, not to provide the ruler with a mandate, as if the people were transferring their own sovereignty onto him.

86 *Ibid.*, 319-20.
87 John Fitzpatrick, 'Some more theology about tyranny. A reply to Prof. O'Rahilly', *Irish Theological Quarterly*, 16 (1921), pp. 1–15, at p. 2.
88 *Ibid.*, pp. 2–3.
89 Bride, 'Tyran', p. 1958. See also Peter Donnelly, 'Bishops and violence. A response to Oliver Rafferty', *Studies. An Irish Quarterly Review*, 82:331 (1994), pp. 331–40, at p. 335.

This teaching allowed Leo to consolidate his predecessors' rejection of popular sovereignty while offering an ingenious escape clause for democracies such as the French *troisième république* with which he was keen to realise a rapprochement. However, as Professor Fitzpatrick pointed out, this doctrine left precious little room for the notion of legitimate revolt against tyranny. In fact, the only remedy for tyranny Leo had to offer was to remind the tyrant that he would have to answer to God for his actions, and the pope pointed out that the early Christians had obeyed and prayed for their emperors even as they were being persecuted.[90] As early as 1919, Walter McDonald had already raised another objection to the argument later advanced by O'Rahilly, namely to question whether British rule in Ireland could really qualify as usurpation. Not only did the Anglo-Normans find no single sovereign polity whose powers could be usurped when they arrived in the twelfth century, but McDonald also argued that the centuries-long acquiescence of the 'Irish people' in British rule had supplied the Castle with any legitimacy that may originally have been lacking.[91] Although O'Rahilly did not convince his clerical opponents, his argument was gratefully adopted by supporters of the IRA campaign, both clerical and lay. Tom Barry recalled that O'Rahilly had 'completely clarified the position for anyone in doubt'.[92]

A number of other topical issues were also discussed in the theological journals. The most prominent of these was a debate on the morality of hunger-strike as a political weapon. This controversy took place first in the *Irish Ecclesiastical Record* between August 1918 and May 1919, and was then continued from January to July 1921 in the *Irish Theological Quarterly*.[93] In this rather repetitive debate, three theologians sympathetic to the republican

---

90 God's judgement: Leo XIII, 'Epistola encyclica de civitatum constitutione christiana' (*Immortale Dei*), 1 November 1885, *Acta Sanctae Sedis*, 18 (1885), pp. 161–80, at p. 163; early Christians: Leo XIII, 'Diuturnum illud', 29 June 1881, *Acta Sanctae Sedis*, 14 (1881), pp 3–14, at p. 9.
91 McDonald, *Questions*, pp. 3–38.
92 Barry, *Days*, p. 57.
93 Stuart Mews, 'The hunger-strike of the lord mayor of Cork, 1920: Irish, English and Vatican attitudes', in W. J. Sheils and Diana Wood (eds), *The Churches, Ireland and the Irish. Papers Read at the 1987 Summer Meeting*

hunger-strikers unsuccessfully tried to convince Canon Waters of Clonliffe College that hunger-strike was not suicide and was not therefore gravely sinful. And as has been seen, the *Irish Ecclesiastical Record*'s canonical expert, Professor Jeremiah Kinane, discussed the question of whether priests were allowed to sit on arbitration courts in 1921.

In the April 1919 issue, Kinane moreover replied to a query about whether the new *Code of Canon Law* had changed the provisions of the 1869 bull *Apostolicae sedis* with regard to secret societies. *Apostolicae sedis* had regulated the use of excommunication in the Catholic church before the promulgation in 1917 of the *Code of Canon Law*. Kinane responded that *Apostolicae sedis* had excommunicated members of secret societies, those who 'show favour to these societies, and ... those who fail to denounce the secret leaders in them'. The new code altered these provisions slightly by removing favouring or failure to denounce as grounds for excommunication, although those who caused others to become members still qualified. He added, however, that 'clerics and religious who become members of such societies should be denounced to the Holy Office'. Ever careful to allow manoeuvring space to his republican brethren, Kinane stressed that both *Apostolicae sedis* and the code defined secret societies as organisations that 'plot against the church or against legitimate civil authority'.[94] Whether the IRA was a secret society consequently depended on whether it could be said to be plotting against legitimate civil authority. Those who argued that the Dáil administration was the legitimate civil authority and the British government was an oppressive foreign usurper clearly did not believe that such was the case, and thus Kinane's diplomatic answer offended no one. The *Irish Ecclesiastical Record* and the *Irish Theological Quarterly* endeavoured to please readers from all camps.

Impact of clerical support

The small group of priests who supported the IRA campaign through their words and actions provided moral reassurance and

---

and the *1988 Winter Meeting of the Ecclesiastical History Society* (Oxford and New York: Basil Blackwell, 1989), pp. 385–400.
94 J. Kinane, 'Changes in the bull "Apostolicae sedis" and in the Index legislation', *Irish Ecclesiastical Record*, 13 (1919), pp. 332–5.

practical aid and thus helped to further its efforts. As Patrick Murray has contended plausibly with regard to the Civil War, they also helped to avoid wholesale alienation of republicans from the Catholic religion.[95] Their presence allowed Volunteers to defy clerical denunciations of violence without adopting an anti-clerical or anti-religious outlook. It would require a study of IRA members rather than the clergy to measure fully the impact of clerical support, but a number of clues must be discussed here. The very fact that IRA members were aware of the existence of republican priests who supported their actions helped to boost morale. Thus the Kerry veteran Billy Mullins recalled that although the Volunteers were refused the sacraments by 'a number of our bishops ... not all were of that mind', suggesting that it was important to them to have the backing of at least a section of the clergy.[96] And Liam Deasy praised Father O'Connell, parish priest of Enniskean, who 'never made any secret about his disapproval of the pastoral of Dr Coholan [sic], ... and in this he shared the feeling shown privately by many other priests in the diocese'.[97] Similarly, Seán Healy, an IRA veteran from Cork, recalled that, after the 'bewildering blow' of Cohalan's decree, their chaplain Father Dominic 'put our minds at rest by a suitable explanation of the matter'.[98] Frequent references in the Bureau's witness statements and in other republican sources to 'good' priests, 'staunch supporters' and 'great friends' confirm the importance of their presence.[99]

These comments suggest that the significance of supportive priests was that they offset the damage done to Volunteer confidence by the condemnations issued by other clerics. Supportive priests assuaged consciences, reconciled difficulties and boosted morale. This was aiding and abetting rather than taking the lead. None of the priests who supported the IRA during the War of Independence much resembled Father Murphy of Boolavogue, the

---

95 Murray, *Oracles*, p. 147. See also Harris, 'Parnell', p. 218.
96 Billy Mullins, *Memoirs of Billy Mullins. Veteran of the War of Independence* (Tralee: Kenno, 1983), p. 169.
97 Deasy, *Free*, p. 193.
98 MA, BMH, WS1479, Seán Healy, pp. 58–9.
99 UCDA, O'Malley papers, P17b/109, John Duffy; MA, BMH, WS1516, P. H. Doherty, p. 12, and WS1348, Michael Davern, p. 21.

famed leader of the 1798 rebellion in Wexford. Priests did not lead the guerrilla war, but they helped the campaign by smoothing out moral and physical difficulties for the fighting men. The clerical minority that supported the IRA was important because it cleared the Volunteers' paths of moral obstacles that had first been placed there by other priests.

III
The clergy and the crown

7

Priest and victim: British measures against the clergy

While there were abundant grounds for condemning the British campaign in Ireland after the escalation of violence in mid-1920, Catholic priests nonetheless had some specific reasons of their own for doing so. The old RIC's traditional rapport with the parish clergy became increasingly strained as normal relations between the constabulary and society broke down. Moreover, the newly arrived Black and Tans and Auxiliaries had none of their Irish colleagues' lingering inhibitions with regard to the way priests should be treated. On the contrary, they widely believed that Irish priests were agitating against them. As a result, the crown forces increasingly turned their attention to ecclesiastical persons and buildings. By the summer of 1921 there was scarcely a monastery left in the country that had not been searched, and arrests of priests had become a frequent occurrence. More sinister encounters with the crown forces also began to take place. From the spring of 1920 onwards, there were reports of priests being harassed, intimidated and even tortured. These were eventually followed in November by the killing of a priest in Galway. Many clerics regarded this as the crossing of a line which the crown forces had hitherto respected. Most priests continued to counsel restraint even after this event and the two subsequent clerical fatalities. But clerical attention turned decisively to criticism of the crown forces.

In examining this issue it is necessary to make some important distinctions. British measures against the clergy were quickly portrayed in sermons and newspapers as a persecution campaign, and as such they caused a shift in clerical attitudes towards the conflict. This raises the question of whether these charges of persecution had a basis in fact. The *Oxford English Dictionary* defines 'persecution' as 'a particular course or period of systematic violent oppression, *esp.* one directed against the members of a particular

… group', with 'oppression' defined in turn as 'prolonged cruel or unjust treatment'.[1] To the extent that raids and arrests were carried out on genuine suspicion of seditious activity, it is rather doubtful whether they must count as 'cruel or unjust', and consequently whether they should be regarded as proof of persecution. By contrast, molestation of priests by crown forces either during or outside these raids certainly qualifies as cruel and unjust treatment. It remains to be judged, however, as it will be in this chapter, whether these acts of violence constituted a prolonged or systematic campaign and whether they were specifically directed at the clergy as a distinct group.

Important as it is to determine whether or not the charge of persecution was justified, it is even more pertinent to acknowledge the crucial role of publicity as a factor in its own right. In guerrilla wars the propaganda effects of violence often outweigh its military results, and victimhood brings certain public relations benefits to the injured parties. Publicity-minded priests succeeded in capitalising on raids and arrests to tell a tale of sacrilege and desecration, while the priestly victims of the Black and Tans became symbols of how British oppression went hand in hand with persecution of the Catholic religion. An image was forged of anti-Catholic sectarianism. This in itself served a purpose, namely to allow priests to ignore the divisive issue of republican violence and focus instead on British atrocities.

Raids on churches and other ecclesiastical buildings

After the war, an RIC document dated July 1920 was discovered in a Waterford police barracks, instructing county and district inspectors not to search 'convents, monasteries and churches' without the inspector general's authority.[2] Rather than proving that ecclesiastical buildings were thenceforth relieved of government interference, this document shows that the RIC command was trying to manage the problem of bad publicity surrounding these searches by tightening central control.[3] All private houses, including those

1 *Oxford English Dictionary* (1989).
2 NLI, MS 31,225, district inspector in divisional commissioner's office, Cork, to county and district inspectors, 23 July 1920.
3 Cf. Augusteijn, *Defiance*, p. 309.

of clergymen, could still be freely searched if there were grounds for suspicion, and convents, monasteries and churches could be searched once the inspector general's permission had been obtained. Tomás Ó Fiaich has contended in his 1970 article that 'so many priests' houses were raided ... that even the list of those which found their way into the daily press would be too long for inclusion'.[4] The research carried out for this book has uncovered 130 instances, all but four from mid-1920 onwards, and it is quite likely that the true number was even higher.[5] The chronological distribution shows very clearly that the arrival of the Black and Tans and Auxiliaries initiated a new phase in the crown forces' dealings with the clergy.

A very common tactic from the summer of 1920 onwards was to surround a church during Sunday mass and then search the entire congregation, or its male half, as it left the building. Thus in late 1920, crown forces surrounded the chapel in Ballagh, County Roscommon, while mass was in progress, entering the building with revolvers in hands. The parish priest went outside to speak to the commanding officer, and then came back in to tell the congregation that the men would be searched. The event passed without further incident as column members in the church passed revolvers to some girls who were not searched.[6] Other examples of this phenomenon in the newspapers came from counties in all four provinces, with County Cork leading the tally. Ulster counties were well represented, the tactic being favoured by the 'B Specials'.[7]

Crown forces also raided presbyteries very frequently. The parish priest of St Joseph's, Berkeley Road, Dublin, told Archbishop Walsh in a telegram in September 1920 that the house of the parish priest of Fairview had been raided by soldiers during the night.[8] He added that 'should I be honoured I will wire you'. In October Fathers Michael Walshe, Laurence Hearne and Maurice Egan, curates of Dungarvan, County Waterford, were compelled to get out of bed

4 Ó Fiaich, 'Clergy', p. 495.
5 See Appendix 4.
6 MA, BMH, WS770, Frank Simons, p. 15.
7 See for instance *Irish Independent*, 20 December 1920, 4 January, 8 January and 10 March 1921.
8 DDA, Walsh papers, 380/3, Downing to Walsh, 2 September 1920.

at night while their residence was subjected to a thorough search by soldiers.[9] And Father Michael Carney, curate in Cong, County Mayo, wrote to Archbishop Gilmartin's secretary in December 1920 that the military had searched his rooms a month ago.[10] The number of cases in which incriminating objects or documents were actually found during these raids was quite small and allegations sometimes followed that such items were planted.[11]

Despite the warning contained in the July 1920 instruction, monasteries were also frequently searched. Mount Melleray was raided in the autumn of 1920, as were a number of religious houses in Dublin. A Capuchin house and two Carmelite priories in Dublin were raided in December 1920, while Dominican and Jesuit houses in the centre of the city followed in February 1921.[12] The army also visited convents on a number of occasions from late 1920 onwards. The first of these raids in Dublin took place on the night of 29 December 1920 in a convent of the sisters of Mary Reparatrix on Merrion Square.[13] And St Joseph's Carmelite convent in Ranelagh, County Dublin, was visited no fewer than three times in December 1920 and January 1921 after the gatekeeper's son was found to have republican sympathies.[14]

Clerical schools and colleges were also raided on numerous occasions. Most of the country's prominent colleges were visited, such as Rockwell College, Cashel, St Columb's College, Derry, Blackrock College and St Mary's College, Rathmines. Some were visited more than once, such as Crescent College, Limerick, St Flannan's College, Ennis, Terenure College, Dublin,

---

9 *Irish Independent*, 11 October 1920.
10 TDA, Gilmartin papers, B4/8-ii/4, Carney to Walsh, 12 December 1920.
11 See for instance *Irish Independent*, 21 October 1920.
12 Mount Melleray: *Catholic Bulletin*, 10:11 (November 1920), pp. 650–1; Capuchins: TNA, WO35/81; Carmelites: TNA, WO35/81, and *Irish Catholic*, 25 December 1920; Dominicans: *Irish Independent*, 1 March 1921; Jesuits: *ibid.*, 19 February 1921.
13 TNA, WO35/70. See also Michael Hopkinson, *The Last Days of Dublin Castle. The Mark Sturgis Diaries* (Dublin and Portland, OR: Irish Academic Press, 1999), p. 104.
14 *Irish Catholic*, 8 January 1921.

and St Malachy's College, Belfast.[15] Raids on St Patrick's College, Maynooth, were conspicuously avoided, despite the shelter its residents gave to republican fugitives.[16] The college's obvious status as the symbolic centre of the Irish church and the fear of public outcry no doubt shielded it from this fate. The Oblate novitiate at Belmont House, Galloping Green, County Dublin, was raided on 5 January 1921, the Auxiliaries and RIC having a list of names of novices suspected of illegal activities. The house was searched, including the papers of a retired missionary bishop living there. Two students were taken away by the raiding party, only to be released from their lorry when it got to Donnybrook.[17] St Patrick's College, Thurles, the Cashel diocesan seminary, was nearly commandeered by the crown forces in January 1921. Archbishop Harty told John Hagan in Rome that 'if they proceed with their intention I shall send you a wire, so that you may tell His Holiness if you think it well to do so'.[18] He protested to General Macready, no doubt mentioning the possibility of international publicity, and the move was cancelled.

As has been seen, a few of these raids yielded significant results, but most of them were fruitless. Not only does this confirm that active clerical support for the IRA was a small-scale phenomenon, but the raids also demonstrate that the crown forces had come to harbour strong suspicions regarding the clergy.

Priests under arrest

These suspicions are also evident from the relatively high number of arrests of priests. 'Arrest' in the context of the War of

---

15 Rockwell: *Irish Independent*, 21 September 1920; St Columb's: *ibid.*, 21 October 1920; Blackrock: *ibid.*, 1 June 1921; St Mary's: TNA, WO35/81; Crescent: IJA, Crescent College papers, SC/CRES/4/2/2, 12 and 15 November 1920; St Flannan's: *Irish Independent*, 24 December 1920, and *Nenagh Guardian*, 9 July 1921; Terenure: TNA, WO35/81 and WO35/82; St Malachy's: *Irish Catholic*, 2 April 1921, and TNA, WO35/126.
16 Corish, *Maynooth*, p. 303.
17 *Irish Catholic*, 8 January 1921.
18 AICR, Hagan papers, HAG1/1921/19, Harty to Hagan, 13 January 1921.

Independence is not a straightforward term. In official police and military records, it is employed in the usual sense, meaning that a person was taken into custody on the basis of a suspicion that he or she had broken the law. But in newspaper reports and witness accounts, it also occasionally refers to the deprivation of liberty by the crown forces during reprisals, where it belonged more to the repertoire of intimidation than of legal prosecution. Thus according to the *Irish Catholic*, a curate in Kiltimagh, County Mayo, was 'placed ... under arrest' in March 1921 and 'marched ... for some distance through the streets at the point of a bayonet'.[19] Since it is often impossible to determine on the basis of these sources how the events mentioned must be classified, in this chapter they have all been included in a single category. 'Arrest' has thus been understood simply as any deprivation of liberty by the crown forces. A search of the sources reveals forty-three cases of arrests of clerics during the War of Independence, including one seminarian who was already a deacon. All but two of these occurred after September 1920, with most of them – twenty-five – taking place during the first half of 1921.[20] It is clear that most of the clerics arrested had republican sympathies, and nine of the arrested priests also appear in the list of priests who gave material support to the IRA.[21]

As can be seen from Table 7.1, the authorities found it difficult to gather sufficient evidence to secure convictions. The one priest who was charged with knowledge of an ambush was acquitted. Many of the others were charged with possession of arms and/or ammunition. Although this charge carried sentence of death in the counties subject to martial law, in fact the priests convicted for it were just fined.[22] This category included priests who had forgotten to hand over their fowling pieces, as well as priests who stored arms and ammunition for the IRA. Others were charged with relatively

---

19 *Irish Catholic*, 9 April 1921.
20 See Appendix 5 for details. Ó Fiaich, 'Clergy', pp. 497–8, counted twenty-two. One priest – Father Eugene Coyle, curate in Clontibret, County Monaghan – was arrested twice.
21 See Appendices 2 and 5: Patrick Delahunty, Patrick Gaynor, Louis Gerhard, Michael McKenna, Patrick Markey, John Meehan, Michael Morley, Walter O'Neill, Patrick Walsh.
22 Hopkinson, *War*, p. 93.

Table 7.1 *Charges preferred against arrested clerics, January 1919 – July 1921*

Charge	Number of clerics
Possession of arms and/or ammunition	10
Unlawful assembly	7
Possession of seditious documents	6
Driving a car without a military permit	2
Knowledge of an ambush	1
Refusing to be searched	1
Using language disloyal to the king	1 (army chaplain)
'Aiding a supposed Sinn Féiner'	1
Writing a threatening letter	1
Inciting disobedience towards the crown forces	1
Unknown	8
Not charged	5
Total	44[a]

[a] See Appendix 5 for sources. The total is forty-four because one priest was charged with more than one crime.

Table 7.2 *Results of arrests of clerics, January 1919 – July 1921*

Result of arrest	Number of clerics
Released without trial	16
Acquitted	4
Convicted, sentenced, released immediately, apparently without execution of the sentence	4
Convicted, sentenced, fined	5
Convicted, sentenced, imprisoned/hard labour	4
Detained without trial	1
Unknown	9
Total	43

minor offences, such as unlawful assembly and possession of seditious documents.

The cases brought against these priests were rarely successful. As can be seen from Table 7.2, only four priests were convicted and sentenced to imprisonment. Five others were convicted and fined, but most priests were released without charge, acquitted or released upon sentencing.

When cases did go to court, the main beneficiaries were usually the priests themselves, who gloried in their martyrdom. As has been seen, the first priest to be arrested was the Australian army chaplain Thomas O'Donnell in October 1919.[23] Coming as it did quite early in the conflict, at a time when arrests of priests were still uncommon, the case received a lot of high-profile press attention. The *Irish Independent* found much to complain about in the conditions of O'Donnell's imprisonment. When he was taken to the Tower of London to await court-martial, the newspaper made the most of his brief sojourn in a cell beside that once occupied by Roger Casement.[24] From September 1920 the number of arrests started to rise sharply, with sixteen arrests before the end of the year, and another twenty-five in the first half of 1921. The impact which this new development had on clerical opinion cannot be seen apart from the killing of two priests in November and December 1920, nor from the increasing number of raids and incidents of violence against priests. To clerics and to many lay Catholics, these events, considered together, seemed indisputable evidence of sectarian targeting of Catholic clergy.

Coming shortly after the first killing of a priest, the arrest of Father Patrick Delahunty on 30 November 1920 on charges of possession of seditious documents also attracted considerable press attention. Court-martialled and convicted in Waterford in December, he was sentenced to two years' imprisonment with hard labour, the sentence being commuted to two years' imprisonment without hard labour in January.[25] The sentence was considered very harsh and the editor of the *Irish Independent* called it excessive, accusing the government of being vindictive, as well as stupid for making Delahunty into a political martyr.[26]

Another high-profile case was the arrest of Fathers Dominic and Albert at Church Street Capuchin priory in December 1920. As has been seen, Dominic had become a public figure during the MacSwiney hunger-strike. The instructions issued for the raid had been to arrest the two friars in the priory together with, ambitiously, Michael Collins, Richard Mulcahy and Cathal Brugha.[27] It was

23 *Irish Independent*, 21 and 29 October 1919.
24 *Ibid.*
25 TNA, WO35/120, Register of cases tried, 3 September 1920.
26 *Irish Independent*, 10 January 1921.
27 TNA, WO35/81.

personally approved by the chief secretary. Dominic's arrest was ordered because the crown forces had obtained a letter by him containing seditious statements.[28] None of the wanted lay men were found on the premises, but Dominic and Albert were apprehended amid a mass of incriminating documents strewn about their rooms. They were taken to Dublin Castle. The superior warned the commanding officer several times that Albert was 'a very delicate man and [that] his nerves and digestive organs [were] not in a healthy condition'.[29] The officer recommended that Albert be seen by a doctor as soon as possible, but this did not happen, and Albert himself subsequently claimed that he had been threatened and led to believe that Dominic had been shot.[30] According to his confrere Father Aloysius Travers, Dominic was kept in solitary confinement between his arrest and his transfer to an English prison in January 1921, although Ernie O'Malley claimed to have shared a cell with him in December.[31] Albert was released without charge, but Dominic was sentenced by court-martial to five years' penal servitude for 'making statements[,] spreading false reports [and] having documents, the publication of which would be likely to cause disaffection'.[32] This conviction was also widely regarded in the press as an instance of victimisation of the clergy.[33]

The crown forces selected some priests for arrest to make a public example of them. The previous chapter has mentioned Father Eugene Coyle of Clontibret. This republican priest was arrested for the first time in September 1920 for refusing to be searched at a checkpoint. Coyle had been carrying incriminating documents, but because neither the soldiers at the checkpoint nor an officer at the barracks where he was taken wished to have the

---

28 Hopkinson, *Castle*, p. 93; MA, BMH, WS207, Aloysius Travers, p. 3; and CPA, O'Connor papers, CA/IR/1/5/3/8, Travers, 'Account'.
29 TNA, WO35/81.
30 NLI, Maurice Moore papers, MS 10,556, 'Rough statement of Father Albert of the Franciscan Friars'.
31 MA, BMH, WS207, Aloysius Travers, p. 4; CPA, O'Connor papers, CA/IR/1/5/3/8, Travers, 'Account', and O'Malley, *Wound*, p. 272.
32 Sentence: MA, BMH, WS207, Aloysius Travers, p. 5; charge: TNA, WO35/93B.
33 See quotations from newspapers in CPA, O'Connor papers, CA/IR/1/5/3/8, Travers, 'Account'.

'unpleasantness of searching a priest', he was released without the papers being discovered. Coyle had appealed to his clerical status to avoid the search: he told the officer that 'as a priest I [object] to being searched by either military or police officers'.[34] In May 1921, Coyle was arrested a second time after a raid on his house, and was subsequently kept in prison for a number of weeks. Bishop McKenna of Clogher told him after his release in June or July 1921 that he had heard from contacts in Dublin Castle that Coyle's had been a test case because the government had become concerned about the involvement of younger priests in IRA activities.[35]

The last high-profile case during the war was the arrest of Father William O'Kennedy, president of St Flannan's College, Ennis, in July 1921.[36] Crown forces raided the college during the Killaloe diocesan clergy's annual retreat and arrested O'Kennedy in the presence of Bishop Fogarty, the canons and many other priests.[37] Recognising the public relations potential of the arrest, the clergy present immediately published a strongly-worded protest, calling it an 'uncalled for and shameful outrage on religious decency, and good order'.[38] O'Kennedy was held in a military prison on Bere Island in County Cork until he was released on parole in December 1921. Soon after the arrest, Fogarty appointed O'Kennedy a canon and chancellor of the diocese.[39] Having made this gesture, the bishop quickly began to urge O'Kennedy to request parole. The college needed him back and Fogarty had difficulty in 'having to explain to the pope why [O'Kennedy was] not entering upon office', presumably as chancellor. O'Kennedy's reply shows that he was sensitive to the necessity of dealing with this practical consequence of his incarceration, emphasising the opportunities for pastoral work which he had in jail. He replied that he was 'very useful here to the men – I do quite a lot of work for them – spiritually – when

---

34 MA, BMH, WS325, Eugene Coyle, pp. 7–8. In his statement Coyle claimed that this arrest took place 'early in the year 1921', but the newspaper report of the events appeared in September 1920: see *Irish Independent*, 28 September 1920.
35 MA, BMH, WS325, Eugene Coyle, p. 14.
36 Ó Haichir, *Rebel*, p. 8.
37 *Irish Catholic*, 9 July 1921.
38 *Nenagh Guardian*, 9 July 1921.
39 Ó Haichir, *Rebel*, p. 6.

I get out I'll have much to tell you'.[40] Even republican bishops evidently felt that republican priests must not allow the making of political statements interfere with their pastoral responsibilities.

Ó Fiaich has remarked that the number of priests arrested during the war was quite high.[41] The arrest of forty-three priests during a period of two and a half years was indeed quite exceptional when compared with the figures for most periods of that duration in modern Irish history, and the marked upsurge after July 1920 is clear evidence of a change in attitude on the part of the crown forces. The forty-three priests amounted to 1.2 per cent of the total clerical population in Ireland. This was a higher percentage than that applying to the general population: 1.2 per cent of a population of about 4.4 million would have represented more than 50,000 arrests in total, hardly a realistic number.[42] This discrepancy shows that priests were more likely to be arrested than average lay people, indicating that they were under special scrutiny from the crown forces. But the arrest of a mere 1.2 per cent of the clergy also demonstrates that there was no widespread lock-up of priests. The main consequence of the policy was that the public indignation which it aroused helped to further the notion that British oppression in Ireland had a sectarian connotation. Moreover, at the same time as priests began to be arrested more frequently, they also began to fall victim to the rougher tactics employed by the crown forces. This inevitably coloured the perception of the arrests.

Intimidation

Violent reprisals for IRA actions began to occur regularly from mid-1920 onwards.[43] As D. M. Leeson has shown, Black and Tans and Auxiliaries were not the only section of the crown forces responsible for these incidents.[44] Irish constables also participated. Intimidation of civilians suspected of republican activism had occurred before the new recruits from Britain arrived, and Irish

---

40 KDA, Fogarty papers, F5A17, O'Kennedy to Fogarty, 28 November 1921.
41 Ó Fiaich, 'Clergy', pp. 497, 501.
42 The size of the total population is based on the 1911 census.
43 Leeson, *Black and Tans*, pp. 156–222.
44 *Ibid.*, pp. 191–2.

Catholic constables continued to be involved in police violence afterwards. But priests rarely had much to fear from the 'old RIC'. In fact there are a number of instances where constables prevented their newly arrived colleagues from harming clerics. IRA members occasionally disguised themselves as priests, a further indication that the clergy was regarded as immune from interference by the old RIC. Dan Breen called the cassock a common disguise and contended that the 'old Peelers ... gave the benefit of the doubt even to suspicious-looking clergy'.[45] Although this benevolence began to falter as an embattled RIC responded to the effects of its ostracism from local society, the greater threat to clerical safety came from the Black and Tans and Auxiliaries. These frequently suspected the clergy of incitement to violence and had considerably fewer qualms than the 'old Peelers' about treating priests accordingly.

A search of the sources used for this book has yielded eighty instances of intimidation and violence against priests allegedly at the hands of the crown forces.[46] The vast majority of these incidents took place from mid-1920 onwards. It included such things as physical assault, firing shots and death threats. The latter soon became a common feature of the conflict. Father T. Curtayne, a curate in Ballybunion, County Kerry, and a Sinn Féin member, received a threatening letter in May 1920 from the 'Black Hand', stating that in God's sight 'all priests are murderers who encourage and incite murder and crime in those who know no better'.[47] The same author sent a similar notice to other priests in the area, who were then given armed IRA protection.[48] A few days later, Father Charles Culligan, curate in Kilmihil, County Clare, received a threatening letter from the 'Brotherhood of Irish Avengers' stating that he had been condemned to death for complicity in a recent murder.[49]

The conflict claimed its first ecclesiastical victim in July 1920, when a Redemptorist lay brother called Michael Morgan was

45 Breen, *Fight*, p. 74.
46 See Appendix 6.
47 *Irish Independent*, 10 May 1920, and MA, BMH, WS1212, Liam McCabe, p. 5.
48 MA, BMH, WS1212, Liam McCabe, pp. 5–6, and WS1011, Patrick Garvey, p. 11.
49 *Irish Independent*, 13 May 1920.

shot dead through the window of Clonard monastery on the Falls–Shankill border in Belfast. During an outbreak of sectarian violence the monastery had become the target of gunmen, and while shooting was in progress, Morgan looked out of a window on the top floor and was immediately shot dead.[50] He was probably mistaken for a sniper, and the killing was not generally ascribed to the specific targeting of clergy or religious, although the community was divided over whether the killer had been a soldier or an Orangeman.[51] The following night, the house of Father Malachy Brennan, the Sinn Féin priest in Ballinasloe, County Galway, was fired into by 'policemen'.[52] In September a Black and Tan struck the parish priest of Dunkerrin, King's County, on his chest as he was walking to the church for a parish mission with a group of other priests. An Irish constable among the party that assaulted the priest told them that he 'did not want to insult the clergy', but that the police were being burned out of house and home. According to one of the witnesses, the English Black and Tans were very hostile to the priests, and it was one of them that had hit the parish priest.[53]

Apart from such chance encounters that turned ugly, attacks were also intentionally aimed at particular priests. Father John O'Malley, parish priest of Turloughmore, County Galway, reported that crown forces had fired shots outside his house for more than two hours on three nights, causing him and his co-residents to 'shelter behind a wall away from windows and doors'. After that, RIC lorries from Galway had passed O'Malley's residence almost every day for about a fortnight, firing shots on each occasion.[54] A curate in Feakle, County Clare, Father Patrick O'Reilly, suffered a similar ordeal, as he testified in a letter to the *Irish Independent*

---

50 CMA, box 'T. The Troubles and Clonard, 1920–2000', envelope 'T1. Br. Michael's killing', Cleary to Burke, 26 July 1920.
51 Sniper and soldier: James Grant, *One Hundred Years with the Clonard Redemptorists* (Blackrock: Columba Press, 2003), p. 97, and CMA, box 'T. The Troubles and Clonard, 1920–2000', envelope 'T1. Br. Michael's killing', Cleary to Burke, 26 July 1920; Orangeman: CMA, 'Domestic chronicle', p. 302.
52 *Irish Independent*, 24 July 1920.
53 *Ibid.*, 29 September 1920.
54 TDA, Gilmartin papers, B4/8-ii/4, O'Malley to Walsh, 3 December 1920.

in October 1920. After an ambush in his parish had left two RIC men dead, a district inspector and a group of soldiers arrived at his door and took him out. They dragged him to a wall and 'proceeded "to thrash" [him] with a stock of a rifle' and threatened his life. Throughout that night and for a number of subsequent nights, shots were fired at O'Reilly's house and explosives thrown in through the broken windows. Finally, all his belongings were taken out, piled up in front of the house and burned.[55] The cause of this was that soldiers had discovered that O'Reilly had ministered to the victims on the scene of the ambush.[56] They evidently concluded from this that he had known of the attack in advance.

Senior clergy were not immune from harsh treatment. When Archbishop Patrick Clune of Perth visited Ireland in 1920, his secretary Father J. T. McMahon travelled with him. Black and Tans raided McMahon's parents' house in Ennis while he was staying there. As the victim later recounted, they 'dragged me out into the street, and what would have happened then, heaven knows, had not my mother followed them down the stairs and clung on to me, despite their efforts to shake her off'. After kicking McMahon 'around the street', they took Mrs. McMahon's money and left.[57] Bishops were also threatened personally. Thus Bishop Fogarty received a notice in October 1920 telling him that he and his house and property would be held responsible if two kidnapped constables were not delivered up within forty-eight hours.[58] And in the same month, a Tipperary IRA man, James Leahy, obtained a police list containing twelve names of prominent people 'marked down for shooting by the Thurles RIC "Murder Gang"' in case any more crown forces should be killed.[59] Second or third on the list was Archbishop Harty of Cashel, despite the fact that he was a strong critic of the IRA.

The martyr boy priest

In November 1920 this catalogue reached its highpoint with the killing of a priest. The tally of clerics killed by British forces

55 *Irish Independent*, 15 October 1920.
56 MA, BMH, WS983, Thomas Tuohy, pp. 18–20.
57 MA, BMH, WS362, J. T. McMahon, p. 34.
58 KDA, Fogarty papers, F3A23, anon. to Fogarty, 18 October 1920.
59 MA, BMH, WS1454, James Leahy, pp. 50–50A.

during the War of Independence came to three, or, if the canonical meaning of that term is disregarded and Brother Michael and two seminarians are included, to six.[60] By far the most famous of these was the 'martyr boy priest', Father Michael Griffin (1892–1920), a Clonfert cleric working as a curate in Rahoon in the diocese of Galway.[61] The shock which his death caused to public consciousness changed the clergy's outlook on the conflict and ensured him an enduring place in republican martyrology. Griffin's status was reinforced by such hagiographical portrayals as John Rushe's article in the 1961–62 edition of *Vexilla Regis* – a journal published by the eponymous association of lay Maynooth alumni – and by commemorative pictures sold at fairs and markets by 'ballad men'.[62] In the days after the killing, Griffin's bishop, O'Doherty of Clonfert, even hinted at the possibility of canonisation.[63]

Around midnight on Sunday 14 November 1920, men came to the house on Montpellier Terrace in Galway city where Griffin and his fellow curate Father John O'Meehan lived. O'Meehan was not at home. After a short while, Griffin left with them, fully dressed and apparently without offering resistance.[64] Nothing more was heard of the unfortunate twenty-eight year-old until his body was found buried in a bog at Cloughscoiltia, west of the city, a week later. Two doctors performed a post mortem on the body and concluded that Griffin had been shot through the head.[65] Despite

---

60 The *Code of Canon Law* defined as clerics those who had been advanced to the sacred ministry 'at least by first tonsure'; see *CIC*, canon 108. This excluded lay religious and seminarians during the early stages of their studies. Finbar Darcy, an Alexian brother killed in Cork in January 1921 according to Ó Fiaich, 'Clergy', p. 496, was in fact an ex-Alexian: *Irish Independent*, 7 January 1921.
61 John Rushe, 'The martyr boy priest. Father Michael Griffin', *Vexilla Regis. Maynooth's Laymen's Annual*, 9 (1961–62), pp. 60–72. For a recent account of the Griffin killing, see Leeson, *Black and Tans*, pp. 51–2.
62 Rushe, 'Martyr'. For an example of a commemorative picture featuring Griffin and the other two priests killed during the War of Independence, see Pádraic Ó Laoi, *Fr. Griffin 1892–1920* (n.p.: Connacht Tribune, 1994), p. 95.
63 *Irish Catholic*, 11 December 1920.
64 *Connacht Tribune*, 20 November 1920.
65 Ó Laoi, *Griffin*, pp. 38–43.

the claim made by the RIC county inspector that Griffin had been 'slain by Sinn Feiners', in fact there has been always been unanimity that the men who abducted and killed Griffin were members of the crown forces.[66] This was the view expressed by Griffin's parish priest, Father Peter Davis, and by a conference of the bishops of Galway and Clonfert and the senior priests of Galway city at the time of Griffin's disappearance. Bishop O'Dea of Galway repeated it after Griffin's body had been found.[67] Subsequent statements from IRA veterans and from General Frank Crozier, head of the RIC's Auxiliary Division, confirm that the killers were Auxiliaries.[68]

There has been some speculation about the motives which the killers may have had for targeting Griffin in particular. This question is especially relevant, since his fellow curate O'Meehan had much the stronger public profile as a republican. O'Meehan had been the recipient of no fewer than five threatening notices.[69] His sister asserted that he had been actively involved in the Irish Volunteers in Kinvara, County Galway, where he had been a curate before moving to Rahoon. This assertion is confirmed by a complaint in May 1916 from General Maxwell to Bishop O'Dea that O'Meehan had helped with the drilling of Irish Volunteers in Kinvara.[70] Because of these threats, O'Meehan no longer slept at home, taking refuge instead in a local nursing home. O'Meehan believed that he had been the real target of the killers and that they had taken Griffin instead because he refused to tell where O'Meehan could be found.[71]

66 TNA, CO904/113, IGMR, November 1920, p. 479.
67 Father Davis's comments: *Irish Catholic*, 20 November 1920; statement of the bishops of Galway and Clonfert and senior priests of Galway city: GDA, O'Dea papers, 32/15, statement, undated; O'Dea's repetition: GDA, O'Dea papers, 31/7, O'Dea to Greenwood, 25 November 1920.
68 IRA veterans: MA, BMH, WS1729, Joseph Togher, p. 9, and WS1126, Michael-Francis Kelly-Mor, pp. 1–2; Crozier: F. P. Crozier, *Ireland for Ever* (London and Toronto: J. Cape, 1932), p. 107. See also MA, BMH, WS1050, Vera McDonnell, pp. 5–6.
69 *Irish Catholic*, 27 November 1920, and GDA, O'Dea papers, 31/7, O'Dea to Greenwood, 25 November 1920.
70 MA, BMH, WS1034, Mary Leech, p. 1; Maxwell's complaint: GDA, O'Dea papers, 40/224, 6 May 1916. For O'Meehan's activities in Kinvara see also McMahon (ed.), *Ó Fathaigh*, p. 7.
71 MA, BMH, WS1034, Mary Leech, p. 3.

But an incident that took place in Galway some weeks before the killing provides significant clues that point in a different direction. In October, the IRA apprehended a man called Patrick Joyce, a teacher at Barna national school in Griffin's parish, who had been caught sending letters to the British authorities with information about local Volunteers.[72] One of these letters contained a list of names, including Griffin's. Griffin's own involvement with the IRA is not in doubt. In fact, some of Joyce's letters, which had been intercepted by a friendly postman, were handed in to the brigade by Griffin himself.[73] Joyce was taken away for court-martial by the IRA on 15 October and was killed after another priest heard his confession; probably Father Thomas Burke, a curate in Glencorrib who was well connected with the IRA.[74] Joyce was buried in a bog near Galway, and his grave was not discovered until 1998.[75] It is likely that local crown forces believed that Griffin had been the priest who had attended Joyce before his killing.[76] This belief was apparently shared by Joyce's son, who was closely linked to the Auxiliaries.[77] A number of IRA veterans conjectured that Joyce's son accompanied Auxiliaries on the night when Griffin was abducted.[78] This circumstance, rather than the refusal to tell where O'Meehan was, provides the most probable motive for Griffin's killing.

From Father Griffin to Canon Magner

The Griffin killing was an important turning point. In the immediate aftermath, local clerics responded by urging calm and restraint, and by calling for prayers for the killers' conversion. Bishop O'Doherty told a congregation at Loughrea cathedral that he would pray that

---

72 MA, BMH, WS1718, Mícheál Ó Droighnáin, p. 17.
73 *Ibid.*, p. 18. For Griffin's connections with the IRA, see also MA, BMH, WS1729, Joseph Togher, p. 4, and Ó Laoi, *Griffin*, p. 20.
74 MA, BMH, WS1718, Mícheál Ó Droighnáin, pp. 19–20. Ó Droighnáin does not mention Burke's name, but says that a priest was collected from Shrule, where Burke was a curate at the time. Ó Laoi does mention Burke: Ó Laoi, *Griffin*, pp. 68–70.
75 *Galway City Tribune*, 10 July 1998.
76 MA, BMH, WS714, Thomas Hynes, p. 20.
77 MA, BMH, WS1729, Joseph Togher, p. 8.
78 *Ibid.*; see also MA, BMH, WS714, Thomas Hynes, p. 20.

'on the great accounting day ... the murderers ... and their victim may meet in eternal friendship at the right hand of God. This, and this alone, will be our reprisal.'[79] Griffin's parish priest, Father Davis, also called for prayers for the murderers, and Bishop O'Dea said that 'it is wise to be prudent as well as just in pressing even the most righteous of claims'.[80] But the killing had a huge impact on the clerical attitude towards the British authorities. There was a feeling, in O'Dea's words, that 'the worst has happened', and that the killing marked 'a new departure in the campaign, the beginning of an attack on the church and religion'.[81] What little had been left of the clergy's regard for the authorities was now rapidly disappearing.

This perception was strengthened by the fact that a number of clerics – including O'Dea himself – received anonymous letters threatening them with Griffin's fate.[82] As has been seen, there had been death threats before, but these naturally appeared in an entirely different light after Griffin's murder. Thus a few days after the discovery of Griffin's body, Father Bernard Crehan, curate in Grange, County Sligo, received a threatening notice.[83] The letter, signed 'Black [and] Tans', stated pointedly that 'surely your conscience are [sic] troubling you, if not they will in future as you can prepare for the same end as Fr. Griffin'. The authors also explained why Crehan merited this fate: 'we hold you responsible for the murder of the Cliffoney police by your sermons preached each Sunday to the congregation'.[84] Crehan told his bishop that he was not aware of having done anything wrong, unless it was 'the holding of views professed by the nations at the time of the Great War – the right of any nation to self-determination, [and] the Irish word for that is Sinn Féin'.[85]

---

79 *Irish Catholic*, 11 December 1920.
80 *Ibid.*, 27 November 1920.
81 *Ibid.*, 4 December 1920.
82 *Ibid.* See also Leeson, *Black and Tans*, p. 164.
83 Elphin Diocesan Archives, Sligo (hereafter EDA), Bernard Coyne papers, box 'Bishop Coyne, 1913–1919', folder 'Jan–Dec '20', Crehan to Crowe, 25 November 1920.
84 EDA, Coyne papers, box 'Bishop Coyne, 1913–1919', folder 'Jan–Dec '20', letter signed 'Black & Tans' enclosed in Doorly to Crowe, 30 November 1920.
85 EDA, Coyne papers, box 'Bishop Coyne, 1913–1919', folder 'Jan–Dec '20', Crehan to Crowe, 25 November 1920.

In December, Father P. Ryan, curate in Bournea, Roscrea, County Tipperary, wrote to Bishop Fogarty that he had been visited at home by 'masked men with foreign accents' who had searched his house. 'When the search was completed I was taken out, tied hands and feet to a gate about a mile from the house and my life was threatened.' The men accused Ryan of having been an agitator and said that unless he severed his connection with the arbitration courts and left the district his life would be taken.[86] In the same month, it was reported that Bishops Fogarty and MacRory were no longer living in their houses for fear of attack.[87] Westbourne, Fogarty's Ennis residence, became the target of 'four Auxiliaries with blackened faces' on the night of 3 December 1920. Fogarty happened to be absent when the four men arrived at the door late that night and asked to see him. They made a thorough search of the house and went through some papers in the library before sampling whiskey in the cellar.[88] According to rumours later published by General Crozier, some members of the crown forces had decided to kill Fogarty that night by drowning him in a sack in the Shannon.[89] Questions were asked about the case in the House of Commons.[90]

A second priest was killed a month and a day after Griffin's disappearance, this time in County Cork. On the afternoon of Wednesday 15 December 1920, Resident Magistrate P. S. Brady was driving near Dunmanway when his car broke down.[91] The septuagenarian parish priest of Dunmanway, Thomas Canon Magner (1850–1920), was walking along the road when he came across Brady, who was trying to start his car. He offered assistance and

---

[86] KDA, Fogarty papers, F5A20, Ryan to Fogarty, 1 December 1920.
[87] AICR, Hagan papers, HAG1/1920/462, O'Kelly to Hagan, 13 December 1920.
[88] KDA, Fogarty papers, F3A23, typescript statement by Bishop Fogarty, undated.
[89] Crozier, *Ireland*, p. 107.
[90] David Lloyd George responded to a question by Walter Smith, MP for Wellingborough, 7 April 1921: Hansard, series 5 (Commons), vol. cxl, col. 466W.
[91] The following account is taken from *Freeman's Journal*, 17 December 1920 and *Irish Independent*, 17 December 1920. See also Enright, *Trial*, pp. 27–33, whose account is based on the *Cork Constitution*.

helped Brady push the vehicle. A young man from the locality called Timothy Crowley then passed by on a bicycle, and Magner asked him for help. Then two lorries of Auxiliaries arrived, one of which drove past while the other stopped. An armed cadet called Vernon Hart emerged and asked Brady who he was, making threats to shoot him. Hart, who was in charge of the party, then turned to Crowley, while Brady took the opportunity to take cover out of Hart's sight near the lorry. Brady and the Auxiliaries in the lorry then heard a shot. When they went to look, they saw Crowley lying on the ground with a gunshot wound to his head. According to the *Irish Independent*, Hart then forced Magner onto his knees, and interrogated him for some time before shooting him in the head too. Brady, who understandably feared for his life, made good his escape. After his departure, the lorry which had driven past returned, carrying the district inspector.[92] The latter managed with some difficulty to persuade Hart to put his gun away. The party then flung Crowley's and Magner's bodies over a ditch adjoining the road and returned to Dunmanway workhouse, where Hart was disarmed and placed under arrest. Original press reports stated that Magner had been shot when trying to intervene on Crowley's behalf, but later newspaper articles did not repeat this claim.[93]

The crime was discovered when Magner's curate, Father Michael Carmody, was told that there had been a shooting. He cycled to the scene of the crime, but could not find the bodies. Carmody then went to a cottage in the vicinity, where he found Brady. The magistrate brought Carmody to the dead men, finally managed to start his car and drove it to Macroom, where he reported events to the RIC.[94] While Carmody was attending to the bodies, another lorry with Auxiliaries passed by and stopped. The officer in charge expressed regret to Carmody and informed him that the killer had been arrested. The lorry then brought the bodies to the workhouse mortuary in Dunmanway.[95] It became clear afterwards that when the district inspector had tried to disarm Hart at the barracks, the

---

92 Donal O'Donovan, *The Murder of Canon Magner and Tadhg O'Crowley* (n.p., 2005), pp. 8–9.
93 *Freeman's Journal*, 16 December 1920.
94 T. M. Healy, *Letters and Leaders of my Day* (New York: Frederick A. Stokes, 1929), ii, p. 620–1.
95 *Irish Independent*, 17 December 1920.

cadet had first threatened to shoot him too.[96] The culprit was taken under escort to Cork, where he was reportedly out of his mind. He was court-martialled in early January and found guilty but insane.[97] Despite this verdict, and in an obvious attempt to show that the government was not engaging in a cover-up, the chief secretary announced to the House of Commons that Hart had been sentenced to a period of detention. In fact, he was committed to a lunatic asylum.[98]

The day after the murder, Bishop Cohalan received a telegram from T. J. Smyth, the inspector general of the RIC, who asked him to accept his sympathy on the death of Canon Magner and to convey 'an expression of my deep sorrow and sincere sympathy' to his relatives. Cohalan had just issued his excommunication decree three days before Magner's death and was not keen to encourage the perception that he favoured the government. He cabled back that he would have accepted the sympathy of the inspector general of the old RIC, but that he could not accept or convey the sympathies of Smyth, 'whose men are murdering my people and have burned my city'.[99]

Despite these exchanges, and despite the fact that the Magner killing was no less tragic than the Griffin one, it did not capture subsequent imagination to the same degree as the death of the 'boy-priest'. The under-secretary wondered shortly after the incident why 'the murder of Canon Magner had aroused so little storm'.[100] Whereas fatalities in County Galway were a relative rarity, Cork had been so badly affected by violence that this murder seemed just one of many in the general conflagration that enveloped the county.[101] The shock of a murdered priest was less keenly felt in areas where murder had become a regular occurrence. Moreover, Galway had a relatively high level of clerical support for Sinn Féin, whereas Cork had a high percentage of priests who condemned the IRA. Galway priests were more likely than their Cork counterparts to put these events to good use publicity-wise.

96 Enright, *Trial*, p. 30.
97 *Ibid.*, p. 33.
98 *Ibid.*
99 *Freeman's Journal*, 17 December 1920.
100 Hopkinson, *Castle*, p. 97.
101 Hart, 'Geography', p. 147.

From Canon Magner to Father O'Callaghan

Most of the eighty incidents of violence and intimidation against priests found took place in the first half of 1921, seemingly vindicating O'Dea's contention that Griffin's killing had been the beginning of a specific 'attack on the church and religion'. On the night after an ambush near Ballinhassig, County Cork, in February 1921, the curate, Father Laurence Callanan, was about to go to bed when he saw someone trying to push back the shutter of his dining room window. When he went outside he was told by a voice in the darkness to go back into the house but to stay away from the dining room. As soon as he was back inside, an explosive device was detonated which destroyed the window. Earlier that day, Callanan's servant boy had been arrested in connection with the ambush and Callanan himself had been questioned about his own knowledge of the attack.[102]

Further death threats demonstrate that crown forces – including the army – had come to regard the clergy in a hostile light. In March 1921 two soldiers were seriously wounded during an ambush near Partry, County Mayo. As soon as news of the event reached him, the parish priest, Father Thomas O'Malley, went to the place where the wounded men were lying. On his way he met the captain of the party that had been attacked and some of his soldiers. O'Malley told Archbishop Gilmartin afterwards that the infuriated soldiers 'threatened me, pointed revolvers [and] rifles at me, charged me with being the whole cause of the ambush. I was in real peril of my life'. Although the captain forbade him to proceed, O'Malley waited until the man had gone before going up to the lorry with the wounded soldiers. When he found out that both were Catholics, O'Malley administered extreme unction and had them conveyed to his house on a cart.[103]

And in May, Bishop Fogarty's house in Ennis was visited again by anonymous callers who set fire to the building. The bishop's housekeeper noticed the fire in time and two priests staying at the house successfully fought the flames with the aid of a Minimax fire extinguisher.[104]

---

102 *Irish Independent*, 10 February 1921.
103 TDA, Gilmartin papers, B4/8-ii/4, O'Malley to Gilmartin, 11 March 1921.
104 KDA, Fogarty papers, F3A23, Fogarty to O'Reilly, 30 November 1928.

The third priestly fatality took place in Cork and, just like Magner's death, it was more the result of an unhappy convergence of circumstances than of premeditation. The victim was a young curate called Father James O'Callaghan. O'Callaghan had spent some years as a chaplain to the Good Shepherd convent in Sunday's Well, Cork, before being appointed curate in the North Cathedral in October 1920.[105] His new appointment left him without living quarters. O'Callaghan was friendly with the Sinn Féin TD Liam de Róiste, who lived on Upper Janemount, Sunday's Well. He asked de Róiste for hospitality, and was invited to stay at his house. According to a statement which de Róiste sent to Cohalan after O'Callaghan's killing, crown forces raided his house only a few days after O'Callaghan had moved in and treated the priest roughly.[106] At the elections held in May 1921 under the provisions of the 1920 Government of Ireland Act, de Róiste was an unopposed Sinn Féin candidate for the Cork borough constituency. Fearing that this would attract further adverse attention from the crown forces, he did not sleep in his house at night, leaving O'Callaghan there together with his wife, his mother-in-law and a servant girl.

In the early hours of Pentecost Sunday, 15 May 1921, the residents were awoken by shouting and knocking at the door. Armed men believed to be Black and Tans demanded to see 'Mr. Roche' and sought entry. Both de Róiste's wife Norah and O'Callaghan shouted to them that the man they sought was not at home and that the only residents were three women and a priest. Eventually the intruders – who were inebriated according to the unanimous verdict of all witnesses – gained entry and struggled both with Norah de Róiste and with O'Callaghan. According to the servant's statement, O'Callaghan shouted: 'I am a priest, for God's sake don't shoot me' while struggling with one of the intruders.[107] The man who was holding O'Callaghan nevertheless shot him in the back, and fired again as the priest fell on the ground. When the attackers

---

105 This and the following details are derived from a statement accompanying a letter sent to Bishop Cohalan by Liam de Róiste, TD. CDA, Cohalan papers, box i, De Róiste to Cohalan, 19 May 1921. See also NLI, Moore papers, MS 10,556, for statements from Norah de Róiste, Bridget O'Brien and Kate Kearney.
106 CDA, Cohalan papers, box i, De Róiste to Cohalan, 19 May 1921.
107 *Ibid.*

had disappeared, O'Callaghan, who remained conscious, was taken to hospital, where he lived until the afternoon. The administrator of his parish, Michael Canon O'Sullivan, later swore an affidavit to say that O'Callaghan had described his killer as 'a tall lanky fellow with a clean shaven face, a Black and Tan I've often seen at the North Gate Bridge'.[108] O'Callaghan's funeral, presided over by the bishop, took place under large public interest on the Wednesday after his death.[109] But this killing impinged on public consciousness to an even lesser degree than Canon Magner's. County Cork had become accustomed to killings, and, as has been seen, the murder of a priest did not have the same resonance it had had in County Galway a few months previously.

Three fatalities represented 0.08 per cent of the total clerical population in Ireland. If this figure is extrapolated to the population in general, it would mean more than 3,500 deaths. In fact, Eunan O'Halpin has counted 2,141 fatalities between January 1917 and December 1921, 898 of whom were civilians.[110] As with arrests, priests were thus at a higher risk of being killed than the general population, but with an absolute total of three the evidence certainly does not point to a murder campaign against the clergy. It is more difficult to compare figures for intimidation and non-lethal forms of violence, as these are not available for the wider population in general. Nonetheless it is evident that after mid-1920 priests were exposed to interference by the crown forces to a higher degree than the general population.

Members of the crown forces had a specific motive to single out priests for harassment. Father Curtayne was told that 'all priests are murderers who encourage and incite murder and crime', and Crehan's threatening notice said that he bore responsibility for the

---

108 NLI, Moore papers, MS 10,556, O'Sullivan affidavit, 29 June 1921. The de Róiste statement gives a slightly different version of O'Callaghan's response to the question: 'A Black and Tan policeman. He was from Shandon barrack': CDA, Cohalan papers, box i, De Róiste to Cohalan, 19 May 1921.
109 *Irish Independent*, 17 May 1921.
110 O'Halpin, 'Counting', p. 153. O'Halpin's time frame is wider than this book's, but since it is certain that there were no clerical fatalities between January 1917 and January 1919 and between July and December 1921, the comparison is valid.

death of policemen 'by [his] sermons preached each Sunday to the congregation'. Father O'Malley was charged with 'being the whole cause of the ambush' when he was threatened, and Father Ryan was told that he was an agitator. Similarly, D. M. Leeson has recounted that on one occasion English members of the crown forces in Galway refused to call a priest before killing a republican, saying: 'Your priests are worse than you are yourselves.'[111] These incidents confirm that there was a perception among members of the crown forces that priests were complicit in the rebellion in a way that lay civilians were not, and that they therefore merited extraordinary punishment.

But there is evidence to show that this singling-out of priests happened primarily in specific parts of the country. Appendix 7 shows the geographical distribution of intimidation of and violence against priests by the crown forces. As has been seen, the fighting was generally more intense in Munster than elsewhere. The fact that all civilians in this province were consequently at a higher risk of falling victim to violence also explains the significantly higher figures for intimidation of Munster priests.[112] By contrast, the county with the highest figure was Galway, which had relatively low levels of violence. This points to the specific targeting of the clergy there in a way that did not happen in Munster or in more peaceful parts of the country. The particular hostility to priests in Galway was probably due to the county's culture of strong clerical links with Sinn Féin. The Galway clergy's reputation for republicanism caused members of the crown forces there to perceive priests as being responsible for inciting to violence against them.[113]

Sacrilege

In the narrative of persecution that came to be favoured by clerical commentators even relatively insignificant examples of British

111 Leeson, *Black and Tans*, p. 49; see also p. 164.
112 In the absence of specific figures for violence by the crown forces, 'levels of violence' here are measured by levels of IRA violence. Hart, 'Geography', p. 151.
113 See the high number of priests in leadership positions in the Galway Sinn Féin constituency executives: NLI, MS 5649, List of Sinn Féin officers, 1920.

aggression were useful. This was especially true for acts that could give rise to accusations of sacrilege. Catholics were quite familiar with the concept of sacrilege at the beginning of the twentieth century. Its most common use was in the context of the unworthy reception of the sacraments. Persons who received communion while in a state of mortal sin were deemed to have committed sacrilege. As weekly or even daily communion became standard practice during the pontificate of Pope Pius X (1903–14), this doctrine caused an upsurge of frequent confession in order to avoid 'sacrilegious communions'. But originally the term referred to the violation of a sacred object or person, and it was this meaning that provided for the charge of sacrilege against the crown forces. Doubtless acts of sacrilege were actually committed by members of the crown forces, although these are likely to have resulted more often from ignorance or indifference than from the intention to offend religious sensibilities. Thus aggressive or insensitive behaviour during raids of churches could easily result in the accusation of sacrilege.

The most celebrated case happened during a raid by the military on a temporary church in Dunmore, County Galway, in October 1920. Dean Thomas Macken, the parish priest, was celebrating mass in a school building used as a church in an outlying part of his parish. He was addressing the congregation after the conclusion of mass, when a soldier brandishing a revolver entered the building and told everyone present to leave. Macken refused this and went out to speak to the commanding officer, telling him that the interruption of a religious service was 'outrageous conduct' that was unknown in any civilised country.[114] The commanding officer claimed later that it had not been obvious from the outside that the school building was being used as a church, and when he saw men running away as the patrol approached, he believed that the building was being used for an illegal assembly. He stated: 'Dean Macken came up rather upset and rather lost control of himself. Told him why I came there: not for purpose of upsetting religious ceremony and then I left.'[115]

114 TDA, Gilmartin papers, B4/8-ii/4, Macken to Gilmartin, 16 October 1920.
115 TDA, Gilmartin papers, B4/8-ii/4, unsigned and undated statement from soldier.

Macken was well aware of the public relations significance of the incident. He informed Archbishop Gilmartin that 'this is the first instance of stopping a religious service [and] I am sending a wire to the press.'[116] In a second letter, he told Gilmartin that 'the report sent to the *Independent* was carefully corrected by the [curates] before being sent, [and] it is perfectly correct and quite full.'[117] The newspaper report did not mention that the building was a school and was unrecognisable as a church from the outside, nor that men had fled when they saw the military approaching. Although the *Irish Independent* said that the service 'had almost concluded' when the soldier entered for the first time, it emphasised that it had been 'a station of confessions, including mass and holy communion'.[118] This gave the impression that the military had interrupted while mass was being said. In fact mass was over and the dean had been addressing the people. Macken was clearly keen on making the most of the affair.

Other incidents of sacrilege involved nightly visits to church buildings by members of the crown forces. They forced their way into the sacristy and threw vestments and sacred vessels around the floor. This happened in St Joseph's church, Berkeley Road, Dublin, in October 1920 and in St Mary's church, Killanena, County Clare, in November 1920.[119] A more serious incident took place in Galway city in November 1920. IRA prisoners kept by British authorities in the town hall in November 1920 discovered that tape recorders had been hidden under the carpet of a room where a priest usually heard their confessions.[120] And Father Michael McKenna of Mullagh said at his court-martial in May 1921 that the door of the tabernacle of Mullagh parish church had been forced open on the day of his arrest and 'frightful desecration' had been committed.[121]

---

116 TDA, Gilmartin papers, B4/8-ii/4, Macken to Gilmartin, 16 October 1920.
117 TDA, Gilmartin papers, B4/8-ii/4, Macken to Gilmartin, 18 October 1920; *Irish Independent*, 16 October 1920, and *Irish Catholic*, 23 October 1920.
118 *Irish Independent*, 16 October 1920.
119 St Joseph's: *Irish Independent*, 1 November 1920; St Mary's: *ibid.*, 15 November 1920.
120 MA, BMH, WS1330, John Costello, p. 7.
121 *Irish Independent*, 24 May 1921.

A similar incident took place at Creeve parish church, County Roscommon, in January 1921. As has been seen, the searching of congregations upon exiting was a relatively common, if much-resented procedure. But this time 'the officiating priest was subjected to a search, during the progress of which he was compelled to keep the sacred host, which was in his custody at the time, in his outstretched hand, in order to prevent desecration'. The raiding party then searched the church and the sacristy, forced the priest to open the door of a tabernacle, peered into an empty ciborium and broke open the door of another tabernacle.[122] In another incident, four women praying in the Catholic church of Claudy, County Derry, saw a man wearing a uniform and smoking a cigarette emerge from the sacristy and ascend the altar steps before mass one Sunday morning in May 1921. The man's conduct led the women to believe that he was drunk. As he was wearing a uniform and the Ulster 'Specials' had just visited the grounds of the church, they assumed that he was one of them. After 'a mock display on the altar' the man opened the tabernacle and searched it. He then 'approached the women and asked them what they were doing there' before departing.[123]

Two incidents of gunshots fired at churches while services were in progress also understandably aroused religious indignation. The first of these happened in St John's church, Tralee, although accounts vary as to whether the offending bullets came from the crown forces or from the IRA. On 26 March 1921, a number of people were assembled in the church as Dean David O'Leary and his curates were hearing confessions, when a burst of machine-gun fire was heard just outside the church. Those present threw themselves on the ground and a bullet entered the roof of the church precisely over the dean's confessional. O'Leary mentioned afterwards that he had been hearing a woman's confession when the shooting took place. She retired during the fusillade, but returned again after fifteen minutes and continued her confession where she had left off, 'like a true, brave Irishwoman'. He said that 'the event

---

122 *Irish Catholic*, 12 March 1921. Questions were asked in the House of Commons, 3 March 1921, see Hansard, series 5 (Commons), cxxxviii, col. 1981.
123 *Irish Catholic*, 28 May 1921.

would be heard of throughout the world, and everywhere humanity would be shocked'.[124]

A similar incident happened in Kilmoyle, County Roscommon, a few months later. While mass was being celebrated in the parish church, machine-gun fire from close by caused a panic, especially when one bullet 'perforated the roof above the priest's head and scattered mortar over the altar and sacristy'. The *Irish Catholic* reported keenly that when the celebrant interrupted mass to administer general absolution to the faithful, 'immediately a perfect quiet was restored'. After mass the men of the congregation were searched, and the explanation was proffered that men had been 'seen running away when the forces were about a quarter of a mile from the church'.[125] Both O'Leary's story about his penitent and the *Irish Catholic*'s emphasis on the miraculous effect of the sacraments show that the incidents were promptly assimilated into a persecution narrative reminiscent of penal times.

---

124 *Irish Independent*, 28 March 1921. See *Kerryman*, 2 April 1921, for the assertion that the shots came from 'civilians'.
125 *Irish Catholic*, 9 July 1921.

8

The reign of frightfulness: clerical responses to the British campaign

As the conflict progressed, clerical criticism of the British campaign became ever more vociferous. The bishops gave a clear lead in their October pastoral of 1920. This document blasted the 'terrorism' perpetrated by the crown forces and compared the British 'reign of frightfulness' to the 'horrors of Turkish atrocities, or ... the outrages attributed to the red army of bolshevist Russia'.[1] These sentiments were broadly shared by the Irish clergy, and animosity towards the crown forces only increased when it became apparent, as the previous chapter has shown, that 'neither sacred places nor sacred persons were spared', as Pope Benedict XV put it in a public letter to Cardinal Logue in April 1921.[2] This new focus on British atrocities enabled the clergy to shift their attention away from the moral dilemmas that republican violence presented. However, it also created fresh problems. Clerical condemnations of IRA violence had often included protestations of the innocence of Catholic RIC members. Now that denunciations began to focus on the wrongdoings of the crown forces, the question of the moral status of Catholic constables needed resolving. This chapter examines the development of clerical responses to the British campaign, charting the emergence of the discourse of persecution described in the previous chapter. It also looks at the small number of priests who continued to support the crown forces even in the later stages of the conflict, and analyses their motives.

1 *ICD 1921*, pp. 556–61, at p. 556.
2 Benedict XV, 'Epistola ad Michaëlem S.R.E. Card. Logue, Archiepiscopum Armachanum de necessitate et ratione pacis intra fines Hiberniae reconciliandae', 27 April 1921, *Acta Apostolicae Sedis*, 13 (1921), pp. 256–8, at p. 257. English translation in *ICD 1922*, p. 593.

Double condemnations

As Chapter 2 has established, clerical condemnations of IRA violence increased up to the end of 1920, and declined from that point on as the crown forces began to target priests more frequently. This is does not mean, however, that condemnation of British violence only began in December 1920. Ever since the conscription crisis of 1918, criticism of the British government and its supposed misrule of Ireland had been an acceptable and common theme in clerical pronouncements. When IRA attacks began in 1919, many clerics started issuing 'double condemnations', combining denunciations of republican violence with continued criticism of the British government or the crown forces. During 1919 such criticism often focused on the 'militarisation' of Ireland, and the bishops complained in a joint statement in June of having 'the evils of military rule exhibited at our doors'.[3] Now and then a distinction was made between the authorities and ordinary soldiers, who were only doing their duty. When a soldier was seriously injured by the IRA near Macroom, County Cork, in January 1919, the local curate condemned the attack and said that 'the soldiers were there against their will, and were as little responsible for the provocative policy of the government in this country as they were for the discussion at the peace conference'.[4] This attitude changed as soon as soldiers began to hit back after IRA attacks. This happened for the first time during the 'sack of Fermoy' in County Cork in September 1919, when soldiers went through the town smashing windows and damaging property in revenge for the killing of a comrade.[5] This first reprisal of the War of Independence elicited a strong denunciation from Bishop Browne of Cloyne, who condemned the IRA attack and then called the military's behaviour disgraceful. He wrote that 'the military seem to have been let loose to wreak their frenzied vengeance on the unoffending people of Fermoy. ... We cannot refrain from condemning the outrageous conduct of the soldiers.' The administrator of Fermoy parish echoed Browne's statement and said that 'it is evident from what we have seen and heard that it was no mad act, but a deliberate

---

3 *ICD 1920*, p. 518.
4 *Irish Catholic*, 8 February 1919.
5 Cottrell, *War*, p. 47.

and well thought-out plan of destruction'.[6] These denunciations mentioned both IRA ambushes and subsequent reprisals. Such double condemnations became a standard part of the repertoire of denunciation.

From the beginning of 1920 onwards, reprisals by the RIC became gradually more frequent.[7] This situation presented the clergy with a new dilemma. The pattern that had been set at Soloheadbeg was to condemn the killing of constables as murder, and to praise the victims as 'martyrs to duty'.[8] With constables beginning to engage in reprisals against innocent people, it became more difficult to maintain this image of the RIC as inoffensive victims of unprovoked attack. Archbishop Harty introduced a distinction between well-meaning RIC authorities and unruly constables in January 1920. When constables carried out a reprisal in Thurles after a colleague was killed by the IRA, Harty condemned both the IRA attack and the reprisal and emphasised that the policemen who had engaged in the violence had done so without approval from their superiors. At mass in the cathedral he said: 'it is ... shocking that a number of policemen, whose special duty it is to protect life and property, should break away from their authorities, indulge in an orgy of violence, and endanger the lives of many innocent people'.[9] One of the curates in Thurles cathedral concurred, saying that 'even [the RIC's] most ardent supporter and warmest sympathiser cannot defend, and must necessarily condemn, the conduct of these men on Tuesday night'.[10]

Official episcopal statements continued to focus on the government's ultimate responsibility for the state of the country, but also began to be more critical of the RIC. A joint pastoral issued in January 1920 spoke of 'an iron rule of oppression as cruel and unjust as it is ill-advised and out of date', which was, moreover, the cause of 'violent collisions and retaliations between exasperated sections of the people and the forces of oppression'. The bishops clearly counted the RIC among the latter and wrote that the police were 'diverted from their proper functions as the guardians of

6 *Irish Catholic*, 20 September 1919.
7 Hopkinson, *War*, pp. 79–80.
8 *Irish Catholic*, 1 February 1919.
9 *Ibid.*, 31 January 1920.
10 *Ibid.*

civil order'.[11] At the same time, Harty complained publicly that 'our homes are raided by armed forces of the British crown, our streets are paraded by the army of occupation'.[12] And Bishop Cohalan responded to the killing of the lord mayor of Cork, Tomás MacCurtain, in March by lamenting the fact that the police, 'the official guardians of life and property', were now under the charge and even the suspicion of organised murder. He hoped that the charge would be disproved.[13]

As Auxiliaries and Black and Tans began to arrive from early summer 1920, the dilemma of the 'old RIC' engaging in atrocities resolved itself quickly. Clerical criticism shifted to the new recruits while continuing to focus on the authorities in Dublin Castle.[14] John Canon Doyle, parish priest of Ferns, County Wexford, warned a congregation in July that 'the police' – meaning the Black and Tans and Auxiliaries – 'were strangers, and it was the business of the people to keep away from them and give them no provocation'.[15] It was not uncommon for the clergy to draw an explicit distinction between the 'old RIC' and the new paramilitary troops. When reprisals took place in Trim, County Meath, in September 1920, after an IRA attack, Bishop Gaughran of Meath presided over a conference of the clergy of his diocese in Navan. The meeting issued a statement condemning the attack and protesting 'against the conduct of the British "Black and Tan" troops in burning and sacking Trim after the regular military and police force had withdrawn, satisfied with the guarantee given by the priests that they would be responsible for the peace of the town'.[16]

This distinction was also apparent in the way John Canon Gunning responded to the reprisal following the killing of a district inspector by the IRA in October 1920. Gunning, parish priest of Tobercurry, County Sligo, read a letter at mass from the father of the dead man, assuring the canon that he and his wife 'were deeply grieved to learn of the reprisals that have taken place in your parish. ... If anything could now make my poor boy unhappy

---

11 *ICD 1920*, p. 524.
12 *Irish Catholic*, 31 January 1920.
13 *ICD 1921*, p. 513.
14 See Leeson, *Black and Tans*, p. 193.
15 *Irish Independent*, 13 July 1920.
16 *Irish Catholic*, 2 October 1920.

it would be to know that he was the innocent cause of injury to anyone.'[17] Gunning contrasted the innocent, Catholic 'old RIC' with the foreign Black and Tans who were interfering in the affairs of the Irish Catholic community by exacting a revenge which the victim's relatives had not sought. D. M. Leeson has argued that the arrival of the new British recruits allowed republicans to marginalise the old RIC, making it easier to depict the crown forces in their entirety as enemies rather than 'half-brothers'.[18] As this chapter will show, however, priests did not abandon the idea that Catholics in the RIC belonged to the Irish Catholic community. Instead, they emphasised that the foreign elements of the crown forces were to blame for the outrages. Far from weakening their new emphasis on British atrocities, this position reinforced hostility to the British oppressor by its implication that the old Irish 'Peelers' had been outmanoeuvred by the 'strangers'. The fact that victimisation of priests themselves was mainly the work of Black and Tans and Auxiliaries gave this view the force of personal conviction.

The government's ultimate responsibility for the new regime also remained an important theme. Father D. J. Fitzpatrick, curate in Adare, County Limerick, wrote to the *Irish Independent* in September 1920 criticising General Macready's condemnation of reprisals by crown forces. He argued that 'it is apparent that the government of England is at the back of the reprisals'.[19] Similarly, in a private letter to the chief secretary, Cardinal Logue lambasted the Castle administration for setting up the mainly Protestant 'B Specials' in Ulster. Logue criticised the arming of Orangemen: 'It was hard to believe that any responsible government ... would arm and cast them loose among their Catholic neighbours.'[20] And Dean Roderick Gearty, parish priest of Strokestown, County Roscommon, said in October 1920 that 'what some people thought were passionate outbursts were nothing of the kind, and that orders or instructions had been issued regarding them'.[21]

17 *Ibid.*, 16 October 1920.
18 Leeson, *Black and Tans*, p. 193.
19 *Irish Independent*, 25 September 1920.
20 ADA, Logue papers, ARCH9/5/1, Logue to Greenwood (draft), undated.
21 *Irish Independent*, 9 October 1920.

References to the army also began to be more critical. As has been seen, there had been disapproving references to the British 'militarisation' policy in clerical commentary ever since 1918, but these had frequently distinguished between the government and the soldiers. When soldiers became implicated in acts of violence, including intimidation of priests, this contributed to a change of attitude. Even Catholic unionists were critical. Father M. J. Doyle of Kingstown, County Dublin, a former army chaplain, wrote to the *Freeman's Journal* in September 1920 that he had refused the honorary chaplaincy bestowed on him by the War Office for services rendered during the First World War. He would not associate himself with the British uniform, 'owing to the disgrace and degradation into which that uniform has been brought by some of those who wear it in Ireland'. This state of affairs would continue until the British government would 'come to its senses and, not only [save] Ireland for the empire, but also [restore] discipline and dignity to the army'.[22]

Civil disobedience

Chapter 4 has already shown that republican priests made many symbolic gestures to show their support for the republican movement, such as declining to take off their hats in court or refusing to pay fines. When directed specifically at the crown forces, these acts of what is best described as civil disobedience were significant not only as a measure of support for republicanism, but also as a gauge for attitudes towards the British campaign. Their object was to be seen to be defying the authority of the crown forces, usually on some minor matter of public order. After the summer of 1920 even minor acts of civil disobedience became hazardous ventures with potentially serious repercussions, and they consequently became much less frequent. Father P. Sharkey, a curate in Liscannor, County Clare, was approached by a British officer in September 1920 as he was overseeing a sports match. The officer told him to take down the republican flag which fluttered proudly above the pitch. Sharkey refused, prompting the officer to withdraw and return with a larger detachment of men. The curate then told the officer that 'if he fired upon the flag he would be held accountable

22 *Freeman's Journal*, 20 September 1920.

for his life if he shot him'. The tenor of this somewhat confused message was unmistakeably discouraging. After a while the crown forces withdrew without securing the removal of the flag, but it was a sign of the times that the episode was followed by the searching, some days later, of Sharkey's residence by the military.[23] In 1919, priests had still survived their defiance of police instructions without suffering personal consequences.

In the propaganda war that was the War of Independence, clerical support for the hunger-strike of Terence MacSwiney in September and October 1920 was also an important symbolic way of highlighting the odiousness of British rule. MacSwiney's sister Mary wrote to Cardinal Logue and Archbishop Walsh asking for a 'pronouncement from the Catholic hierarchy, condemning the action of the government on the grounds of Christianity and civilization'.[24] Bishop Cohalan's subsequent statement calling for MacSwiney's release was perhaps a result.[25] In any case, the attendance of many bishops at MacSwiney's funeral rites in London and afterwards in Cork was a clear Catholic protest against the foreign oppressor.[26]

The October pastoral and beyond

The bishops' most important pronouncement during the war was a joint statement issued after a plenary meeting in Maynooth in October 1920. The letter was a full-blown attack on British rule in Ireland, saying that 'terrorism, partiality, and failure to apply the principles which its members have proclaimed' were its main characteristics. The bishops stated that they had 'warned the government that the oppressive measures, which they were substituting for their professions of freedom, would lead to the most deplorable consequences'. The warning had been in vain, however, and 'never in living memory has the country been in such disorder as it is now'. With the old RIC restored somewhat to its former reputation by the arrival of the Black and Tans and Auxiliaries, the bishops felt able to state that for the 'reign of frightfulness' established by

23 *Irish Independent*, 6 September 1920.
24 DDA, Walsh papers, 380/4, MacSwiney to Walsh, undated.
25 Morrissey, *Walsh*, p. 337.
26 Mews, 'Hunger-strike', pp. 389–90, and *Irish Independent*, 1 November 1920.

the crown forces 'not the men, but their masters [were] chiefly to blame'. They argued that British violence in Ireland was not simply a matter of the lashing-out of individual men under extreme provocation. Rather, 'outrage has been connived at and encouraged, if not organised, not by obscure and irresponsible individuals, but by the government of a mighty empire, professing the highest ideals of truth and justice'. Another important grievance was the fact that the government had turned a blind eye to the persecution of Catholics in Ulster, and had in fact furnished 'a corner of Ulster with a separate government, or its worse instrument, a special police force, to enable it all the more readily to trample underfoot the victims of its intolerance'. The bishops contended that the government's 'grossly partial course' with regard to Ulster was 'more potent than even the rule of brute force' in reducing the country to anarchy.[27]

Just as the Tipperary clergy's condemnations of the Soloheadbeg ambush had set a pattern for responses to violence up to October 1920, the pastoral provided a framework for the same afterwards. As has been seen, a month later the killing of Father Griffin suggested that there was a 'new departure in the campaign, the beginning of an attack on the church and religion'.[28] In the eyes of the clergy, this amply vindicated the pastoral's emphasis on denouncing British violence. A very public illustration of this view was the letter which Bishop O'Dea of Galway wrote a few days after the Griffin killing to the chief secretary, Sir Hamar Greenwood. O'Dea supported the pastoral's special criticism of British rule because 'government outrages have been incomparably greater in volume than those on the other side', and because the 'armed forces of the government' had themselves began 'to terrorise and murder inoffensive and unarmed civilians', thus poisoning the 'very well-springs of order'. Since then, the Galway diocese had 'suffered exceptional ill-usage from government forces', culminating in the shooting of Father Griffin, while he himself and a number of priests had received death threats. O'Dea asserted that he and his priests had always 'publicly denounced attacks on the police, and in our clerical conferences ... I have urged [my priests] to use all their influence against these attacks.'[29]

27 *ICD 1921*, pp. 556–61.
28 *Irish Catholic*, 4 December 1920.
29 *Ibid.*

A tangible result of the new direction was the bishops' decision to start a propaganda campaign of their own to highlight British atrocities. On 1 December 1920, some ten days after the Griffin killing, Bishop O'Doherty wrote to Archbishop Walsh to remind him of a recommendation made at the hierarchy's last meeting that 'each bishop should get compiled a list of the outrages committed in his diocese by the agents of the British crown'. According to his letter, a 'publication committee' had been established, consisting of O'Doherty as secretary and a number of other bishops, apparently one from each ecclesiastical province. According to O'Doherty 'the English are spreading broadcast everything that can tell against Ireland while concealing or denying their own evil deeds', and the committee's task was to set the record straight.[30]

O'Dea and O'Doherty wrote to each of their colleagues to invite them to compile lists of outrages. Archbishop Harty replied to O'Dea on 3 December that 'unfortunately my diocese can supply very many cases', and Bishop Fogarty wrote later that month that 'the sort of list you mention is already being made out in this diocese'.[31] Bishop Morrisroe of Achonry provided O'Doherty with two relevant statements in January. They were signed by the bishop himself and gave details of reprisals in Ballaghaderreen, County Roscommon, and Tobercurry, County Sligo, in September 1920. Morrisroe added a note to the statement concerning the Ballaghaderreen reprisals, saying that it

> gives an accurate account, in my opinion, of what has occurred there. It does not exaggerate, nor does it describe the terror and panic infused into the inhabitants by the burnings and the fearful noise that accompanied them.[32]

A file kept in the Tuam diocesan archives containing numerous statements from parishioners who witnessed atrocities committed

---

30 DDA, Walsh papers, 380/1, O'Doherty to Walsh, 1 December 1920, and *Irish Independent*, 22 November 1920.
31 GDA, O'Dea papers, 39/193, Harty to O'Dea, 3 December 1920, and 39/194, Fogarty to O'Dea, 23 December 1920.
32 GDA, Thomas O'Doherty papers, Morrisroe to O'Doherty, 7 January 1921.

by Black and Tans was probably connected to this project.[33] Priests had invited parishioners to make these statements, which were taken down and countersigned by the clergy. Most of them were from Tuam and were signed by the administrator of the cathedral, Father Owen Hannan. Hannan probably sent them to Archbishop Gilmartin to provide him with material for O'Doherty's list. This list was never actually published, but the fact that the bishops began to organise it in December 1920 testifies to their mindset at the time.

Nor did they change their views subsequently. Bishop MacRory of Down and Connor told a congregation in Belfast in March 1921 that the state of the country was 'a disgrace not only to Christianity, but to civilisation'. Referring to the recent Belfast 'pogroms', he summed up the situation:

> houses were burned, large parts of cities, towns, and villages were wrecked and reduced to ruins, creameries were destroyed, innocent lives were taken daily, and thousands of their young men were hunted like wild beasts.[34]

According to MacRory, the British government was the main culprit. He blamed the 'age-long denial of [the Irish people's] unquestionable rights' for this state of affairs and said that 'this tyranny and perfidy and denial of their rights' was teaching their young men to spurn constitutional action in favour of violence.[35]

Priests of all political persuasions followed the hierarchy's lead. Often they did this in much the same terms as those in which republican violence had been denounced. Thus the parish priest of Drogheda, Monsignor Patrick Segrave, said at the funeral of two victims of British violence in February 1921 that the crime was 'most cold-blooded murder, without any warning or provocation'. He claimed that there had been no town or district in the country so peaceful as Drogheda, and that his parishioners had borne all manner of provocations by the crown forces with restraint. 'It was', he said, 'scarcely conceivable that such a diabolical intent as to

---

33 TDA, Gilmartin papers, B4/8-ii/6 and B4/8-ii/4, files of lay witness statements. See Kieran Waldron, *The Archbishops of Tuam 1700–2000* (Tuam: Nordlaw Books, 2008), p. 106.
34 *Irish Catholic*, 2 April 1921.
35 *Ibid.*

incite the population could be harboured', but if it was, he 'prayed to God that it be frustrated'.[36]

The discourse of persecution of the clergy initiated in the aftermath of the Griffin killing caused clerics and journalists to seize eagerly upon any incident that could provide further corroboration. In the disturbed state of the country such occurrences were rarely difficult to find. The setting up of security cordons or checkpoints by the crown forces provided ample opportunity for accusations of anti-clerical victimisation. Like all others, priests had to submit to being searched when passing through such cordons. Thus unnamed clergymen 'of both denominations' in Mitchelstown, County Cork, in March 1921 were stopped and searched as they attempted to leave the market square, which had been surrounded by military. All males were questioned and had to remove their hats as they approached their interrogator – a requirement which caused the headline 'Clergymen humiliated' in the *Irish Independent*.[37]

The potential for publicity was exponentially greater when the clergyman involved was a bishop. This had already been clear in the summer of 1920 when two bishops were held up by soldiers in County Cork. William Barry, an Irish-born Australian archbishop, barely escaped being frisked when his car was stopped near Mogeely one day. He was eventually allowed to proceed 'without a word of apology', as the *Irish Independent* crossly observed.[38] And a few days later, Bishop Cohalan was submitted to the same treatment near Rushbrooke.[39] After the Griffin killing, such incidents became much more sensitive. From December 1920 onwards, the 'B Specials' made quite a habit of stopping Cardinal Logue and searching his car, each time providing him with the opportunity of 'being difficult' and causing embarrassment to the government.[40] Ó Fiaich included one such incident among his list of 'attacks on the clergy by the British'.[41] This was also the way in which such occurrences

---

36 *Ibid.*, 19 February 1921.
37 *Irish Independent*, 17 March 1921.
38 *Ibid.*, 2 August 1920.
39 *Ibid.*, 11 August 1920.
40 John Privilege, *Michael Logue and the Catholic Church in Ireland, 1879–1925* (Manchester and New York: Manchester University Press, 2009), pp. 180–3.
41 Ó Fiaich, 'Clergy', p. 496.

were portrayed in press reports at the time. John Privilege's account of the Logue searches has shown that the incidents were mostly a matter of pure chance, with rank-and-file soldiers or policemen unaware of whom they were dealing with. He has also demonstrated that government authorities were at pains to ensure that troops on the ground would not search any ministers of religion at all in order to avoid the negative publicity which the procedure engendered.[42]

Ministering to the crown forces

Catholic policemen and soldiers continued to require the ministrations of the clergy even after the Griffin killing. This provided an important motive for priests to distinguish between Irish Catholic constables and foreign Black and Tans and Auxiliaries, with the former generally portrayed as victims and the latter held responsible for the persecution of the clergy. There were exceptions to this rule. The veteran RIC officer John Regan recounted in his memoir that he once accompanied a party of crown forces to the house of the parish priest of Drimoleague, County Cork, to arrest the priest's nephew. He went to mass the following Sunday. During the sermon, the curate launched into a colourful diatribe against Regan personally, calling him a 'myrmidon of the British government' and asking for how much longer it was to be tolerated that the houses of priests were violated by people such as Regan. As there were two IRA officers sitting in the church just opposite Regan, the sermon made him fear for his safety and he left, commenting later that the curate's remarks had amounted to 'an incitement to murder'.[43] But such examples of public clerical hostility towards Catholic constables were very rare. Head Constable John McKenna declared that between 1920 and 1922 he 'went to mass daily, unarmed and in uniform, and no person ever molested' him, which implies at least that none of the celebrants he encountered were guilty of incitement to murder.[44] Some RIC members made

---

42 Privilege, *Logue*, pp. 180–3.
43 Joost Augusteijn (ed.), *The Memoirs of John M. Regan. A Catholic Officer in the RIC and RUC, 1909–1948* (Dublin and Portland, OR: Irish Academic Press, 2007), p. 126.
44 John McKenna, *A Beleaguered Station. The Memoir of Head Constable John McKenna, 1891–1921* (n.p.: Ulster Historical Foundation, 2009), p. 32.

specific efforts to foster good relations with the local clergy. Thus Father John Considine, curate in Gort, County Galway, received a delegation of the police to thank him for his emotional denunciation from the pulpit of an ambush that killed a constable in October 1920.[45]

Most priests were guided by pragmatism in their dealings with Catholics in the army or the RIC. Thus Dean Gearty of Strokestown, whose condemnation of authorised reprisals has been quoted above, a few months later agreed to preside at the funeral of an army officer killed in ambush, referring to the deceased 'in touching terms'.[46] Sometimes the crown forces' appeals for spiritual assistance made considerable demands on the diplomatic skills of the priest in question. In May 1921 an ambush near Tourmakeady, County Mayo, resulted in the deaths of two constables and one IRA man. Remarkably, the remains of all three were removed to the same church in Ballinrobe. The parish priest, Edward Canon D'Alton, had the IRA victim's coffin placed in front of the high altar and the RIC coffins before the side altars on either side of the nave. This irked the RIC, and the officer in charge protested, but the canon did not budge. To complete this impressive balancing act, D'Alton accompanied Archbishop Gilmartin to Ballinrobe RIC barracks to offer his condolences, 'describing the victims as men of excellent character'.[47]

However, when the required ministrations implied endorsement of the British government it proved more difficult to obtain clerical cooperation. In April 1921 a new lord lieutenant was appointed in the person of Viscount Fitzalan of Derwent, the first Catholic to accede to that position since the seventeenth century. Fitzalan had received permission from the Holy See to establish a chapel in the viceregal lodge. Fitzalan wrote to Bishop Edward Byrne, auxiliary bishop of Dublin and vicar capitular of the diocese since Archbishop Walsh's death, that he had contacted the Jesuit

45 *Irish Catholic*, 6 November 1920.
46 *Ibid.*, 9 April 1921.
47 Seán Ó hÓgáin, 'The Tourmakeady ambush, May 1921 – part II', *Cathair na Mart. Journal of the Westport Historical Society*, 23 (2003), pp. 44–59, at p. 54, and Donal Buckley, *The Battle of Tourmakeady. Fact or Fiction. A Study of the IRA Ambush and its Aftermath* (Dublin: Nonsuch Publishing, 2008), p. 83.

provincial to ask for a chaplain.[48] Father Thomas Nolan had discussed this request at a provincial consultation, which concluded that it would be difficult for the province to let an Irish Jesuit take the position.[49] Instead he tellingly suggested that Fitzalan should approach the English provincial. Fitzalan wrote to Byrne that he was disappointed that 'the provincial in Dublin does not find it possible to spare me one of his Fathers'.[50] The *Irish Catholic* commented that 'it would be hard to find in Ireland at present any priest, either secular or religious, who has the least ambition to fill [the] office'.[51] But the lord lieutenant had papal permission and had to have a chaplain. Byrne commiserated with him on the Jesuits' refusal and appointed the parish priest of Aughrim Street parish, who lived adjacent to the Phoenix Park.[52]

Supporting the crown forces

A small number of priests gave active support to the crown forces. The most common way of doing this was by informing on IRA activities that had come to their knowledge. Only a handful of such cases have come to light in research for this book.[53] These priests had diverging motives for their deeds. The distinction made between malicious Black and Tans and benign Catholic constables allowed them to reconcile strong hostility towards the British enemy in general with an accommodating approach towards individual members of the RIC. Chapter 3 has recounted how Father Brennan, curate in Castleisland, County Kerry, tried to stop an IRA operation from going ahead by threatening to tell the local barracks that an ambush had been planned.[54] Brennan was a Sinn

---

48 DDA, Edward Byrne papers, box 'Government 1922–39, 2', folder 'Lord Lieutenant, 1921–22', Fitzalan to Byrne, 15 April 1921.
49 IJA, Provincial consultations, ADMIN/57/3, 19 May 1921.
50 DDA, Byrne papers, box 'Government 1922–39, 2', folder 'Lord Lieutenant, 1921–22', Fitzalan to Byrne, 29 April 1921.
51 *Irish Catholic*, 18 June 1921.
52 DDA, Byrne papers, box 'Government 1922–39, 2', folder 'Lord Lieutenant, 1921–22', Byrne to Fitzalan (copy), 2 May 1921.
53 But see Hart, *Enemies*, p. 304. The eight spies Hart classified as 'priest/minister' could have included Protestant clergymen.
54 MA, BMH, WS 882, Thomas McEllistrim, pp. 19–20.

Féin supporter, and his motive in thwarting the ambush was not to strengthen British rule, but to avoid violence in his parish. There were more priests who did the same, and some carried out the threat that Brennan uttered.

There is much evidence that republicans regarded this motive as more or less acceptable in a priest. The Tipperary IRA veteran Thomas Ryan recalled that his company became concerned during the war that there was frequent leakage of information about operations to the enemy. An investigation concluded that the commandant 'was keeping company with the daughter of a local publican who was very friendly with the local parish priest'. This priest, in turn, had close links with the local RIC sergeant, and information from the commandant had been passed on through these channels to the sergeant. Ryan emphasised that the priest in question was not motivated by anti-republican sentiments: he had 'no political leanings of any kind and was anxious to avoid any bloodshed in his parish'.[55] In August 1919 two brothers in the parish of Cooraclare, County Clare, had been attacked, because they had given information to the 'local parish priest and the police', suggesting that the local IRA also suspected this priest, Father Michael Hehir, of conspiring with the RIC.[56] Significantly, the brothers were disciplined rather than Hehir. And a Tipperary priest was observed knocking at the door of Ballingarry RIC barracks in spring 1921, minutes after he passed by an IRA ambush party waiting for a patrol to come out.[57] His actions also resulted from the desire to avoid bloodshed between the two opposing sections of his parishioners, and he was left unhindered by the IRA.

A crass case was recounted to Ernie O'Malley by the Mayo IRA veteran Brodie Malone. Malone recalled that a colleague had blamed a priest for informing the police of an ambush planned by their company near Louisburgh, County Mayo. One of the men in the company had gone to confession to this priest and mentioned the ambush, which was subsequently foiled by the RIC.[58] In another case in County Galway in 1921, a priest who had heard of

---

55 MA, BMH, WS783, Thomas Ryan, pp. 62–3.
56 TNA, CO904/109, IGMR, August 1919, p. 742.
57 MA, BMH, WS1335, James Leahy, pp. 21–2.
58 UCDA, O'Malley papers, P17b/109, Brodie Malone. See also Augusteijn, *Defiance*, p. 307.

an intended IRA ambush on an RIC lorry invented a ruse which caused the police to call off its journey, but without revealing that he knew an ambush had been planned. The priest was attending the district inspector's sick daughter and told the inspector that the patient was much worse than she really was. Hearing this, the district inspector decided to postpone the journey and the ambush failed.[59] In all of these cases, the priests in question were evidently motivated by the desire to prevent violence rather than by any political considerations.

However, other priests who passed on information were conservative clerics who 'thought in the old groove' politically and who clearly resented the IRA's new power. Father Michael Hayes, parish priest of Feakle, County Clare, threatened at mass on one occasion 'that any information which he could get would be readily passed on to the British authorities and that he would not desist until the last of the murderers was swung by the neck'. Hayes's motives were clear: he was later described by an IRA veteran as 'a violent imperialist who regularly entertained members of the enemy forces'.[60] Presumably the competent British authorities had priests such as Hayes in mind in December 1920 when martial law was proclaimed in most of Munster. The proclamation also decreed that 'the surrender of arms can be made either to an officer of the crown or the police, or to a military officer, or to the parish priest, provided the parish priest surrenders them afterwards to the proper officer in the area'.[61]

As the example of the Dominican Father Hyacinth Collins shows, a healthy awe of British military power was often an important motivation even for 'imperialist' priest-informers. Collins, a former army chaplain, caused the local IRA brigade in April 1921 to take action against him when he told the crown forces about a lay person in Tralee whom he had heard endorsing a recent IRA killing.[62] Collins was not so much a staunch loyalist

---

59 MA, BMH, WS1490, Roger Rabitte, p. 7.
60 MA, BMH, WS983, Thomas Tuohy, p. 20. Hayes experienced the repercussions for his anti-republican stance, see TNA, CO904/113, IGMR, 19 November 1920, and *Irish Independent*, 26 October 1920.
61 *Irish Independent*, 12 December 1920.
62 I am grateful to Rev. Hugh Fenning, OP, for providing me with details of Collins's chaplaincy. IRA intervention: MA, BMH, WS1413, Tadhg Kennedy, pp. 99–102.

as a man eager to keep on friendly terms with the crown forces in Tralee. His past as a British army chaplain did not prevent him from having been 'at one time a *grate* [sic] republican'. In fact, after Terence MacSwiney's death Collins had argued that the hunger-strike victim should be canonised. When Auxiliaries and Black and Tans entered Kerry, Collins had simply 'changed with the times'.[63]

Another priest accused of passing on information to the crown forces was Father John Maguire, curate in Tulla, County Clare. He was accused posthumously by a fellow priest of his own diocese of Killaloe. As has been seen, Father Patrick Gaynor of Mullagh was arrested in April 1921 and put on trial in Limerick for the possession of seditious documents.[64] In his memoir, Gaynor wrote that Maguire had been sent away from his former parish because of suspicions that he was a spy. He also blamed Maguire for his arrest, apparently on the grounds that Maguire was the only priest who was present at Gaynor's court-martial, the date of which had been kept secret by the authorities.[65] Gaynor concluded from this that Maguire had been informed about the date by the authorities and that the curate had had some part in occasioning his arrest.[66] This last assumption is certainly not warranted by the simple fact that Maguire was present at the court-martial. It is likely, however, that Maguire did make some representations to the RIC urging stricter measures against Gaynor. In his memoirs, the RIC officer John Regan probably referred to Maguire when he mentioned a 'somewhat odd' curate who came to see him before Gaynor's trial. Regan, who was based in Limerick at the time, described a visit by a curate who asked him to secure a severe sentence for the clerical 'blackguard' who was in custody in Limerick jail.[67] Regan named neither the curate nor the 'blackguard', but it is likely that he was referring to Maguire and Gaynor. Regan's comment about Maguire also shows that the curate was not a regular contact of his. Maguire was probably motivated by some personal animosity

---

63 AICR, Hagan papers, HAG1/1921/298, O'Murray to Hagan, 1 June 1921.
64 TNA, WO35/136, Register of cases tried, p. 125.
65 NLI, Gaynor papers, MS 19,826, 'Sinn Fein days', p. 529.
66 *Ibid.*, p. 506.
67 Augusteijn (ed.), *Regan*, p. 167.

against Gaynor – a feeling that was clearly mutual – rather than by the desire to crush rebellion against the crown. The context of a guerrilla war gave people of all backgrounds tempting opportunities to settle old scores under the pretext of ideological differences.

9

Preserving the peace: mediation, relief work and political activism

The previous chapters have looked at explicitly 'partisan' clerical responses to political violence: the ways in which priests either condemned or supported the IRA or the crown forces. Only a minority of priests are on record as having expressed such a partisan response. While giving due regard to the limitations of the sources used, it is not an improbable supposition that a majority of the clergy simply tried to avoid becoming involved at all.[1] This was an unremarkable course of action in areas of the country where violence was rare. But even in violent counties such as Cork, it must have been a common attitude. There were approximately 380 priests in County Cork, and yet the public condemnations of just thirty-three clerics have been recorded, including Bishop Cohalan's, while only six Cork priests are known to have given material support to the IRA.[2] Even if it is recognised that many comments never reached the press, it is still very likely that the majority of Cork priests simply tried to keep out of the conflict.

The most pressing concern for most priests most of the time was how to avoid bloodshed in their parishes, and, if bloodshed had already taken place, how to relieve the suffering of their parishioners. This relief work was humanitarian and ostensibly non-partisan, but its emphasis on shared victimhood at the hands of a foreign power was intended to reinforce the message of Irish Catholic unity. The current chapter will examine a number of humanitarian clerical responses to political violence and will assess their meaning. It will also look at the wider context. Priestly involvement did not happen in a vacuum. There were other political issues at

1 See for a similar conjecture Augusteijn, *Defiance*, p. 307.
2 See Appendix 3.

play, related only indirectly to the struggle for independence, but of crucial importance to the clergy.

Mediation

One Irish-born bishop in particular earned the qualification of peacemaker when he visited his native country in December 1920. The Australian Archbishop Patrick Clune came to act as an intermediary, and although his proposals for a truce failed, they proved to be a prelude to talks that did succeed a few months later.³ At parish level, many priests were also involved in mediation.⁴ There were numerous instances during 1919 and early 1920 of priests calming rowdy crowds at political meetings, thus avoiding potentially violent stand-offs with the British forces. During an *aeridheacht* in Inch, near Thurles, County Tipperary, in May 1919, police and military demanded that the speakers on the platform stop addressing the crowds and threatened that they would otherwise clear the platform. According to a newspaper report, the crowd then became 'wildly excited', and it was not until a local priest calmed them down that the situation was defused.⁵

It was, no doubt, much of an exaggeration to say, as one Kerry priest did in January 1920, that the clergy were 'the final, and, indeed, now the only mainstay of whatever law and order English misrule has not already destroyed in this country'.⁶ But priests did assume responsibility for some of the community's self-regulatory functions when normal policing duties were suspended. This was especially the case in Ulster, where the crown forces proved unable or unwilling to contain sectarian rioting. When street battles were being fought out in Derry on 17 April 1920, the administrator of Long Tower church, Father Walter O'Neill, was sent for, and he 'exerted his influence very successfully in pacifying a section of the

---

3 Michael Hopkinson, 'The peace mission of Archbishop Clune', in Laurence M. Geary and Andrew J. McCarthy (eds), *Ireland, Australia and New Zealand. History, Politics and Culture* (Dublin: Irish Academic Press, 2008), pp. 199–210.
4 Ó Fiaich, 'Clergy', p. 490.
5 *Irish Independent*, 27 May 1919.
6 *Irish Catholic*, 24 January 1920.

crowd'.[7] Two priests were said to have 'patrolled the thoroughfares' of the city one night, advising the people to stay indoors, with the result that the streets were empty when night fell.[8]

Outside Ulster, priests were active in trying to minimise damage to people and property during reprisals. They cleared people from the streets to avoid confrontation with police or military. When the IRA killed a constable near Clonakilty, County Cork, in July 1920, the parish priest, Monsignor John O'Leary, and his curate, Father John Collins, went through the town to advise the people to stay indoors. As a result of their endeavours, the streets of Clonakilty were deserted by the time large bodies of police and military arrived to carry out a reprisal.[9] When crown forces detonated two 'bombs' in Earl Street, Mullingar, County Westmeath, in November 1920, five local priests arrived on the scene and advised the panicked people to go indoors.[10] And Father Florence McCarthy, administrator of Skibbereen pro-cathedral, once told all local publicans to close their premises at nine o'clock in the evening and everybody in Skibbereen to 'remain indoors to avoid threatened conflicts between the rival forces'.[11]

Archbishop Gilmartin of Tuam harked back to the medieval concept of the *treuga Dei*, the 'truce of God', when he declared a truce his diocese on Sunday 25 July 1920. After two constables had been shot in Tuam, Gilmartin called for a truce, praying that

> God's justice tempered with mercy may, for the good of society and the salvation of his soul, strike the first man – whether he be a policeman, civilian, or soldier – who fires a criminal shot within the precincts of this diocese.[12]

Of course his qualification that the truce prohibited only 'criminal' shots gave casuists in either camp a wide escape clause. But

---

7 *Irish Independent*, 19 April 1920. See Mary Harris, *The Catholic Church and the Foundation of the Northern Irish State* (Cork: Cork University Press, 1993), p. 81.
8 *Irish Independent*, 21 April 1920. For another example, see MA, BMH, WS1107, Louis O'Dea.
9 *Irish Independent*, 30 July 1920.
10 *Ibid.*, 30 November 1920.
11 *Irish Catholic*, 19 February 1921.
12 *Ibid.*, 31 July 1920. See also Waldron, *Archbishops*, pp. 106–11.

the archbishop took the truce very seriously and repeated his call for it on a number of occasions during the following months. He claimed in September that 'so far as he knew there was no criminal shot fired since in the locality', although he had to acknowledge in December that, while the people had kept the truce, the crown forces had broken it on three occasions.[13] In January 1921, Gilmartin conceded that the truce had then also been broken by 'civilians' with an ambush near Headford.[14] This did not stop him, however, from renewing his call in a public letter to the parish priest of Clifden, and in an address from the pulpit in Tuam cathedral in March 1921.[15]

Priests also negotiated with the commanders of local crown forces to obtain guarantees, particularly that they would not take revenge after IRA acts of violence had taken place. Thus when troops broke their barracks in Limerick in April 1920 after Ballylanders RIC barracks had been captured by the IRA, the cathedral administrator, Father W. Dwane, went to see the military governor. He asked the governor to confine the military to their barracks, which the latter agreed to do.[16] Similarly, when lorries of soldiers arrived in Trim, County Meath, in late September 1920 after the police barracks had been attacked, two local priests sought out some of the officers and assured them that the town would be quiet and that everybody would be indoors by eight o'clock in the evening. Having received this assurance the military withdrew from the town.[17] After the IRA attacked the military barracks in Mallow, County Cork, in the same month, the local population was afraid that the town would be destroyed in reprisal. The parish priest, C. W. Canon Corbett, consulted with businesspeople of both religious denominations and conveyed their concerns to the local resident magistrate and the county inspector. These spoke to the military commanders in the locality, who promised that no damage would be done if the people would keep off the streets after dark. In order to ensure this, Corbett and his curates walked the streets of the town together with a number of prominent lay people and had

---

13 *Irish Catholic*, 25 September and 4 December 1920.
14 *Ibid.*, 29 January 1921.
15 *Ibid.*, 26 March and 2 April 1921.
16 *Irish Independent*, 29 April 1920.
17 *Irish Catholic*, 2 October 1920.

the streets cleared by nine o'clock.[18] And John Canon McDonnell, parish priest of Dingle, County Kerry, called on the local district inspector in November 1920 after two 'military policemen' had been shot and wounded in the town. McDonnell's parishioners feared reprisals too. According to the *Irish Independent* 'a general exodus from the town' was in progress, including people taking refuge in boats in the harbour. Canon McDonnell spoke to the district inspector and obtained an assurance that there would be no reprisals.[19] In the same month, Thomas Canon Barrett, parish priest of Passage West, County Cork, successfully intervened to stop a reprisal by speaking to the local district inspector in the wake of an attack on an RIC patrol.[20]

Sometimes clerics tried to get protection for their parishioners from one part of the crown forces against some other section of the police or military. When a military motor lorry was attacked by the IRA with lethal effect near Midleton, County Cork, in August 1920, soldiers went on the rampage in Queenstown, causing damage to property. On the day after the reprisal, Bishop Browne led a deputation of townspeople to ask Admiral Sir Reginald Tupper of Queenstown, the Royal Navy's commander-in-chief of the western approaches, to offer the town protection. As a result Queenstown was patrolled at night by marines.[21] And a few months before his episode with the IRA, Father Hyacinth Collins obtained a guarantee from the military in Tralee that they would protect life and property in the town after the IRA had killed two constables. When the troops were eventually withdrawn, 'armed uniformed men' – presumably Black and Tans – descended upon the town and a reprisal took place after all.[22]

Averting reprisals was a major preoccupation for many priests, and this explains the attempts made by some priests to influence the IRA. Some examples have already been mentioned in Chapter 3. In October 1920, Patrick Canon Glynn, parish priest of Kilkee, County Clare, managed to prevent a reprisal by persuading local

18 *Irish Independent*, 30 September 1920.
19 *Ibid.*, 6 November 1920.
20 MA, BMH, WS1506, Henry O'Mahony, p. 5. For another example see WS1712, Michael Cordial, p. 5.
21 *Irish Independent*, 30 August 1920.
22 *Ibid.*, 4 and 5 November 1920.

IRA men to release the body of Captain Alan Lendrum, a resident magistrate killed by the IRA a month before.[23] However, Father Lee of Kilfinane tried unsuccessfully to secure the release of an IRA prisoner to save his parish from reprisals in February 1921. The Volunteer guarding the prisoner found it very difficult to refuse a request from this 'saintly man', but eventually found an excuse not to comply.[24]

In view of this refusal, it is all the more remarkable that interventions to stop crown forces from attacking people suspected of supporting the IRA were sometimes successful. The Carlow Cumann na mBan member Brigid Ryan recounted that Black and Tans and soldiers were once approaching her house with the intention of setting it on fire, when Father John Killian, curate in Carlow, accosted them and managed to dissuade them from their plans.[25] And in May 1920 the parish priest and curate of Kilmurry, County Cork, Patrick Canon Tracey and Father M. Cotter, succeeded in preventing the shooting by constables of a county councillor suspected of having organised an attack on Kilmurry RIC barracks. According to the newspaper report, Councillor John Murphy had been told to 'prepare for his doom' by the two constables on account of his alleged involvement in the attack. A man accompanying him was told to get away, and one of the policemen was loading his gun when Tracey and Cotter arrived. The priests reasoned with the constables, who, after some tense minutes, were persuaded to forgo their intention.[26] Similarly, when the military commander in Enniscorthy, County Wexford, announced that the chairman of the town council would be arrested following the defacement of martial law pronouncements in January 1921, the administrator of the cathedral, Father James Rossiter, successfully intervened.[27] These examples show that despite clerical rhetoric of an attack on the church, crown forces – including the army – continued to be amenable to pressure from the clergy even in the later stages of the conflict.

---

23 MA, BMH, WS809, David Conroy, p. 3. For another example see WS970, John Ahern, p. 2.
24 MA, BMH, WS883, John MacCarthy, p. 86, and WS1435, Daniel O'Shaughnessy, p. 68.
25 MA, BMH, WS1573, Brigid Ryan, p. 4.
26 *Irish Independent*, 14 May 1920.
27 *Ibid.*, 18 January 1921.

Finally, priests also took other precautions to ensure that the peace was preserved. The *Irish Independent* reported in August 1919 that Father John Glynn, parish priest of Mullagh, had announced the formation of a 'vigilance committee' in his parish for the preservation of the peace, since the police had withdrawn from the area.[28] This committee was possibly the same body as the republican police of which Glynn's curate Patrick Gaynor took charge some months later.[29] Father Peter Hill, parish priest of Rosscarbery, County Cork, also tried to stop threats to the safety of his parishioners in April 1921. He was reported to have been among a group of local inhabitants who 'attacked and drove off' a party of raiders who were proceeding to Rosscarbery after having ravaged the residence of the prominent Catholic lawyer A. M. Sullivan. The village had acquired a reputation for loyalism because its inhabitants had given support to the RIC when the local barracks was under attack from the IRA.[30]

Relief work

In April 1921 Pope Benedict XV finally addressed the Irish question in a public letter that had been expected but feared by republicans for a long time. In the event, the pope avoided saying anything that could give offence to either of the opposing parties and devoted a large portion of his letter to the relief of suffering. Benedict noted with pleasure that Cardinal Logue had been 'at pains to establish and zealous to foster an association known as the White Cross', which had as its object 'to collect alms for the relief of those reduced to straits by the devastation of property or other acts of violence'.[31] The pope also pledged 200,000 Italian lire, or approximately £2,500, towards the provision of relief to the victims.[32] For many priests the pope's emphasis on a humanitarian response was familiar. They worked to provide support for those families whose source of income had been destroyed or who had to make ends meet after the breadwinner had died or disappeared.

28 *Ibid.*, 20 August 1919.
29 NLI, Gaynor papers, MS 19,826, 'Sinn Fein days', p. 473.
30 *Irish Independent*, 16 April 1921.
31 Benedict XV, 'Epistola', 27 April 1921, p. 258.
32 See exchange rate in *Irish Times*, 27 April 1921.

Yet this solicitude for the victims conveyed the same message contained in the discourse of persecution of the clergy. Priests and people were united in their suffering at the hands of non-Catholic foreigners.

Although Logue was the president of the Irish White Cross, he was not its instigator. The organisation was in fact a non-denominational body set up by the lord mayor of Dublin and supported by senior Christian and non-Christian clerics.[33] The White Cross had been established to relieve the distress of people affected by British violence. It drew its funds from donations, which were sent to the society's headquarters in Dublin. Parish committees were formed which reported to headquarters about the need for relief in their localities, and headquarters then distributed the funds accordingly.[34]

Logue was not the only bishop to become involved in this kind of humanitarian work. Bishop Charles McHugh of Derry set up a 'Catholic relief fund' in the spring of 1920 for victims of sectarian attacks in his city.[35] And when Balbriggan, County Dublin, was damaged by crown forces after an ambush in September 1920, Archbishop Walsh sent a telegram to the parish priest telling him to draw on him for a considerable amount of money.[36] The priest, Eugene Canon Byrne, wrote back thanking Walsh, but saying that there was no immediate want.[37] Byrne wrote to the archbishop again in early October thanking him for his 'princely munificence' but reiterated that there was 'no immediate want for your substantial cheque'. Byrne was clearly playing a successful role in organising relief for his parish, because he mentioned that the 'money is

33 For the Irish White Cross, see Ann Matthews, *Renegades. Irish Republican Women 1900–1922* (Dublin and Cork: Mercier Press, 2010), pp. 255–9. For Logue's role see Privilege, *Logue*, p. 155, and *Irish Catholic*, 29 January 1921.
34 Áine B. É. Ceannt, *The Story of the Irish White Cross, 1920–1947* (Dublin: Three Candles, n.d.), p. 10.
35 Philip Donnelly, 'Bishop Charles McHugh of Derry diocese (1856–1926)', *Seanchas Ard Mhacha. Journal of the Armagh Diocesan Historical Society*, 20:2 (2005), pp. 212–44, at p. 239.
36 DDA, Walsh papers, 380/3, Walsh to Byrne (telegram), undated but 22 September 1920.
37 DDA, Walsh papers, 380/3, Byrne to Walsh (telegram), 22 September 1920.

coming in, [and] the relief fund promises to be a great success'.[38] Walsh could not be dissuaded from a show of solidarity with the victims, however, and Byrne wrote to him a third time in December thanking him for an additional contribution.[39]

Bishop Cohalan of Cork wrote to an acquaintance after the burning of his city in December 1920 that he had called a number of meetings with the parish priests and administrators of the city parishes in order to 'get accurate statistics of the distress and to procure relief for urgent cases'. Although the priests had assured him that there was no pressing distress yet, they believed this would soon follow as the impact of the loss of income made itself felt. Cohalan ordered a collection in all the churches of his diocese for this purpose and expected to collect some £1,500.[40] Similarly, Archbishop Gilmartin wrote at the same time that, although there was no acute humanitarian crisis in his diocese, he was asking the parish priests of Connemara to warn him if distress were to arise.[41]

Bishops also showed their support for victims in other ways. Thus after the 'sack of Fermoy' in September 1919, Bishop Browne went to inspect houses that had been damaged.[42] Similarly, Walsh paid a visit to Balbriggan some days after the reprisal, giving the townspeople 'the greatest pleasure' according to Canon Byrne.[43] In his capacity of chancellor of the National University of Ireland, Walsh also visited University College, Dublin, after it had been subjected to a military raid in November 1920.[44] Moreover, Logue, Walsh and Cohalan made unsuccessful but well-publicised attempts to have the sentences commuted of political prisoners condemned to death. This happened in February 1921, when a number of prisoners were executed in Cork, and again in March 1921 when executions were carried out in Mountjoy prison in Dublin.[45]

---

38 DDA, Walsh papers, 380/3, Byrne to Walsh, 9 October 1920.
39 DDA, Walsh papers, 380/3, Byrne to Walsh, 21 December 1920.
40 NLI, Shane Leslie papers, MS 22,838, Cohalan to Leslie, 29 December 1920.
41 NLI, Leslie papers, MS 22,841, Gilmartin to Leslie, 29 December 1920.
42 *Irish Catholic*, 27 September 1919.
43 DDA, Walsh papers, 380/3, Byrne to Walsh, 9 October 1920.
44 *Irish Independent*, 4 November 1920.
45 *Irish Catholic*, 5 and 19 March 1921.

Priests also gave direct aid to victims of violence. Thus Father M. McCabe, parish priest of Drumshanbo, County Leitrim, gave shelter in his home to a local businessman and his son who had fled their own residence when it was torched by 'disguised, uniformed men, armed with rifles and bombs' in September 1920.[46] And Canon Corbett, parish priest of Mallow, recounted a week or two later that there had been 'a rush of frantic women and children to his door at midnight asking him, for God's sake, to provide them with some place of refuge' when the town was attacked by the army in reprisal for the killing of a soldier. Some women had fled to the local cemetery, where they sat on the family graves clutching their children. Corbett managed to give them shelter in local convent schools.[47] There are also numerous examples of priests risking personal safety to attend to victims of violence perpetrated by both sides. Thus the Redemptorist Father Michael McLaughlin of Clonard monastery in Belfast crossed the line of fire between rioting groups of civilians in July 1921 to reach a number of Catholic victims of violence so that he could administer the last rites.[48] Clerical involvement in relief work gave material and spiritual support to victims of violence, and simultaneously served a publicity goal by presenting an image of the clergy as sustainers of the Irish people in their suffering.

The campaign against the Education Bill

One aspect of the British 'reign of frightfulness' that caused the bishops very great concern in 1919 and the first half of 1920 was the government's attempt to reform the Irish education system.[49] The bishops regarded it at this time as important evidence for the oppression of the Irish people, and it contributed in no small measure to the hierarchy's alienation from the Castle administration. As several historians have remarked, the bishops' decision to concern themselves so publicly with this issue also marked out education as a primary ecclesiastical interest that the rival contender

---

46 *Irish Independent*, 23 September 1920.
47 *Irish Catholic*, 9 October 1920.
48 CMA, 'Domestic Chronicle', pp. 318–19.
49 'Reign of frightfulness': *ICD 1921*, p. 556.

for Irish sovereignty would likewise do well to respect.[50] The standing committee of the bishops asserted in a public statement in December 1919 that 'after religion and its immediate requirements no interest of the people so deeply concerns their pastors as does the interest of education'.[51] On the same day, the parish priest of St Joseph's church, Berkeley Road, Dublin, wrote to Archbishop Walsh complaining that the Irish people were being 'menaced with the [chief secretary's] plans ... to supply us with our spiritual pabulum'. He went on to quote Walsh's own words that these plans would not 'gradually ... undermine the whole fabric of the faith', but would 'by one bill ... destroy – forsooth the "soul of Ireland"'.[52] The menacing plans in question consisted of the Education (Ireland) Bill, which the chief secretary, Ian Macpherson, had introduced in the House of Commons in November 1919.[53] This bill, which was the government's response to the reports of two committees of inquiry, was intended to remedy deficiencies in the Irish education system. Foremost among the latter was the inadequate remuneration of teachers in primary and secondary schools.[54]

The bishops took exception to some other aspects of the reorganisation of the education system that were also included in the plans. The bill proposed that an Irish department of education be established to replace the existing boards responsible for national, intermediate and technical schooling.[55] County education committees

50 See R. V. Comerford, 'The British state and the education of Irish Catholics, 1850–1921', in Janusz Tomiak *et al.* (eds), *Schooling, Educational Policy and Ethnic Identity* (New York: New York University Press, 1991), pp. 13–33 and Séamas Ó Buachalla, *Education Policy in Twentieth Century Ireland* (Dublin: Wolfhound Press, 1988), pp. 209–11.
51 *ICD 1920*, p. 520.
52 DDA, Walsh papers, 386/6, Downing to Walsh, 8 December 1919.
53 Hansard, series 5 (Commons), cxxi, co. 1451 (24 November 1919). See also R. B. McDowell, 'Administration and the public services, 1870–1921', in W. E. Vaughan (ed.), *A New History of Ireland*, vi: *Ireland under the Union, II* (Oxford: Oxford University Press, 1996), pp. 571–605, at pp. 600–1.
54 E. Brian Titley, *Church, State, and the Control of Schooling in Ireland 1900–1944* (Kingston, Montreal and Dublin: McGill-Queen's University Press and Gill and Macmillan, 1983), pp. 55–61.
55 R. W. Dudley Edwards, 'Government of Ireland and education, 1919–1920', *Archivium Hibernicum*, 37 (1982), pp. 21–8, at pp. 23–4.

were to be set up, consisting of county councillors and persons nominated by the new department. Moreover, local authorities were to be made responsible for the cost of maintaining school buildings. The bishops objected to this strengthening of lay power, because, as they candidly admitted, 'it would deprive the bishops and clergy of such control of the schools as is necessary for that religious training of the young which [is] a chief part of the care of souls'.[56] The hierarchy was entirely justified in suspecting that the curbing of its control was one of the bill's main objectives. Robert Dudley Edwards has suggested that the bill was part of an attempt by the government to secure Irish unionist acceptance of home rule.[57]

The standing committee of the bishops issued a statement in December 1919 condemning the proposed legislation and connecting the matter with the national question by arguing that 'education ... should be a native plant of native culture ... It should be a growth from within, not an importation from without. Its bloom and fragrance and fruit should be racy of the soil.'[58] This statement was followed by a second one issued by all the bishops at a meeting in January 1920, which announced that they would 'resist by every means in our power' any attempts to abolish the existing boards of education.[59] They also threatened that they would issue instructions to Catholic parents concerning the education of their children in case a department of education should be established. These statements formed the prelude to a campaign to move the government to relinquish its plans. The highpoint was a solemn novena in March 1920. The bill received some support from teachers, who naturally took a more favourable view of the measures, but the government quietly shelved it later that year.[60]

The campaign was instigated by the bishops, but it had to be carried out by priests. Bishop O'Sullivan of Kerry wrote to the vicars forane of his diocese in February 1920 to set the wheels in motion. He said the bishops had suggested 'that the priests of each deanery should meet together with a view to securing combined

---

56 *ICD 1920*, p. 523.
57 Dudley Edwards, 'Education', p. 22.
58 *ICD 1920*, p. 520.
59 *Ibid.*
60 Miller, *Church, State*, p. 440, and Titley, *Schooling*, p. 128. For the dropping of the bill, see Dudley Edwards, 'Education', pp. 27–8.

opposition' to the bill. O'Sullivan set a date and asked his vicars to call a conference of the priests of their deanery for that day. At this conference, the vicars were to discuss the holding of public meetings 'to give the people an opportunity of expressing their views on this important question'. Lay speakers should hold pride of place at these meetings. Priests were quite at liberty to speak about the issue from the altar, 'as this is primarily a religious question'. When doing so, and lest any lay persons should still waver, priests were expected 'to explain to their flocks how objectionable and insidious this bill is, and how essential it is from every point of view that we should oppose it by all the means in our power'.[61]

Apart from denouncing the bill from the pulpit and organising public meetings, priests at the deanery conferences were also expected to take steps to secure the opposition of local government. This was especially important, as the bill envisaged an active role for county, urban and rural councils in the management of local schools. O'Sullivan wanted priests to do 'quiet work' among the councillors resident in their parishes to ensure that councils would pass resolutions opposing the bill and 'declaring that if it is forced on this country [they] will refuse to strike a rate in connection with it'.[62] In the event, many councils were already withdrawing their allegiance from the Castle government and declaring support for the Dáil, thus making fanciful any thoughts Macpherson may have had of implementing the measure.[63] O'Sullivan returned to the topic in a circular letter to the clergy of his diocese on 18 March 1920. He asked priests 'for the signatures of as many parents as possible' for a mass protest which had been planned for Sunday 21 March. The clergy were expected to organise petitions for lay people in their parishes to give them the opportunity to record their abhorrence. He added that

> while anything like compulsion would be undesirable, no effort should be spared to bring home to your people the disastrous results to faith, nationality and parental rights, that may ensue if the bill is forced on our country.[64]

---

61 KyDA, O'Sullivan papers, 'Ad clerum', O'Sullivan to vicars forane, 9 February 1920.
62 *Ibid.*
63 Miller, *Church, State*, p. 440.
64 KyDA, O'Sullivan papers, 'Ad clerum', O'Sullivan to clergy, 18 March 1920.

David Miller has emphasised the publicity value of this petition, which did not apparently materialise.[65] The anti-Education Bill campaign was a clear signal to all parties concerned – teachers and parents, as well as Dublin Castle and the Dáil – that educating the youth of the Irish nation was a task that belonged by rights to the Catholic clergy. The identification of 'faith, nationality and parental rights' in O'Sullivan's letter shows that the campaign attempted to consolidate the dominant position of the clergy in society at a time that a transfer of sovereignty seemed imminent.

---

65 Miller, *Church, State*, p. 440.

Epilogue

The Civil War and beyond

When the Irish Free State was established in 1922 by virtue of the Anglo-Irish treaty, the bishops quickly rallied to the new government. In their support for the new institutions of state, they were willing to overlook examples of coercion on the part of the Free State government that they would have decried as state terror during the War of Independence. As Patrick Murray has established, there was a sizeable anti-treaty minority among the clergy during the Civil War.[1] But the bishops and the majority of the priest adopted a strong position in favour of the southern government's legitimacy. This stood in marked contrast to the hierarchy's studied ambiguity on either the Castle's or the Dáil's constitutional status during the War of Independence. What had been an exception between 1919 and 1921 – the excommunication of republican fighters – became the rule during the Civil War. In Northern Ireland, meanwhile, bishops and priests regarded the new unionist state and its constables with the same hostility they had shown Dublin Castle and the British sections of the crown forces during the War of Independence.

The bishops' strong support for the pro-treaty side at the time of the Civil War was an important factor in shaping subsequent perceptions of the clergy's role during the War of Independence. If the new state's legitimacy was beyond question, as the bishops and the majority of the clergy maintained, it was necessary to explain that the guerrilla campaign that had led to its establishment was very different from the anti-treaty campaign. The result was a certain forgetfulness of clerical opposition to the IRA between 1919 and

1 Murray, *Oracles*, p. 139.

1921. The new interpretation contrasted the 'nobility and glory of the fighting in the War of Independence with the ignobility of the Civil War', as Catherine Candy has observed with regard to an early fictionalised account of the clergy's role.[2] Joseph Canon Guinan's 1928 novel *The Patriots*, about a parish priest and his curate in the fictional village of Druminara in the midlands, portrayed the anti-treaty republicans much as the Black and Tans.[3]

As Patrick Maume has observed, an important theme of the book is the 'indissoluble union of priests and people'.[4] This union was never stronger than in their common victimhood at the hands of the enemy, but it was threatened by the anti-treaty republicans. The image that Guinan portrayed of the clergy's role during the War of Independence was that of clerical martyrdom at the hands of the British forces. His book shows that this trope, developed in 1920 by the clergy itself, had become the enduring image of priests during the war. Clerical condemnation was successfully elided from the narrative, with counterexamples such as the denunciation of the Soloheadbeg ambush and Bishop Cohalan's decree consigned to oblivion.

Two important episodes in Guinan's novel were inspired by actual incidents from the War of Independence. The first is reminiscent of the killing of Canon Magner, with the two main clerical protagonists narrowly escaping murder at the hands of a Black and Tan. The killings of Magner and Griffin were described as 'crimes that will rankle in the brooding memory of Ireland for ever'.[5] The second was modelled on the incident in Dunmore in October 1920, when devotions in a temporary church building were disturbed by crown forces.[6] Guinan dramatised the scene considerably. Unlike in Dunmore, the curate-protagonist is searched while still wearing his

---

2 Catherine Candy, *Priestly Fictions. Popular Irish Novelists of the Early 20th Century* (Dublin and Harpenden: Wolfhound Press, 1995), p. 110.
3 Joseph Guinan, *The Patriots* (New York, Cincinnati and Chicago: Benziger, 1928).
4 Patrick Maume, 'A pastoral vision. The novels of Canon Joseph Guinan', *New Hibernia Review*, 9:4 (2005), pp. 79–98, at p. 95.
5 Guinan, *Patriots*, p. 196.
6 *Ibid.*, pp. 203–12.

vestments, and one of the raiders profanes a consecrated host, thus making Jesus himself a victim of the Black and Tans.[7]

Admittedly Guinan's parish priest and curate both held that killing RIC constables was immoral.[8] But the discourse of clerical victimhood which his book advanced nonetheless served to supplant the memory of clerical condemnation of IRA violence during the War of Independence. In his 1949 witness statement to the Bureau of Military History, Bishop Fogarty of Killaloe said that he had believed at the time that 'the national interest would over-ride such unpleasant happenings as the shooting of policemen'.[9] He asserted that he had condoned these killings insofar as they 'were carried through by authorization of at least de facto government'.[10] It is true that Fogarty was the strongest republican sympathiser among the bishops during the War of Independence, and that he had made statements at the time to the effect that 'mistakes and sorrows are ... inevitable' in the struggle that was underway. But he had also condemned republican violence on more than one occasion, saying that it was 'useless and wrong' and calling it 'criminal madness'.[11] Moreover, he was a signatory to a number of joint episcopal statements that denounced republican violence.[12] Fogarty had been a very strong opponent of the anti-treaty camp during the Civil War. His acceptance of the contrast between 'good fighting' during the War of Independence and 'bad fighting' during the Civil War coloured his memory of the period before 1922.[13]

Twenty years after Fogarty's statement, contemporary developments in Northern Ireland became the prism through which the past was viewed. Ó Fiaich's portrayal of the clergy's role in the War of Independence reads almost like a programme of action for priests in the Northern Ireland of his own day:

> Indictment of the British régime, denunciation of the atrocities committed by the crown forces, pleas on behalf of prisoners sentenced to death or on hunger-strike and visits to them, charitable work

---

7 *Ibid.*, pp. 209–10.
8 *Ibid.*, pp. 131–6.
9 MA, BMH, WS271, Michael Fogarty, p. 2.
10 MA, BMH, WS271, Michael Fogarty, Fogarty to Hayes, 24 May 1949.
11 *Irish Catholic*, 8 May and 2 October 1920 and 30 April 1921.
12 See for instance *ICD 1920*, pp. 517–19, 524–5, 556–61.
13 Murray, *Oracles*, pp. 238–40.

on behalf of those who suffered, peace-making and peace-keeping efforts at local level, avoidance of sectarian strife ... .[14]

For some historians, clerical opposition to the use of violence had become a cause of regret. Thus the Trappist Father Colmcille Ó Conbhuidhe, writing in the same edition of the *Capuchin Annual* as Ó Fiaich, contended that condemnations of IRA attacks were due to the fact that priests had been unable to 'adapt themselves to the altered situation resulting from the setting up in Ireland by the Irish people [of] a native government'.[15] But for Ó Fiaich the 'question-mark' that existed in the minds of the majority of priests concerning the use of physical force was normal for clergymen, having been 'implanted by the teaching of Christ' itself.[16] This priestly peculiarity did not, however, detract in any way from the clergy's fundamental solidarity with their people's cause.

More recent ecclesiastical assessment of the fighting between 1919 and 1921 has often tacitly accepted its legitimacy, while contrasting it sharply with the morally unacceptable use of violence in Northern Ireland. Thus Cahal Cardinal Daly, then archbishop emeritus of Armagh, said in a homily at the reburial of 'old IRA' men in 2001 that 'the true inheritors today of the ideals of the men and women of 1916 to 1922 are those who are explicitly and visibly committed to leaving the physical force tradition behind'.[17] And three years later, Archbishop Diarmuid Martin of Dublin remarked at the annual state commemoration of the Easter rising in Arbour Hill that the 'historical memory' of the rising must be 'lived out today as a rejection of violence ... anywhere, for whatever reason'.[18] It is an irony of commemoration that these bishops' eagerness to abjure physical force in their own day caused them to assess political violence in the past more positively than their predecessors did at the time.

---

14 Ó Fiaich, 'Clergy', p. 490.
15 Colmcille [Ó Conbhuidhe], 'Tipperary's fight in 1920', *The Capuchin Annual* (1970), pp. 255–75, at p. 261.
16 Ó Fiaich, Clergy', p. 501.
17 *Irish Times*, 14 October 2001.
18 *Ibid.*, 6 May 2004.

Conclusion

The purpose of this book has been to examine how Catholic priests responded to the use of political violence in Ireland during the War of Independence. It has found that the most common clerical response to republican violence was simply to ignore it, especially in areas unaffected by large-scale fighting. But when priests did respond publicly, they condemned it. Up to the last quarter of 1920, denunciations rose in number as violence increased, being most frequent in areas where violence was most common. Denunciations were forthcoming from conservative priests who mourned the demise of the Irish Parliamentary Party, but equally from sympathisers of Sinn Féin. The Sinn Féin priest was a very common phenomenon, with many clerics playing an active role in the republican party. There were strong links between local IRA units and the parish clergy, with many a priest the founder of the local company. As some Volunteers became radicalised in early 1920 and began to engage actively in guerrilla warfare, a small minority of priests also underwent radicalisation and became supporters of the IRA campaign. A handful of them considered themselves 'column chaplains', while at least seventy-one provided material assistance. While senior clerics were clearly overrepresented in reported condemnations of IRA violence, they were proportionally represented among the seventy-one who provided material assistance. Active support for the guerrilla campaign was not the monopoly of wild young curates.

A minority of priests also gave occasional spiritual aid to the guerrilla fighters. This kind of assistance gave the small number of supportive priests their particular significance. Public condemnation did not dissuade many Volunteers already involved in the fighting, although it may have discouraged those who would otherwise have joined. But clerical denunciation did cause problems of conscience for the fighting men, and this is where supportive priests played an important role. They smoothed out conscientious objections raised by clerical condemnations. They gave moral reassurance, thus easing the process of radicalisation and sustaining the fighting.

The key to understanding the clergy's role during the War of Independence, however, was the British campaign. Priests initially emphasised that RIC constables belonged to the Irish Catholic community and that it was wrong to ostracise them. As the RIC responded to IRA attacks in ever more violent fashion, this message lost some of its plausibility. The arrival of new security forces from Britain during the summer of 1920 provided the clergy with conveniently foreign objects of indignation. Moreover, the Black and Tans and Auxiliaries had none of the traditional esteem that the 'old RIC' had had for the parish clergy as fellow members of the local elite. They widely suspected priests of inciting the population to violence against the crown forces, and as a result, raids of ecclesiastical buildings and arrests of priests became very common, and instances of intimidation and terror against priests became frequent. Publicity was pivotal here, and priests proved themselves very able public relations managers. An image was soon created of sectarian anti-Catholic targeting of the clergy, with as its centrepiece the trope of the martyred priest familiar from penal times. In fact there was no widespread persecution of the clergy. But the perception of martyrdom was fuelled by the fact that priests were more prone than the population in general to be targeted by the crown forces. Thus they were more likely to be arrested, and in some areas they were specifically singled out for harassment. An important psychological turning point was the killing of Father Michael Griffin in Galway in November 1920, which appeared to vindicate the notion of a specific British 'attack on the church and religion'.

The result was that condemnations of IRA violence dropped in number, and that the attention of clerics both conservative and republican shifted to denunciation of British violence. This did not mean that bishops and priests suddenly began to view IRA ambushes more benignly. But the new focus on British outrages did provide priests with a convenient reason to ignore the conundrum of killings by the IRA. The ensuing dilemma caused by the continued presence of Catholics in the crown forces was resolved by placing the blame with the Black and Tans and Auxiliaries.

The image of the British enemy, both anti-Irish and anti-Catholic, thus allowed the clergy to endure the strain that breaches of the Fifth Commandment caused on its relationship with the freedom fighters. As has been seen in the Introduction, competition between elites over the power to define and lead the national community was very common in Europe at this time, having replaced the more traditional conflicts between church and state.[19] This was also true for countries such as Ireland where national and confessional identities overlapped in a 'symbiotic' manner.[20] This symbiosis did not happen automatically: unity had to be forged. The Irish War of Independence saw the self-assertion of a new political leadership that successfully challenged the role of an older elite linked to the Irish Parliamentary Party. This challenge also carried with it a potential threat to the authority of the clergy, which had been an important element of the 'old order'. Moreover, priests and bishops had their own agenda, that of mobilising the Irish masses to build a Catholic community. A guerrilla war to overthrow authority – even if it was the authority of the secular power – was not part of this agenda. The forces that had been unleashed threatened to cause a rupture between the clergy and the new leaders, posing a potential threat to the symbiosis between Catholicism and Irish nationalism. This book has shown how these tensions were turned around into an opportunity to strengthen the bond through emphasis on common suffering at the hands of the enemy.

The crisis was overcome, and the relationship with the 'nation under new management' lasted.[21] In the south, this left the clergy in a strong position to shape the policies of the new state. In the north, bishops and priests became a natural rallying point for their community against a government regarded with hostility. Definitions of Irish nationhood in the south began to allow for the inclusion of non-Catholic groups, while there had always been Protestant nationalists and Catholic unionists in both parts of the country. But for the majority of Irish Catholics, it was not until the end of the twentieth century that being Irish ceased to be coterminous with being Catholic.

---

19 Urs Altermatt and Franziska Metzger, 'Einführung', in Urs Altermatt and Franziska Metzger (eds), *Religion und Nation. Katholizismen im Europa des 19. und 20. Jahrhunderts* (Stuttgart: W. Kohlhammer, 2007), pp. 11–13, at pp. 11–12.
20 Altermatt, 'Katholizismus', p. 24.
21 Miller, *Church, State*, p. 426.

Appendices

Appendix 1

Reported instances of clerical condemnation of IRA violence, January 1919 – July 1921

Name	County	Status	I	II	III	IV	V
Ahern, Jeremiah	Cork	J			1		
Brady, Terence	Cavan	S					2
Brew, Maurice	Cork	J	1				
Brophy, Martin	Wicklow	J			1		
Browne, Robert	Cork	S		1	3	1	
Brownrigg, Abraham	Kilkenny	S			1		1
Burke, John	Galway	S	?	?	?	?	?
Byrne, Eugene	Dublin	S			1		
Byrnes, James	Tipperary	S					1
Cahalane, Patrick	Cork	J			1	1	
Callery, Philip	King's County	S				1	
Carpenter, H.	Westmeath	S				1	
Carr, John	Galway	S			1		
Casey, D.	Galway	J				1	
Cassidy, Francis	Clare	S		1			
Codd, William	Wexford	S			1		1
Cohalan, Daniel	Cork	S	1		1	4	
Cohalan, Jeremiah	Cork	S				1	
Collins, John	Cork	J			1		
Columba	Westmeath	J				1	
Condon, William	Tipperary	J	1				
Connolly, Michael	Tipperary	J	?	?	?	?	?
Considine, Anthony	Galway	S				1	

Name	County	Status	I	II	III	IV	V
Considine, John	Galway	J				1	
Corbett, C.W.	Cork	S				1	
Cosgrave, John	Longford	J			1		
Coveney, P.	Cork	S		1			
Cregan, James	Limerick	S			1		
Dalton, Edward	Leitrim	J			1		1
Daly, Eugene	King's County	J				1	
Delaney, William	Dublin	S				1	
Dennehy, Denis	Cork	J				1	
Dooley, T.	Tipperary	J			1		
Duggan, John	Cork	J			1		
Farrell, Patrick	Meath	S		1			
Finegan, Patrick	Cavan	S			3	1	2
Finnegan, John	Westmeath	J				1	
FitzPatrick, Bartholomew	Dublin	S		1			
Flynn, Denis	Meath	S			1		
Fogarty, Michael	Clare	S				1	
Foley, Patrick	Carlow	S			1	3	1
Fortune, William	Wexford	S				1	
Gallagher, Thomas	Roscommon	J				1	
Gaughran, Laurence	Westmeath	S		1		1	
Gearty, Roderick	Roscommon	S				1	1
Gilmartin, Thomas	Galway	S	3	1	4	2	5
Gleeson, John	Tipperary	S		1			
Godley, John	Cork	S				1	
Hackett, Bernard	Waterford	S				1	1
Halpin, James	Clare	S				1	
Hannon, John	Clare	S					1
Harty, John Mary	Tipperary	S	3		3	1	
Hayes, Michael	Clare	S				1	
Hayes, Patrick	Cork	S					1
Heany, M.	Galway	S			1		
Hoare, Joseph	Longford	S			2	3	3
Horan, James	Tipperary	S	1				
Houlihan, Joseph	King's County	J				1	
Hughes, Daniel	Kilkenny	J		1			
Hurley, John	Cork	J			1		
Hurley, Timothy	Roscommon	J				1	
Jones, Thomas	Kerry	J				1	

Name	County	Status	I	II	III	IV	V
Jones, T. J.	Wicklow	J				1	
Keenan, Laurence	Monaghan	S					1
Keller, Daniel	Cork	S				1	
Kelly, Denis	Cork	S	1		3	2	1
Kelly, John	Limerick	S			1		
Keogh, William	Tipperary	J	1				
Keville, John	Longford	S			1		
Kiely, Daniel	Tipperary	S	1				
Lawless, Nicholas	Louth	S					1
Logue, Michael	Armagh	S	1			2	3
Lynch, Thomas	Galway	J			1		
McAlister, Daniel	Down	J					1
MacAlpine, Patrick	Galway	S					2
McBrien, Thomas	Armagh	J		1			
McCarthy, Florence	Cork	S			1	1	
McCarthy, Joseph	Tipperary	J				2	
McCotter, Thomas	Antrim	S	1				
MacFeely, William	Derry	S			1		
McGeown, Michael	Tyrone	S					1
McGovern, John	Cavan	S					1
McHugh, Charles	Derry	S					1
McKenna, Bernard	Cork	J			1		
McKeone, James	Louth	S		1		1	1
McMahon, John	Tipperary	S				1	
MacRory, Joseph	Antrim	S				1	
McSwiney, John	Cork	J			1	2	
Maguire, Thomas	Longford	S				1	1
Maher, John	Wexford	S			1		
Morrisroe, Patrick	Roscommon	S				3	1
Moynihan, Jeremiah	Kerry	S					1
Mulhern, Edward	Down	S			1		1
Mullins, William	Clare	J		1			
Murphy, John	Cork	S				2	1
Murphy, Martin	Cork	S			1		
Murphy, Nicholas	Kilkenny	S				1	
Murphy, Philip	Cork	S				1	
Nolan, James	Kerry	S				1	1
Nunan, John	Cork	J		1			
O'Brien, Denis	Tipperary	J			1		

Name	County	Status	Date				
			I	II	III	IV	V
O'Connell, Patrick	Cavan	S				1	
O'Connor, Daniel	Monaghan	S		1			
O'Connor, Denis	Kerry	S					1
O'Connor, Dominic	Cork	J				1	
O'Connor, James	Sligo	S		1			
O'Connor, Patrick	Wexford	S		1			
O'Dea, Thomas	Galway	S		1	1	2	
O'Doherty, Thomas	Galway	S				1	
O'Donnell, Michael	Limerick	S	1		1		
O'Donnell, Patrick	Donegal	S		1		1	2
O'Donoghue, John	Cork	S		1			
O'Donoghue, Michael	Kerry	J					1
O'Farrell, Matthew	Meath	S		1			
O'Farrell, William	Leitrim	J	1				1
O'Flanagan, Michael	Roscommon	J		1		2	
O'Gorman, J.	Clare	J		1			
O'Hare, Francis	Down	J				1	
O'Hea, Timothy	Cork	S			1		
O'Leary, David	Kerry	S			1		
O'Leary, John	Cork	S			1		
O'Leary, Michael	Cork	J			1		
O'Malley, Thomas	Mayo	S					1
O'Neill, Anthony	Donegal	J				1	
O'Neill, Walter	Derry	S			1		
O'Reilly, Edward	Leitrim	J					1
O'Reilly, E. J.	King's County	S				1	
O'Reilly, Patrick	Cavan	S					1
O'Reilly, Thomas	Leitrim	S	1				2
O'Sullivan, Charles	Kerry	S					1
O'Sullivan, C.	Kerry	J				1	
Ryan, Arthur	Tipperary	S	1			1	
Ryan, Innocent	Tipperary	S			1		
Ryan, Michael	Tipperary	S	1		1		
Ryan, Michael K.	Tipperary	J	1		1		
Scanlon, Denis	Cork	J				1	
Segrave, Patrick	Louth	S					1
Sheedy, James	Cork	J		1			
Sheridan, Joseph	Donegal	J					1
Shinkwin, Thomas	Cork	S			1		
Slattery, John	Tipperary	S	1				

Name	County	Status	Date				
			I	II	III	IV	V
Trant, Timothy	Kerry	S			1		
Walsh, John	Wexford	S		1			
Walsh, William	Dublin	S		1			
Unnamed[a]	Cavan	?				1	
Unnamed[b]	Cork	?					1
Unnamed[c]	Cork	?					1
Unnamed[d]	Galway	?		1			
Unnamed[e]	Limerick	?				1	
Totals per period:			22	26	59	79	55
Total incidents: 243[f]							
Total clerics: 149							
Totals status: S: 96; J: 48; unknown: 5.							

Notes:
[a] TNA, CO904/115, IGMR, May 1921.
[b] *Irish Independent*, 8 February 1921.
[c] *Irish Catholic*, 2 April 1921.
[d] TNA, CO904/110, IGMR, October 1919.
[e] *Irish Independent*, 7 December 1920.
[f] This figure includes the totals per period, plus the two incidents that could not be dated.

Legend: S = senior cleric, including bishops, parish priests, administrators and priors of religious houses; J = junior cleric, including curates and members non-priors of religious houses; I = January–June 1919; II = July–December 1919; III = January–June 1920; IV= July–December 1920; V = January–July 1921.

Sources: Irish Catholic, Irish Independent, Meath Chronicle; AICR, O'Riordan papers; MA, BMH, witness statements; TNA, CO: Dublin Castle records; Waterford and Lismore Diocesan Archives, Waterford, Bernard Hackett papers; Maureen Mulryan, 'Bishop Hoare and politics', *Teathba. Journal of County Longford Historical Society*, 3:2 (2007), pp. 32–5.

Appendix 2

Priests who gave material support to the IRA, January 1919 – July 1921

Name	County	Status
Ambrose, Robert	Limerick	S
Behan, William	Kerry	J
Breen, Joseph	Cork	J
Burke, Thomas	Mayo	J
Carmody	USA, on leave in Ireland	?
Connolly, John	Galway	S
Crowley, John	Cork	J
Cunningham, C.	Mayo	S
Curran, Michael	Italy	S
Daly	Cork	S
Darcy, Michael	Wexford	J
Delahunty, Patrick	Kilkenny	J
Doyle, Patrick	Carlow	S
Duggan, Thomas	Cork	J
Fergus, James	Galway	J
Fidelis	Galway	S
Flannery, Francis	Cork	J
Fogarty, John	Tipperary	J
Ford, Patrick	Galway	S
Gaynor, Patrick	Clare	J
Gerhard, Louis	Dublin	S
Hackett, William	Dublin	J
Hayes, Michael	Limerick	J
Hegarty, John	Mayo	S
Hegarty, Martin	Mayo	J
Hobbins, Thomas	Wicklow	J
Keane, Bernard	Sligo	J
Kelly, John	Limerick	J
Langan, Thomas	Westmeath	S
Lanigan, J.	USA, on leave in Ireland	?
Larkin, John	Kilkenny	J
Lee, John	Limerick	S
Lyne, T. J.	Kerry	S
McAdam, Eugene	Monaghan	S
McCarthy, Richard	Limerick	J
McDevitt, C.	Donegal	J

Name	County	Status
McKenna, Michael	Clare	J
McNamara, Patrick	Antrim	J
McNamara	Kilkenny	J
McNamee, B.	Derry	J
Magee, John	King's County	S
Markey, Patrick	Longford	S
Meehan, John	Mayo	J
Montford, Thomas	Longford	J
Moran, Patrick	Galway	S
Morley, Michael	Galway	J
Murray, Michael	Clare	J
Norris, P.	Meath	J
O'Connor, James	Sligo	S
O'Doherty, Philip	Donegal	S
O'Doherty, William	Donegal	S
O'Donnell, Roger	Sligo	J
O'Farrell, Martin	Galway	J
O'Kelly	Kildare	?
O'Meara, L.	Galway	J
O'Neill, John	Antrim	S
O'Neill, Walter	Derry	S
O'Reilly	England, on leave in Ireland	?
Sharkey, Timothy	Roscommon	S
Shinnick, Edward	Cork	S
Smith	Kildare	J
Smyth, James	Antrim	J
Synnott, Henry	Waterford	J
Toner, Arthur	Armagh	J
Walsh, Patrick	Wexford	J
Unnamed[a]	?	?
Unnamed[b]	Dublin	?
Capuchin Priory, Church Street	Dublin	?
Carmelite Priory, Whitefriar Street	Dublin	?
Mount Melleray Abbey	Waterford	?
St. Patrick's College, Maynooth	Kildare	?

Total clerics: 71
Totals status: S: 24; J: 37; unknown: 10.

Notes:
ᵃ MA, BMH, WS1161, Patrick O'Carroll, p. 2.
ᵇ MA, BMH, WS596, George Nolan, p. 9.

Legend: S = senior cleric, including parish priests, an administrator, a college rector and vice-rector, a prior of a religious house and a religious priest who was a 'definitor' (a member of his provincial's council); J = junior cleric, curates, a hospital chaplain and a teacher in a college. The religious houses and Maynooth College have each been counted as one.

Sources: *Irish Independent*; CtDA, O'Doherty papers; IJA, 'Brief lives' papers; MA, BMH, witness statements; NLI, Gaynor papers; TNA, WO: Army of Ireland records; Barry, *Days*; Breen, *Fight*; Corish, *Maynooth*; D'Arcy, *Terenure*; Carmel Hughes, 'Statement of Michael Hughes Castlebar battalion I.R.A.', *Cathair na Mart. The Journal of the Westport Historical Society*, 19 (1999), pp. 77–85; Kautt, *Ambushes*; Ó Fiaich, 'Clergy'.

Appendix 3

Geographical distribution of clerical condemnation of IRA violence and material support for the IRA

County	Number of priests	Percentage of priests with reported condemnation	Percentage of priests who gave material support	Hart's figures for IRA violence (per 10,000 people)
Antrim	122	1.6	2.5	0.2
Armagh	52	3.8	1.9	2.2
Carlow	42	2.4	2.4	3.6
Cavan	85	7	0	1.4
Clare	106	6.6	2.8	8.9
Cork	380	8.7	1.6	15.4
Derry	75	4	2.7	1.4
Donegal	104	2.9	2.9	0.8
Down	83	3.6	0	1
Dublin	531	0.8	0.9	7.7
Fermanagh	n/a	0	0	2.9
Galway	212	5.7	3.8	2.6
Kerry	122	7.4	1.6	9.8
Kildare	114	0	2.6	1.1
Kilkenny	111	2.7	2.7	2.4
King's County	62	6.5	1.6	2.6
Leitrim	54	7.4	0	2.4
Limerick	164	2.4	3	7.1
Longford	43	9.3	4.7	12.3
Louth	104	2.9	0	1.4
Mayo	140	0.7	3.6	2.2
Meath	80	3.8	1.3	2.6
Monaghan	57	3.5	1.8	4.7
Queen's County	n/a	0	0	1.8
Roscommon	83	6	1.2	6.1
Sligo	55	1.8	5.5	3.4
Tipperary	224	7.8	0.4	8.8
Tyrone	85	1.2	0	1.4
Waterford	117	0.9	1.7	2.4

County	Number of priests	Percentage of priests with reported condemnation	Percentage of priests who gave material support	Hart's figures for IRA violence (per 10,000 people)
Westmeath	*90*	4.4	1.1	4
Wexford	*124*	4	1.6	2
Wicklow	*50*	4	2	0.3

Correlation coefficient for condemnation and violence: 0.5885
Correlation coefficient for support and violence: 0.1601

Legend: The numbers of priests per county are needed to obtain the percentages of priests who condemned and gave support per county. They have been given in italics in the second column.

Sources: The figures for reported condemnations have been taken from Appendix 1, those for support from Appendix 2. The numbers of priests per county were calculated on the basis of *ICD 1920*. The figures for IRA violence are based on Hart, 'Geography', p. 147. Hart's figures are for 1920–21 only, even though the clerical figures also include 1919 and exclude 1921 from 11 July onwards. Hart's figures also exclude Belfast, which is included in the figures for clerical condemnations and support in Counties Antrim and Down.

Appendix 4

Chronological distribution of raids on ecclesiastical buildings by crown forces, January 1919 – July 1921

Period	Number
Jan.–June 1919	–
July–Dec. 1919	2
Jan.–June 1920	2
July–Dec. 1920	77
Jan.–July 1921	46
Exact date unknown	3
Total	130

Sources: *Catholic Bulletin*; *Connacht Tribune*; *Freeman's Journal*; *Irish Catholic*; *Irish Independent*; AICR, Hagan papers; CMA, Book A, 'Missionary works'; CtDA, O'Doherty papers; DDA, Walsh papers; IJA, Crescent College papers and Tullabeg papers; KDA, Fogarty papers; MA, BMH, witness statements; TDA, Gilmartin papers; TNA, CO: Dublin Castle records and WO: Army of Ireland records; UCDA, Mulcahy papers; George Maguire, 'Mayo and Sligo – 1920', *The Capuchin Annual* (1970), pp. 396–9; Ó Fiaich, 'Clergy'.

Appendix 5

Clerics arrested by the crown forces, January 1919 – July 1921

Date	Name	County	Status
14/10/1919	Thomas O'Donnell	n/a	J
24/6/1920	Walter O'Neill	Derry	S
8/9/1920	Patrick Walsh	Wexford	J
26/9/1920	Eugene Coyle	Monaghan	J
6/10/1920	Michael Morley	Galway	J
11/10/1920	Michael O'Flanagan	Roscommon	J
11/10/1920	Michael Carney	Mayo	J
11/10/1920	J. Burke	Galway	J
12/10/1920	John Meehan	Mayo	J
17/10/1920	J. J. Glynn	Roscommon	J
17/10/1920	James Roddy	Roscommon	J
2/11/1920	Patrick Markey	Longford	S
18/11/1920	George Culhane	Clare	S
30/11/1920	Patrick Delahunty	Kilkenny	J
2/12/1920	Michael Conroy	Mayo	S
16/12/1920	Albert Bibby	Dublin	J
16/12/1920	Dominic O'Connor	Dublin	J
24/12/1920	Philip Hickey	Tipperary	J
6/1/1921	John Greed	Clare	J
6/1/1921	P. Spain	Clare	J
15/1/1921	Thomas Burbage	King's County	J
20/1/1921	Murray	Kerry	J
21/1/1921	Timothy Mannix	Cork	J
23/1/1921	Louis Gerhard	Dublin	S
24/1/1921	Patrick Scott	Sligo	J
29/1/1921	Patrick Ahern	Cork	J
24/2/1921	Charles Boyce	Donegal	J
2/1921	P. Smith	King's County	J
22/3/1921	Unnamed[a]	Mayo	J
2/4/1921	Patrick Gaynor	Clare	J
2/4/1921	Michael McKenna	Clare	J
9/4/1921	John McCaughan	Antrim	J
18/4/1921	Michael Aherne	Cork	J
4/5/1921	John Power	Waterford	S
21/5/1921	John Loughrey	Tipperary	J
30/5/1921	Eugene Coyle	Monaghan	J

Date	Name	County	Status
4/6/1921	Edward Campion	Carlow	J
26/6/1921	John Nunan	Tipperary	S
26/6/1921	P. O'Dea	Galway	J
26/6/1921	Robert O'Reilly	Galway	J
6/1921	Michael Rice	Kildare	J
6/1921	Unnamed[b]	?	?
6/7/1921	William O'Kennedy	Clare	S

Total arrests: 43
Total priests arrested: 42
Totals status: S: 8; J: 34; unknown: 1

Notes:
[a] *Irish Catholic*, 9 April 1921.
[b] *Irish Independent*, 2 June 1921.

Legend: S = senior cleric, including parish priests, an administrator, the prior of a religious house, and the president of a diocesan college; J = junior cleric, including curates, army chaplains, members non-priors of religious houses, a teacher at a college and a deacon.

Sources: Anglo-Celt; Freeman's Journal; Irish Catholic; Irish Independent; Kerryman; Nenagh Guardian; Kildare and Leighlin Diocesan Archives, Carlow, Foley papers; MA, BMH, witness statements; TNA, CO: Dublin Castle records and WO: Army of Ireland records.

Appendix 6

Chronological distribution of intimidation of and violence against priests by crown forces, January 1919 – July 1921

Period	Number
Jan.–June 1919	1
July–Dec. 1919	–
Jan.–June 1920	6
July–Dec. 1920	42
Jan.–July 1921	31
Total	80

Sources: *Freeman's Journal*; *Irish Catholic*; *Irish Independent*; *Kerryman*; AICR, Hagan papers; CDA, Cohalan papers; CMA, box 'T. The Troubles and Clonard'; EDA, Coyne papers; IJA, Tullabeg papers; MA, BMH, witness statements and contemporary documents; Mount St Alphonsus Redemptorist Monastery Domestic Archive, Limerick, House chronicles (with thanks to Rev. Joe Mac Loughlin, CSsR); KDA, Fogarty papers; KyDA, O'Sullivan papers; TDA, Gilmartin papers; TNA, CO: Dublin Castle records; Martin Dolan, 'Galway 1920–1921', *The Capuchin Annual* (1970), pp. 384–95; Donnelly, 'McHugh'; Martin, 'Hennessy'; Maye, 'Islandeady'; Ó Fiaich, 'Clergy'; Thomas Ryan, 'One man's flying column', *Tipperary Historical Journal* (1991), pp. 19–34.

Geographical distribution of intimidation of and violence against priests by crown forces, January 1919 – July 1921

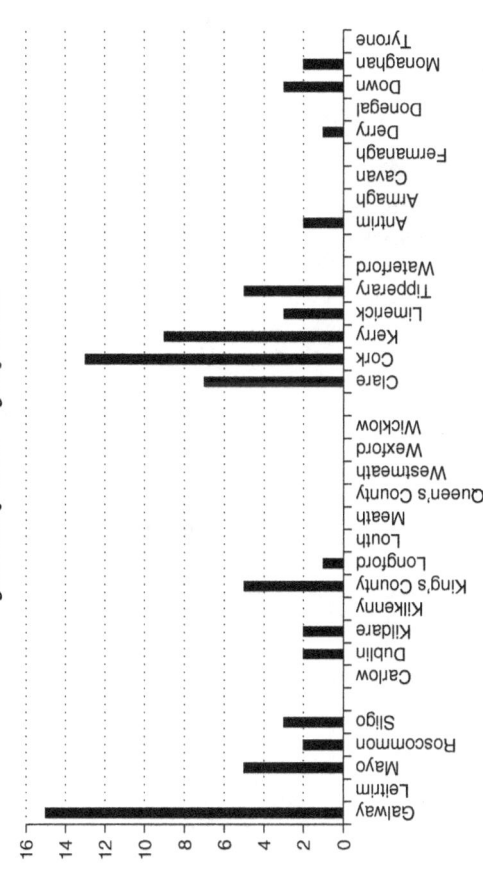

Sources: *Freeman's Journal*; *Irish Catholic*; *Irish Independent*; *Kerryman*; AICR, Hagan papers; CDA, Cohalan papers; CMA, box 'T: The Troubles and Clonard'; EDA, Coyne papers; IJA, Tullabeg papers; MA, BMH, witness statements and contemporary documents; Mount St Alphonsus Redemptorist Monastery Domestic Archive, Limerick, House chronicles (with thanks to Rev. Joe Mac Loughlin, CSsR); KDA, Fogarty papers; KyDA, O'Sullivan papers; TDA, Gilmartin papers; TNA, CO: Dublin Castle records; Martin Dolan, 'Galway 1920–1921', *The Capuchin Annual* (1970), pp. 384–95; Donnelly, 'McHugh'; Martin, 'Hennessy'; Maye, 'Islandeady'; Ó Fiaich, 'Clergy'; Thomas Ryan, 'One man's flying column', *Tipperary Historical Journal* (1991), pp. 19–34.

Appendix 8

Catholic diocesan bishops in Ireland, January 1919 – July 1921

Diocese	Bishop	Appointment to see	Death
Province of Armagh			
Armagh (*archbishop and primate of All Ireland*)	Michael Cardinal Logue (b. 1840)	3/12/1887	19/11/1924
Ardagh and Clonmacnoise	Joseph Hoare (b. 1842)	8/2/1895	14/4/1927
Clogher	Patrick McKenna (b. 1868)	12/6/1909	7/2/1942
Derry	Charles McHugh (b. 1852)	14/6/1907	12/2/1926
Down and Connor	Joseph MacRory (b. 1861)	18/8/1915	13/10/1945 (*tr. to Armagh 22/6/1928*)
Dromore	Edward Mulhern (b. 1863)	19/1/1916	12/8/1943
Kilmore	Patrick Finegan (b. 1858)	4/7/1910	25/1/1937
Meath	Laurence Gaughran (b. 1842)	19/5/1906	14/6/1928
Raphoe	Patrick O'Donnell (b. 1856)	21/2/1888	22/10/1927 (*tr. to Armagh 14/1/1922*)
Province of Dublin			
Dublin (*archbishop and primate of Ireland*)	William Walsh (b. 1841)	3/7/1885	9/4/1921
	Edward Byrne (b. 1872)	28/8/1921	9/2/1940
Ferns	William Codd (b. 1864)	7/12/1917	12/3/1938
Kildare and Leighlin	Patrick Foley (b. 1858)	19/12/1896	24/7/1926

Diocese	Bishop	Appointment to see	Death
Ossory	Abraham Brownrigg, SSS (b. 1836)	28/10/1884	1/10/1928
Province of Cashel			
Cashel and Emly (*archbishop*)	John Mary Harty (b. 1867)	4/12/1913	11/9/1946
Cloyne	Robert Browne (b. 1844)	26/6/1894	23/3/1935
Cork	Daniel Cohalan (b. 1858)	29/8/1916	24/8/1952
Kerry	Charles O'Sullivan (b. 1862)	10/11/1917	29/1/1927
Killaloe	Michael Fogarty (b. 1859)	12/7/1904	25/10/1955
Limerick	Denis Hallinan (b. 1849)	10/1/1918	2/7/1923
Ross	Denis Kelly (b. 1852)	29/3/1897	18/4/1924
Waterford and Lismore	Bernard Hackett, CSsR (b. 1863)	29/1/1916	1/6/1932
Province of Tuam			
Tuam (*archbishop*)	Thomas Gilmartin (b. 1861)	10/7/1918	14/10/1939
Achonry	Patrick Morrisroe (b. 1869)	13/5/1911	27/5/1946
Clonfert	*sede vacante*	10/7/1918	3/7/1919
	Thomas O'Doherty (b. 1877)	3/7/1919	15/12/1936 (*tr.* to Galway 13/7/1923)
Elphin	Bernard Coyne (b. 1854)	18/1/1913	17/7/1926
Galway, Kilmacduagh and Kilfenora	Thomas O'Dea (b. 1858)	29/4/1909	9/4/1923
Killala	James Naughton (b. 1865)	27/11/1911	16/2/1950

Legend: b. = born; CSsR = Redemptorists; *sede vacante* = see vacant; SSS = Congregation of the Blessed Sacrament; tr. = translated to

Source: Benignus Millett and C. J. Woods, 'Roman Catholic bishops from 1534', in T. W. Moody, F. X. Martin and F. J. Byrne (eds), *A New History of Ireland*, ix: *Maps, Genealogies, Lists. A Companion to Irish History, II* (Oxford: Clarendon Press, 1984), pp. 333–91.

Bibliography

Primary sources

Church archives

Armagh

> *Armagh Diocesan Archives, Cardinal Tomás Ó Fiaich Memorial Library and Archive*
> Michael Cardinal Logue papers

Belfast

> *Clonard Redemptorist Monastery Domestic Archive*
> Several uncatalogued items

Carlow

> *Kildare and Leighlin Diocesan Archives*
> Patrick Foley papers

Cork

> *Cork and Ross Diocesan Archives*
> Daniel Cohalan papers

Dublin

> *Capuchin Provincial Archives*
> Albert Bibby papers
> Dominic O'Connor papers
>
> *Carmelite (Calced) Provincial Archives, Gort Muire*
> Uncatalogued item
>
> *Dominican Provincial Archives*
> Letters of provincials

Dublin Diocesan Archives
Edward Byrne papers
William Walsh papers

Irish Jesuit Archives
'Brief lives' papers
Milltown Park papers
Provincial consultations
Sacred Heart (Crescent) College papers
St Ignatius' College papers
Tullabeg papers

Ennis

Killaloe Diocesan Archives
Michael Fogarty papers

Galway

Galway Diocesan Archives
Thomas O'Dea papers
Thomas O'Doherty papers

Killarney

Kerry Diocesan Archives
Charles O'Sullivan papers

Limerick

Mount St Alphonsus Redemptorist Monastery Domestic Archive
House chronicles

Loughrea

Clonfert Diocesan Archives
Thomas O'Doherty papers

Paris

Archives of the Irish College, Centre Culturel Irlandais
Collège papers

Rome

Archives of the Pontifical Irish College
John Hagan papers
Michael O'Riordan papers

Sligo

Elphin Diocesan Archives
Bernard Coyne papers

Tuam

> *Tuam Diocesan Archives*
> Thomas Gilmartin papers

Waterford

> *Waterford and Lismore Diocesan Archives*
> Bernard Hackett papers

British government archives

Kew

> *The National Archives*
> Colonial Office: Dublin Castle records
> War Office: Army of Ireland: Administrative and Easter rising records

Archives holding papers of republicans

Dublin

> *Military Archives*
> Bureau of Military History
> > Contemporary documents
> > Witness statements
>
> *National Library of Ireland*
> Patrick Doyle papers
> Patrick Gaynor papers
> Shane Leslie papers
> Maurice Moore papers
> Florence O'Donoghue papers
> Several loose items
>
> *University College Dublin Archives*
> Mary MacSwiney papers
> Richard Mulcahy papers
> Ernie O'Malley papers

Newspapers and periodicals

> *Anglo-Celt*
> *The Capuchin Annual*
> *The Catholic Bulletin and Book Review*
> *Connacht Tribune*
> *Cork Examiner*
> *Freeman's Journal*
> *Galway City Tribune*

Irish Catholic
Irish Independent
Irish Times
Kerryman
Meath Chronicle
Morning Post
Nenagh Guardian

Other printed primary sources

Acta et decreta synodi plenariae episcoporum Hiberniae habitae apud Maynutiam, an. MDCCCLXXV (Dublin: Browne and Nolan, 1877).

Acta et decreta synodi plenariae episcoporum Hiberniae habitae apud Maynutiam an. MDCCCC (Dublin: Browne and Nolan, 1906).

Augusteijn, Joost (ed.), *The Memoirs of John M. Regan. A Catholic Officer in the RIC and RUC, 1909–1948* (Dublin and Portland, OR: Irish Academic Press, 2007).

Barry, Tom, *Guerrilla Days in Ireland* (reprint; Dublin: Anvil Books, 1989).

Benedict XV, 'Epistola ad Michaëlem S.R.E. Card. Logue, Archiepiscopum Armachanum de necessitate et ratione pacis intra fines Hiberniae reconciliandae', 27 April 1921, *Acta Apostolicae Sedis*, 13 (1921), pp. 256–8.

Breen, Dan, *My Fight for Irish Freedom* (revised edn; Dublin: Anvil Books, 1989).

Catechism Ordered by the National Synod of Maynooth and Approved of by the Cardinal, the Archbishops and the Bishops of Ireland for General Use throughout the Irish Church (reprint; Galway: Firinne Publications, n.d.).

Codex iuris canonici Pii X Pontificis Maximi iussu digestus, Benedicti Papae XV auctoritate promulgatus (Rome: Typus Polyglottis Vaticanis, 1918).

Coffey, Peter, 'The conscription menace in Ireland and some issues raised by it', *Irish Ecclesiastical Record*, 11 (1918), pp. 484–98.

Crozier, F. P., *Ireland for Ever* (London and Toronto: J. Cape, 1932).

Dáil Éireann Debates, vol. 1.

Deasy, Liam, *Towards Ireland Free. The West Cork Brigade in the War of Independence 1917–1921* (Dublin and Cork: Mercier Press, 1973).

Finlay, Peter, 'Irish Catholics and conscription', *Irish Independent*, 14 May 1919.

Fitzpatrick, John, 'Some more theology about tyranny. A reply to Prof. O'Rahilly', *Irish Theological Quarterly*, 16 (1921), pp. 1–15.

Gaynor, Eamonn (ed.), *Memoirs of a Tipperary Family. The Gaynors of Tyone 1887–2000* (Dublin: Geography Publications, n.d.).

Guinan, Joseph, *The Patriots* (New York, Cincinnati and Chicago: Benziger, 1928).

Gury, Ioannes Petrus, *Compendium theologiae moralis* (Regensburg: Georg Joseph Manz, 1862).
Hansard, series 5 (Commons).
Healy, T. M., *Letters and Leaders of my Day* (New York: Frederick A. Stokes, 1929).
Hopkinson, Michael, *The Last Days of Dublin Castle. The Mark Sturgis Diaries* (Dublin and Portland, OR: Irish Academic Press, 1999).
Hughes, Carmel, 'Statement of Michael Hughes Castlebar battalion I.R.A.', *Cathair na Mart. The Journal of the Westport Historical Society*, 19 (1999), pp. 77–85.
The Irish Catholic Directory and Almanac for 1919 with Complete Directory in English (Dublin: James Duffy, 1919).
The Irish Catholic Directory and Almanac for 1920 with Complete Directory in English (Dublin: James Duffy, 1920).
The Irish Catholic Directory and Almanac for 1921 with Complete Directory in English (Dublin: James Duffy, 1921).
The Irish Catholic Directory and Almanac for 1922 with Complete Directory in English (Dublin: James Duffy, 1922).
Kinane, J., 'Changes in the bull "Apostolicae sedis" and in the Index legislation', *Irish Ecclesiastical Record*, 13 (1919), pp. 332–5.
——, 'May clerics be judges in the civil courts?', *Irish Ecclesiastical Record*, 18 (1921), p. 522.
Koch, Antony and Arthur Preuss, *A Handbook of Moral Theology*, ii: *Sin and the Means of Grace* (St Louis, MO, and London: Herder, 1919).
Leo XIII, 'Diuturnum illud', 29 June 1881, *Acta Sanctae Sedis*, 14 (1881), pp. 3–14.
——, 'Epistola encyclica de civitatum constitutione christiana' (*Immortale Dei*), 1 November 1885, *Acta Sanctae Sedis*, 18 (1885), pp. 161–80.
MacBride, Seán, *That Day's Struggle. A Memoir 1904–1951* (Blackrock: Currach Press, 2005).
McDonald, Walter, *Some Ethical Questions of Peace and War with Special Reference to Ireland* (reprint; Dublin: University College Dublin Press, 1998).
McKenna, John, *A Beleaguered Station. The Memoir of Head Constable John McKenna, 1891–1921* (n.p.: Ulster Historical Foundation, 2009).
McMahon, Timothy G. (ed.), *Pádraig Ó Fathaigh's War of Independence. Recollections of a Galway Gaelic Leaguer* (Cork: Cork University Press, 2000).
Mansfield, James, 'The Decies brigade – 1920', *The Capuchin Annual* (1970), pp. 377–83.
Mullins, Billy, *Memoirs of Billy Mullins. Veteran of the War of Independence* (Tralee: Kenno, 1983).

Noldin, Hieronymus, *Summa theologiae moralis*, i: *De principiis theologiae moralis* (Innsbruck: Felix Rauch, 1910).
O'Grady, Brian, 'Old I.R.A. days in Ballylongford', *The Shannonside Annual*, 4 (1959), pp. 33–7.
Ó hÓgáin, Seán, 'The Tourmakeady ambush, May 1921 – part II', *Cathair na Mart. Journal of the Westport Historical Society*, 23 (2003), pp. 44–59.
O'Malley, Ernie, *On Another Man's Wound* (2nd edn; Dublin: Mercier Press, 2002).
O'Rahilly, Alfred, 'Some theology about tyranny', *Irish Theological Quarterly*, 15 (1920), pp. 301–20.
Synodus dioecesana Dublinensis, habita in ecclesia Sanctae Crucis, Dublini, die 25 Nov., 1879 una cum statutis concilii provincialis Dublinensis an. 1853, et synodi dioecesanae Dublinensis an. 1831, necnon aliis documentis usui cleri accommodatis (Dublin: Joseph Dollard, 1879).
Vatican Council II. The Basic Sixteen Documents: Constitutions, Decrees, Declarations, ed. Austin Flannery (Northport, NY, and Dublin: Costello Publishing and Dominican Publications, 1996).
Wister, Owen, *A Straight Deal, or The Ancient Grudge* (New York: Macmillan, 1920).

Correspondence

Late Professor Patrick J. Corish
Rev. Hugh Fenning, OP
Rev. David Kelly, OSA
Dr Brian Kirby
Rev. Joe Mac Loughlin, CSsR

Secondary sources

Altermatt, Urs, 'Katholizismus und Nation. Vier Modelle in europäisch-vergleichender Perspektive', in Urs Altermatt and Franziska Metzger (eds), *Religion und Nation. Katholizismen im Europa des 19. und 20. Jahrhunderts* (Stuttgart: W. Kohlhammer, 2007), pp. 15–33.
Altermatt, Urs, and Franziska Metzger, 'Einführung', in Urs Altermatt and Franziska Metzger (eds), *Religion und Nation. Katholizismen im Europa des 19. und 20. Jahrhunderts* (Stuttgart: W. Kohlhammer, 2007), pp. 11–13.
Anderson, Benedict, *Imagined Communities. Reflections on the Origin and Spread of Nationalism* (revised edn; London and New York: Verso, 1991).
Augusteijn, Joost, 'Accounting for the emergence of violent activism among Irish revolutionaries, 1916–21', *Irish Historical Studies*, 35:139 (2007), pp. 327–44.
——, *From Public Defiance to Guerrilla Warfare. The Experience of Ordinary*

Volunteers in the Irish War of Independence 1916–1921 (London and Portland, OR: Irish Academic Press, 1996).
——, 'The origins of Irish nationalism in a European context', in Brian Heffernan et al. (eds), *Life on the Fringe? Ireland and Europe, 1800–1922* (Dublin and Portland, OR: Irish Academic Press, 2012), pp. 15–38.
Bellenger, Dominic Aidan, 'An Irish Benedictine adventure. Dom Francis Sweetman (1872–1953) and Mount St Benedict, Gorey', in W. J. Sheils and Diana Wood (eds), *The Churches, Ireland and the Irish. Papers Read at the 1987 Summer Meeting and the 1988 Winter Meeting of the Ecclesiastical History Society* (Oxford and New York: Basil Blackwell, 1989), pp. 401–16.
Bernard, 'Fathers Albert and Dominic, O.F.M.Cap. The repatriation of their remains', *The Capuchin Annual* (1959), pp. 380–3.
Beugnet, A., 'Absolution conditionelle ou sous condition', in A. Vacant, E. Mangenot and É. Amann (eds), *Dictionnaire de théologie catholique contenant l'exposé des doctrines de la théologie catholique, leurs preuves et leur histoire*, i:1 (Paris: Letouzey et Ané, 1930), pp. 252–5.
Bew, Paul, 'Moderate nationalism and the Irish revolution, 1916–1923', *The Historical Journal*, 42:3 (1999), pp. 729–49.
Bitter, Gottfried, 'Katholische Predigt der Neuzeit', in Horst Balz et al. (eds), *Theologische Realenzyklopädie*, 27 (Berlin and New York: Walter de Gruyter, 1997), pp. 262–96.
Blanchard, Jean, *The Church in Contemporary Ireland* (Dublin and London: Clonmore and Reynolds and Burns and Oates, 1963).
Borgonovo, John (ed.), *Florence and Josephine O'Donoghue's War of Independence. A Destiny that Shapes our Ends* (Dublin and Portland, OR: Irish Academic Press, 2006).
Bride, A., 'Tyran et tyrannie', in A. Vacant, E. Mangenot and É. Amann (eds), *Dictionnaire de théologie catholique contenant l'exposé des doctrines de la théologie catholique, leurs preuves et leur histoire*, xv:2 (Paris: Letouzey et Ané, 1950), pp. 1948–88.
Buckley, Donal, *The Battle of Tourmakeady. Fact or Fiction. A Study of the IRA Ambush and its Aftermath* (Dublin: Nonsuch Publishing, 2008).
Candy, Catherine, *Priestly Fictions. Popular Irish Novelists of the Early 20th Century* (Dublin and Harpenden: Wolfhound Press, 1995).
Carroll, Denis, *They have Fooled you Again. Michael O'Flanagan (1876–1942). Priest, Republican, Social Critic* (Blackrock: Columba Press, 1993).
Ceannt, Áine B. É., *The Story of the Irish White Cross, 1920–1947* (Dublin: Three Candles, n.d.).
Clancy, Carmel, 'The experiences of a Sinn Féin priest. Father Pat Gaynor and self-government in Clare 1919–1921', *The Other Clare. Annual Journal of the Shannon Archaeological and Historical Society*, 31 (2007), pp. 51–8.

Coleman, Marie, *County Longford and the Irish Revolution 1910–1923* (Dublin and Portland, OR: Irish Academic Press, 2003).
Colmcille [Ó Conbhuidhe], 'Tipperary's fight in 1920', *The Capuchin Annual* (1970), pp. 255–75.
Comerford, R. V., 'The British state and the education of Irish Catholics, 1850–1921', in Janusz Tomiak *et al.* (eds), *Schooling, Educational Policy and Ethnic Identity* (New York: New York University Press, 1991), pp. 13–33.
——, *Ireland* (London: Hodder Arnold, 2003).
——, *et al.* (eds), *Religion, Conflict and Coexistence in Ireland. Essays Presented to Monsignor Patrick J. Corish* (Dublin: Gill and Macmillan, 1990).
Connolly, Sean J., 'Religion and Nationality in Ireland. An Unstable Relationship', in Urs Altermatt and Franziska Metzger (eds), *Religion und Nation. Katholizismen im Europa des 19. und 20. Jahrhunderts* (Stuttgart: W. Kohlhammer, 2007), pp. 119–34.
Corish, Patrick J., *Maynooth College 1795–1995* (Dublin: Gill and Macmillan, 1995).
Corkery, Pádraig, 'Bishop Daniel Cohalan of Cork on republican resistance and hunger strikes. A theological note', *Irish Theological Quarterly*, 67 (2002), pp. 113–24.
Cottrell, Peter, *The Anglo-Irish War. The Troubles of 1913–1922* (Oxford: Osprey Publishing, 2006).
D'Arcy, Fergus A., *Terenure College 1860–2010. A History* (Dublin: Terenure College, 2009).
Dolan, Anne, '"The shadow of a great fear". Terror and revolutionary Ireland', in David Fitzpatrick (ed.), *Terror in Ireland 1916–1923. Trinity History Workshop* (Dublin: Lilliput Press, 2012), pp. 26–38.
Dolan, Martin, 'Galway 1920–1921', *The Capuchin Annual* (1970), pp. 384–95.
Donnelly, Peter, 'Bishops and violence. A response to Oliver Rafferty', *Studies. An Irish Quarterly Review*, 82:331 (1994), pp. 331–40.
Donnelly, Philip, 'Bishop Charles McHugh of Derry diocese (1856–1926)', *Seanchas Ard Mhacha. Journal of the Armagh Diocesan Historical Society*, 20:2 (2005), pp. 212–44.
Doyle, Peter, 'Pastoral perfection. Cardinal Manning and the secular clergy', in W. J. Sheils and Diana Wood (eds), *The Ministry. Clerical and Lay. Papers read at the 1988 Summer Meeting and the 1989 Winter Meeting of the Ecclesiastical History Society* (Oxford: Basil Blackwell, 1989), pp. 385–96.
Dudley Edwards, R. W., 'Government of Ireland and education, 1919–1920', *Archivium Hibernicum*, 37 (1982), pp. 21–8.
Ellison, Robert H. (ed.), *A New History of the Sermon. The Nineteenth Century* (Leiden: Brill, 2010).

Enright, Seán, *The Trial of Civilians by Military Courts. Ireland 1921* (Dublin and Portland, OR: Irish Academic Press, 2012).
Ferriter, Diarmaid, '"In such deadly earnest", *The Dublin Review*, 12 (2003), pp. 36–64.
Fitzgerald, Thomas Earls, 'The execution of "spies and informers" in West Cork, 1921', in David Fitzpatrick (ed.), *Terror in Ireland 1916–1923. Trinity History Workshop* (Dublin: Lilliput Press, 2012), pp. 181–93.
Fitzpatrick, David, 'The geography of Irish nationalism 1910–1921', *Past and Present*, 78 (1978), pp. 113–44.
——, 'Introduction', in David Fitzpatrick (ed.), *Terror in Ireland 1916–1923. Trinity History Workshop* (Dublin: Lilliput Press, 2012), pp. 1–9.
——, *Politics and Irish Life 1913–1921. Provincial Experience of War and Revolution* (Dublin: Gill and Macmillan, 1977; reprint; Cork: Cork University Press, 1998).
Gallagher, John A., *Time Past, Time Future. An Historical Study of Catholic Moral Theology* (New York and Mahwah, NJ: Paulist Press, 1990).
Gay, Oonagh, 'The *House of Commons (Removal of Clergy Disqualification) Bill*. Bill 34 of 2000–01', House of Commons Library Research Paper 01/11, 26 January 2001, www.parliament.uk/documents/commons/lib/research/rp2001/rp01–011.pdf (accessed 26 August 2010).
Gellner, Ernest, *Nations and Nationalism* (2nd edn; Ithaca, NY: Cornell University Press, 2008).
Gilley, Sheridan, 'The Catholic church and revolution', in D. G. Boyce (ed.), *The Revolution in Ireland, 1879–1923* (Dublin: Gill and Macmillan, 1988), pp. 157–72.
Grant, James, *One Hundred Years with the Clonard Redemptorists* (Blackrock: Columba Press, 2003).
Gribling, J. P., *Willem Hubert Nolens 1860–1931. Uit het Leven van een Priester-Staatsman* (Assen: Van Gorcum, 1978).
Hanley, Brian, 'Terror in twentieth-century Ireland', in David Fitzpatrick (ed.), *Terror in Ireland 1916–1923. Trinity History Workshop* (Dublin: Lilliput Press, 2012), pp. 10–25.
Haquin, André, 'The liturgical movement and Catholic ritual revision', in Geoffrey Wainwright and Karen B. Westerfield Tucker (eds), *The Oxford History of Christian Worship* (Oxford and New York: Oxford University Press, 2006), pp. 696–720.
Harris, Mary, *The Catholic Church and the Foundation of the Northern Irish State* (Cork: Cork University Press, 1993).
——, 'The Catholic church from Parnell to partition', in Brendan Bradshaw and Dáire Keogh (eds), *Christianity in Ireland. Revisiting the Story* (Blackrock: Columba Press, 2002), pp. 205–19.
Hart, Peter, 'Definition. Defining the Irish revolution', in Joost Augusteijn

(ed.), *The Irish Revolution, 1913–1923* (Basingstoke: Palgrave, 2002), pp. 17–33.

——, 'The geography of revolution in Ireland 1917–1923', *Past and Present*, 155 (1997), pp. 147–54.

——, *The I.R.A. and its Enemies. Violence and Community in Cork, 1916–1923* (Oxford: Oxford University Press, 1998).

——, *The I.R.A. at War 1916–1923* (Oxford: Oxford University Press, 2003).

Heffernan, Brian, '"It is for a nation of martyrs to cultivate constant self-restraint." The Irish Catholic bishops' attitude to the IRA campaign, 1919–21', *Leidschrift. Historisch Tijdschrift*, 23:1 (2008), pp. 151–69.

Hobsbawm, E. J., *Nations and Nationalism since 1780. Programme, Myth, Reality* (2nd edn; Cambridge: Cambridge University Press, 1992).

Hopkinson, Michael, *The Irish War of Independence* (Dublin: Gill and Macmillan, 2004).

——, 'Negotiation. The Anglo-Irish War and the revolution', in Joost Augusteijn (ed.), *The Irish Revolution, 1913–1923* (Basingstoke: Palgrave, 2002), pp. 121–34.

——, 'The peace mission of Archbishop Clune', in Laurence M. Geary and Andrew J. McCarthy (eds), *Ireland, Australia and New Zealand. History, Politics and Culture* (Dublin: Irish Academic Press, 2008), pp. 199–210.

Hughes, Brian, 'Persecuting the Peelers', in David Fitzpatrick (ed.), *Terror in Ireland 1916–1923. Trinity History Workshop* (Dublin: Lilliput Press, 2012), pp. 206–18.

Joy, Sinéad, *The IRA in Kerry 1916–1921* (Cork: Collins Press, 2005).

Kautt, W. H., *Ambushes and Armour. The Irish Rebellion, 1919–1921* (Dublin and Portland, OR: Irish Academic Press, 2010).

Kearns, Raé, 'Republican justice in Meath 1919–1922', *Ríocht na Midhe. Records of Meath Archaeological and Historical Society*, 9:2 (1996), pp. 154–63.

Kee, Robert, *The Green Flag. A History of Irish Nationalism* (London: Penguin, 2000).

Kenneally, Ian, *The Paper Wall. Newspapers and Propaganda in Ireland 1919–1921* (Cork: Collins Press, 2008).

Keogh, Dermot, *The Vatican, the Bishops and Irish Politics 1919–39* (Cambridge: Cambridge University Press, 1986).

Kotsonouris, Mary, 'The courts of Dáil Éireann', in Brian Farrell (ed.), *The Creation of the Dáil. A Volume of Essays from the Thomas Davis Lectures* (Dublin: Blackwater Press, 1994), pp. 91–106.

Laffan, Michael, *The Resurrection of Ireland. The Sinn Féin Party, 1916–1923* (Cambridge: Cambridge University Press, 1999).

Larkin, Emmet, *The Historical Dimensions of Irish Catholicism* (Washington,

DC, and Dublin: Catholic University of America Press and Four Courts Press, 1984).

——, 'The parish mission movement, 1850–80', in Brendan Bradshaw and Dáire Keogh (eds), *Christianity in Ireland. Revisiting the Story* (Blackrock: Columba Press, 2002), pp. 195–204.

——, *The Roman Catholic Church and the Emergence of the Modern Irish Political System, 1874–1878* (Dublin and Washington, DC: Four Courts Press and Catholic University of America Press, 1996).

Leeson, D. M., *The Black and Tans. British Police and Auxiliaries in the Irish War of Independence, 1920–1921* (Oxford: Oxford University Press, 2011).

Lowe, W. J., 'The war against the R.I.C., 1919–21', *Éire-Ireland. An Interdisciplinary Journal of Irish Studies*, 37:3–4 (2002), pp. 79–117.

MacCarthy, Carthach, *Archdeacon Tom Duggan in Peace and in War* (Tallaght: Blackwater Press, 1994).

McDowell, R. B., 'Administration and the public services, 1870–1921', in W. E. Vaughan (ed.), *A New History of Ireland*, vi: *Ireland under the Union, II* (Oxford: Oxford University Press, 1996), pp. 571–605.

McGrath, Andrew, 'The Anglo-Irish War (1919–1921). Just war or unjust rebellion?', *Irish Theological Quarterly*, 77:1 (2012), pp. 67–82.

Maguire, George, 'Mayo and Sligo – 1920', *The Capuchin Annual* (1970), pp. 396–9.

Martin, F. X., 'Fr. Joseph Hennessy, O.S.A. The patriot', *Limerick Souvenir* (1962), pp. 20–2.

Matthews, Ann, *Renegades. Irish Republican Women 1900–1922* (Dublin and Cork: Mercier Press, 2010).

Maume, Patrick, 'A pastoral vision. The novels of Canon Joseph Guinan', *New Hibernia Review*, 9:4 (2005), pp. 79–98.

Maye, Patrick, 'A short history of the I.R.A. in Islandeady, 1919–1921', *Cathair na Mart. Journal of the Westport Historical Society*, 15 (1995), pp. 106–9.

Mews, Stuart, 'The hunger-strike of the lord mayor of Cork, 1920. Irish, English and Vatican attitudes', in W. J. Sheils and Diana Wood (eds), *The Churches, Ireland and the Irish. Papers Read at the 1987 Summer Meeting and the 1988 Winter Meeting of the Ecclesiastical History Society* (Oxford and New York: Basil Blackwell, 1989), pp. 385–400.

Miller, David W., *Church, State and Nation in Ireland 1898–1921* (Dublin and Pittsburgh, PA: Gill and Macmillan and University of Pittsburgh Press, 1973).

Millett, Benignus, and C. J. Woods, 'Roman Catholic bishops from 1534', in T. W. Moody, F. X. Martin and F. J. Byrne (eds), *A New History of Ireland*, ix: *Maps, Genealogies, Lists. A Companion to Irish History, II* (Oxford: Clarendon Press, 1984), pp. 333–91.

Mitchell, Arthur, *Revolutionary Government in Ireland. Dáil Éireann 1919–22* (Dublin: Gill and Macmillan, 1995).
Morrissey, Thomas J., *William J. Walsh. Archbishop of Dublin, 1841–1921. No Uncertain Voice* (Dublin: Four Courts Press, 2000).
Mulryan, Maureen, 'Bishop Hoare and politics', *Teathba. Journal of County Longford Historical Society*, 3:2 (2007), pp. 32–5.
Murphy, Brian P., *The Catholic Bulletin and Republican Ireland with Special Reference to J. J. O'Kelly ('Sceilg')* (Belfast and London: Athol Books, 2005).
——, 'J. J. O'Kelly, the Catholic Bulletin and contemporary Irish cultural historians', *Archivium Hibernicum*, 44 (1989), pp. 71–88.
Murphy, John A., 'O'Rahilly, Alfred', in James McGuire et al. (eds), *Dictionary of Irish Biography from the Earliest Times to the Year 2002* (Cambridge and Dublin: Cambridge University Press, 2009), vii, pp. 825–6.
——, 'Priests and people in modern history', *Christus Rex. Journal of Sociology*, 23:4 (1969), pp. 235–59.
Murray, Patrick, *Oracles of God. The Roman Catholic Church and Irish Politics, 1922–37* (Dublin: University College Dublin Press, 2000).
Newman, Jeremiah, 'The priests of Ireland. A socio-religious survey. I. Numbers and distribution', *The Irish Ecclesiastical Record*, 98 (1962), pp. 1–27.
Newsinger, John, '"I bring not peace but a sword". The religious motif in the Irish War of Independence', *Journal of Contemporary History*, 13 (1978), pp. 609–28.
Norman, E. R., *The Catholic Church and Ireland in the Age of Rebellion 1859–1873* (Ithaca, NY: Cornell University Press, 1965).
Ó Buachalla, Séamas, *Education Policy in Twentieth Century Ireland* (Dublin: Wolfhound Press, 1988).
O'Callaghan, Edward P., 'Correspondence between Bishop O'Dwyer and Bishop Foley on the Dublin rising, 1916–17', *Collectanea Hibernica*, 18–19 (1976–77), pp. 184–212.
O'Donovan, Donal, *The Murder of Canon Magner and Tadhg O'Crowley* (n.p., 2005).
O'Farrell, Padraic, *Who's Who in the Irish War of Independence and Civil War 1916–1923* (Dublin: Lilliput Press, 1997).
Ó Fiaich, Tomás, 'The Catholic clergy and the independence movement', *The Capuchin Annual* (1970), pp. 480–502.
Ó Haichir, Aodh, *A Rebel Churchman. Very Rev. Canon William O'Kennedy, B. D., St. Flannan's, Ennis* (Tralee: The Kerryman, 1962).
O'Halpin, Eunan, 'Counting terror. Bloody Sunday and *The dead of the Irish revolution*', in David Fitzpatrick (ed.), *Terror in Ireland 1916–1923. Trinity History Workshop* (Dublin: Lilliput Press, 2012), pp. 141–57.

Ó Laoi, Pádraic, *Fr. Griffin 1892–1920* (n.p.: Connacht Tribune, 1994).
Ortolan, T., 'Confession. Questions morales et pratiques', in A. Vacant, E. Mangenot and É. Amann (eds), *Dictionnaire de théologie catholique contenant l'exposé des doctrines de la théologie catholique, leurs preuves et leur histoire*, iii:1 (Paris: Letouzey et Ané, 1938), pp. 942–60.
——, 'Guerre', in A. Vacant, E. Mangenot and É. Amann (eds), *Dictionnaire de théologie catholique contenant l'exposé des doctrines de la théologie catholique, leurs preuves et leur histoire*, vi:2 (Paris: Letouzey et Ané, 1947), pp. 1899–962.
O'Shea, James, *Priest, Politics and Society in Post-Famine Ireland. A Study of County Tipperary 1850–1891* (Dublin and Atlantic Highlands, NJ: Wolfhound Press, 1983).
Patterson, Tony, 'Third Tipperary Brigade, number two flying column, January to June 1921', *Tipperary Historical Journal* (2006), pp. 189–206.
Pollard, John F., *Benedict XV. The Unknown Pope and the Pursuit of Peace* (London and New York: Continuum, 2005).
Privilege, John, *Michael Logue and the Catholic Church in Ireland, 1879–1925* (Manchester and New York: Manchester University Press, 2009).
Raedts, Peter, 'The church as nation state. A new look at ultramontane Catholicism (1850–1900)', *Dutch Review of Church History*, 84 (2004), pp. 476–96.
Rushe, John, 'The martyr boy priest. Father Michael Griffin', *Vexilla Regis. Maynooth's Laymen's Annual*, 9 (1961–62), pp. 60–72.
Ryan, Annie, *Comrades. Inside the War of Independence* (Dublin: Liberties Press, 2007).
Ryan, Thomas, 'One man's flying column', *Tipperary Historical Journal* (1991), pp. 19–34.
Ryle Dwyer, T., *Tans, Terror and Troubles. Kerry's Real Fighting Story 1913–23* (Cork and Dublin: Mercier Press, 2001).
Sherry, Richard, *Holy Cross College, Clonliffe, Dublin, 1859–1959. College History and Centenary Record* (Dublin: Holy Cross College, 1962).
Sievernich, Michael, *Schuld und Sünde in der Theologie der Gegenwart* (Frankfurt am Main: Knecht, 1982).
Taylor, Lawrence J., 'Bás i-nÉirinn. Cultural constructions of death in Ireland', *Anthropological Quarterly*, 62:4 (1989), pp. 175–87.
——, *Occasions of Faith. An Anthropology of Irish Catholics* (Dublin: Lilliput Press, 1995).
Titley, E. Brian, *Church, State, and the Control of Schooling in Ireland 1900–1944* (Kingston, Montreal and Dublin: McGill-Queen's University Press and Gill and Macmillan, 1983).
Townshend, Charles, *The British Campaign in Ireland, 1919–21. The Development of Political and Military Policies* (Oxford: Oxford University Press, 1975).

———, 'The Irish Republican Army and the development of guerrilla warfare, 1916–1921', *The English Historical Review*, 94:371 (1979), pp. 318–45.

———, *Political Violence in Ireland. Government and Resistance since 1848* (Oxford: Clarendon Press, 1983).

Travers, Pauric, 'The priest in politics. The case of conscription', in Oliver MacDonagh, W. F. Mandle and Pauric Travers (eds), *Irish Culture and Nationalism, 1750–1950* (London, Basingstoke and Canberra: The Macmillan Press and Humanities Research Centre, Australian National University, 1983), pp. 161–81.

Waldron, Kieran, *The Archbishops of Tuam 1700–2000* (Tuam: Nordlaw Books, 2008).

Whyte, John H., 'Political problems, 1850–1860', in Patrick J. Corish (ed.), *A History of Irish Catholicism*, v (Dublin and Melbourne: Gill, 1967), pp. 1–40.

Wiel, Jérôme aan de, *The Catholic Church in Ireland 1914–1918. War and Politics* (Dublin and Portland, OR: Irish Academic Press, 2003).

———, 'Monsignor O'Riordan, Bishop O'Dwyer and the shaping of new relations between nationalist Ireland and the Vatican during World War One', *Archivium Hibernicum*, 53 (1999), pp. 95–106.

Williams, Tom, 'Fr. Patrick Walsh – the republican priest', *The Journal of the Taghmon Historical Society*, 4 (2001), pp. 13–22.

Index

Note: 'n.' after a page reference indicates the number of a note on that page.

Ambrose, Robert, PP Glenroe 67–8
Anglo-Irish treaty (6 December 1921) 33, 130, 240
Anglo-Irish truce (11 July 1921) 6, 85, 139
anti-conscription campaign (1918) 3, 16, 28, 98–100, 166, 209
Antrim 89–90, 146
Armagh
  county 49
  town 90, 149
arms and/or ammunition
  in possession of clerics 69–70, 128, 143–8, 156, 184, 223
  stored for IRA by clerics 122, 124, 126, 145–6
  supplied to IRA by clerics 117, 146–8
army, British 50, 213, 231
  arrests clerics 102, 105, 183–9
  asks bishops to discipline priests 15–16, 149
  Catholic members of 63n.109, 200
  chaplains *see* army chaplains
  clerical criticism of 120, 204–5, 209, 213
  at funerals of republicans 114, 136
  protects clerics 112
  raids ecclesiastical buildings 146, 204–5, 214
  relatives of clerics serve in 17
  reprisals 209
  respect for clerical state 188
  responsibility for killing Redemptorist 191
  violence against clerics 192, 200
  see also crown forces; violence by/ascribed to crown forces
army chaplains 17–18, 115, 118, 213, 223–4
arrests of clerics 102, 118, 142, 144–5, 156–8, 165, 179–80, 183–9, 202, 224, 245
  see also prosecution of clerics
Aughagower 72, 135, 163–4
Augusteijn, Joost 3, 27, 48, 53, 66, 138, 140, 145
Augustinians 24, 111, 160, 163
Auxiliaries 50, 61–3, 72, 102, 106, 113, 122, 141, 162, 166–7, 179, 181, 183, 189–90, 194–5, 197–8, 211–12, 214, 219, 224, 245
  see also Black and Tans; crown forces; Royal Irish Constabulary; violence by/ascribed to crown forces

Balbriggan 57, 233–4
Ballina 77
Ballinalee 157
Ballinasloe 101–2, 106, 118, 191

Ballyhahill 129, 142, 147
Barry, Kevin 119–20
Barry, Tom 5, 91–2, 173
Belfast 53, 89–90, 101, 112, 120, 144, 146, 191, 217, 235
Belfast boycott 89, 120
Belvedere College, Dublin 163
Benedictines 143, 161
Benedict XV, Pope 15, 152, 208, 232
Bew, Paul 17, 26, 60
Bibby, Albert, OSFC 129–30, 139, 150, 186–7
bishops 4, 9
  and anti-conscription campaign 16
  and British government 3, 64, 151, 154, 156, 188, 214–19, 235–9
  call for reparation 58–60
  and chaplains to Irish Volunteers 127
  condemn republican violence 35, 47–8, 58–61, 110, 155–6, 242
  condemn violence by crown forces 61, 64, 170, 208–19
  and Easter rising 15
  and excommunication 63–4, 175
  and government requests to discipline priests 15–16, 154–6
  and legitimacy of Irish Free State 7, 240
  pastoral letters 61, 208, 210–11, 214–15, 242
  propaganda campaign 216–17
  and republican priests 151, 154–61, 169
  republican sympathies 158–9, 168
  and Sinn Féin 16, 64, 155
  suspend priests 154, 157, 159–60
  treatment by crown forces 196–7, 218–19
Black and Tans 21, 50, 61, 67, 72, 102, 106, 112, 122, 136, 139, 142, 166, 179–81, 189–92, 196, 201–2, 211–12, 214, 217, 219, 221, 224, 230–1, 241–2, 245
  see also Auxiliaries; crown forces; Royal Irish Constabulary; violence by/ascribed to crown forces
Blackrock College 182
Bloody Sunday (21 November 1920) 61–2
Borgonovo, John 127–8
Boyle, Patrick, CM, rector Irish College, Paris 25, 27, 30, 32–3
Breen, Dan 92, 129, 142, 149, 190
Brennan, Malachy, CC Ballinasloe 102, 106, 118, 191
Brennan, Michael 110, 131–2
Brennan, Patrick, CC Castleisland 66, 68, 221
Browne, James, bishop of Ferns 155–6
Browne, Robert, bishop of Cloyne 64, 113, 209, 230, 234
B Specials *see* Ulster Special Constabulary
Burbage, Thomas, CC Geashill 158
Bureau of Military History 10, 66, 123–5, 129, 132–3, 138, 148, 175, 242
Byrne, Edward, auxiliary bishop of Dublin 220–1
Byrne, Eugene Canon, PP Balbriggan 57, 233–4

Callan 66–7, 117, 147
Candy, Catherine 241
canon law 41–2, 45–6, 60, 63, 106–7, 130–2, 152–4, 174
Capuchin Annual 5, 243
Capuchins 126–7, 129–30, 145–6, 150, 160, 182, 186–7
Carlow
  county 100, 103, 126, 143, 231
  town 55, 231
Carmelites 99, 137, 146, 160, 182
Carney, Michael, CC Cong 105, 157, 182
Carroll, Joseph, CC Fedamore 126, 128

Cashel 54, 81, 112, 182–3
Cashel and Emly diocese 183
Castleisland 66–8, 221
Catholic Bulletin and Book Review
   10–11, 20, 74
Cavan 56, 58, 88
censorship 20, 36, 37
church buildings 20, 59–60, 69, 87,
   89–90, 99, 112, 131–2, 145–6,
   180–1, 204–7
Cistercians *see* Trappists
civil disobedience 213–14
Civil War (1922–23) 7, 33–4, 130,
   175, 240–2
Clare 31, 48, 57, 70, 89, 101, 104,
   107–8, 110, 115–17, 120, 127,
   131–3, 136, 144, 190–1, 205,
   213, 222–4, 230
Clogher diocese 158
Clonard monastery, Belfast 90–1,
   101, 190–1, 235
Clonfert diocese 100, 193
Clonliffe, Holy Cross College, 25,
   172, 174
Cloyne diocese 64, 91
Clune, Patrick, CSsR, archbishop of
   Perth 192, 227
Codd, William, bishop of Ferns 106,
   161
Cohalan, Daniel, bishop of Cork
   226, 234
  and anti-conscription campaign
     fund 100
  calls for reparation 59
  condemns republican violence 60,
     63, 82
  condemns violence by crown
     forces 199, 211
  criticises O'Rahilly 171
  excommunication decree
     (December 1920) 63–4,
     74–5, 82–3, 91–2, 113, 128,
     175, 241
  and Kilmichael ambush 62–3
  and MacCurtain killing 211
  and Magner killing 199
  and O'Callaghan killing 201–2
  and republican courts 108

  says republic is unattainable
     31–2, 62
  stopped on road by crown forces
     218
  supports Sinn Féin 31, 64,
     108–9
  and Terence MacSwiney 62, 214
Collins, Hyacinth, OP 72–3, 162–3,
   223–4, 230
Collins, Michael 61, 72, 101, 103,
   167, 186
communion 51, 123, 130–3, 136,
   204–6
confession 49, 51–2, 77, 123,
   128–36, 138–9, 143, 163, 195,
   204–7, 222
Corbett, C. W. Canon, PP Mallow
   229, 235
Cork
  city 62–3, 82, 92, 109, 114,
     127–8, 147–8, 170–1, 199,
     201–2, 211, 214, 234
  county 28, 40, 49, 57, 59–61,
     63–4, 67, 71, 74, 87, 91–2,
     109, 111, 113–14, 118, 125,
     137, 149, 166, 175, 181,
     188, 197, 199–200, 202, 209,
     218–19, 226, 228–32
  diocese 63, 91–2, 113, 234
Corkery, Pádraig 83
Cosgrave, William 103
Coyle, Eugene, CC Clontibret 158,
   184n.20, 187–8
Coyne, Bernard, bishop of Elphin
   154
Crehan, Bernard, CC Grange 196,
   202
Crescent College, Limerick 27, 144,
   162–3, 182
criticism of the clergy 22–4, 32–3,
   73–7, 151, 166–9
crown forces 8–9, 187, 231
  clerics act as informers for 72–3,
     163, 221–5
  clerics incite/accused of inciting
     to violence against 66, 128,
     159, 163–6, 190, 196–7, 200,
     202–3, 219

crown forces (*cont.*)
  clerics minister to 192, 200, 219–21
  'persecution' of Catholics 179–80, 186, 189, 196, 203–4, 207, 214–15, 218, 226, 231, 241, 245
  raid ecclesiastical buildings 144–6, 162, 179–83, 204–6, 214, 245
  sacrilege 180, 203–7, 241–2
  suspect clerics of aiding IRA 130, 144, 146–7, 157, 166–7, 179, 183, 190–2, 195–6, 200, 202–3, 245
  see also army, British; arrests of clerics; Auxiliaries; Black and Tans; prosecution of clerics; Royal Irish Constabulary; violence by/ascribed to crown forces
Crozier, General Frank 194, 197
curates *see* parish priests and curates
Curran, Michael, secretary Archbishop Walsh, vice-rector Irish College, Rome 24, 27, 32–3, 147, 156, 165
curse, curses 37, 44–5, 55–8

Dáil Éireann 19–20, 33, 74, 83–4, 89, 100–1, 103, 105, 107, 120, 174, 201, 238–40
Dáil loan 100–1
Daly, Cahal Cardinal, archbishop of Armagh 243
Davis, Peter, PP Rahoon 194, 196
Deasy, Liam 137, 175
death, preparation for 44, 50–2, 130–1, 134
  see also last rites
Defence of the Realm Act (1914) 36, 102
Delahunty, Patrick, CC Callan 117, 147, 184n.21, 186
Delaney, William, SJ 30, 102
Derry
  city 93, 182, 227–8, 233
  county 30, 93, 206

de Valera, Éamon 30, 84, 103
Dominicans 18, 72–3, 162, 182, 223
Donegal 67, 93, 131, 140, 149
Donnelly, Stephen 77, 134–5
Down 111
Downing, Daniel Canon, PP St Joseph's, Dublin 119, 181, 236
Doyle, Patrick, CC Naas, rector Knockbeg College 103, 105, 143, 147
Dublin
  city 17–18, 22–5, 32–3, 40, 61–2, 78, 98–9, 103, 108–9, 119, 126–9, 137, 145–6, 149–50, 153, 160, 162–3, 167, 181–2, 205, 221, 233–4, 236
  county 30, 57, 78, 182–3, 213, 233
  diocese 24–5, 27, 41, 220
Dublin Castle administration 37–8, 76, 151, 154, 156, 158, 163, 188, 211–12, 215, 220–1, 235–40
Dublin Metropolitan Police 167
Duggan, Thomas, chaplain Cork 147–8
Dundalk 47, 82, 159
Dungarvan 118–19, 160, 181
Dunmanway 197–8
Dunmore 204–5, 241
Dunne, James Canon, PP Donnybrook 28–9, 33

Easter rising (1916) 6–7, 15, 77–8, 81, 97, 99, 118, 126, 154, 243
education 35, 235–9
elections 16, 18, 36, 98–9, 152, 154, 172, 201
Ennis 101, 133, 146, 159, 182, 188, 192, 197, 200
excommunication 63–4, 74–5, 82–3, 91–2, 113, 128, 131, 134, 174–5, 199, 240–1
extreme unction *see* last rites

female religious 182, 201
  see also women
Fermanagh 101, 105

INDEX

Fermoy 50, 57, 119, 209, 234
Ferns diocese 106
Ferriter, Diarmaid 10
First World War 5, 15, 18, 115, 196, 213
Fitzpatrick, David 17, 107
Fitzpatrick, John, professor Clonliffe College 172–3
Flatley, John, PP Aughagower 72, 163–4
Fogarty, Michael, bishop of Killaloe 242
  appoints chaplain to Irish Volunteers 127
  and bishops' propaganda campaign 216
  criticised for republican stance 168
  criticises non-republican clerics 32
  and excommunication 74
  and Irish Parliamentary Party 15
  life threatened 192, 197, 200
  and republican priests 159, 188–9
  republican views 158–9, 242
  residence attacked 197, 200
Foley, Patrick, bishop of Kildare and Leighlin 17, 55, 158
Freeman's Journal 11, 213
funerals 46, 63, 70, 112–14, 119, 136–7, 214, 217, 220, 243

Gaelic League 71
Gaelic revival 3, 26, 97
Galway
  city 50, 111, 118, 163, 191, 193–5, 205, 245
  county 27, 47, 54, 70, 84, 92, 99–102, 104, 106–7, 110, 125, 136, 140, 145, 149, 161, 179, 191, 195, 199, 202–4, 220, 222
  diocese 48, 193, 215
Gaughran, Laurence, bishop of Meath 26, 48, 211
Gaynor, Patrick, CC Mullagh 104, 107–8, 115–17, 119, 142, 144–5, 159, 164–5, 184n.21, 224–5, 232

Gearty, Dean Roderick, PP Strokestown 212, 220
Gilmartin, Thomas, archbishop of Tuam 29, 200, 205, 217, 220, 234
  calls for truce 228–9
  condemns republican violence 57–8, 84
  condemns sectarian violence 89
  condemns violence by crown forces 64
  criticised by MacNeill 74
  dispute with Macready 54
  on 'misgovernment' 170
  praises Volunteers 110
  on priests and politics 46
  and republican courts 106–7
  and republican priests 156–7, 164, 182
  supports dominion home rule 31–2
Gilmore, James, CC Kilmessan 139
Gleeson, John, PP Lorrha 25, 52, 55, 71, 75–6, 135, 167
Glynn, John, PP Mullagh 164–5, 232
Gorey 143, 161
Greenwood, Sir Hamar 88, 187, 199, 212, 215
Gregory XVI, Pope 172
Griffin, Michael, CC Rahoon
  canonisation contemplated 193
  effects of killing on clerical attitudes 62, 163, 179, 193, 195–6, 215–16, 218–19, 241, 245
  identity of killers 194–5
  impact of killing on public opinion 199, 202, 218, 241, 245
  killed 192–5
  killing overshadows Bloody Sunday 61–2
  links with IRA 195
  portrayed as martyr 193
  see also martyrs, clerics as
Griffith, Arthur 97, 102
Guinan, Joseph Canon 241–2

Hackett, Bernard, CSsR, bishop of Waterford and Lismore 25
Hackett, William, SJ 128, 144, 161–3
Hagan, John, rector Irish College, Rome 22–5, 27, 30, 32, 74, 98, 147, 156, 183
Hamilton, M. 133, 146
Hart, Peter 40, 73, 85, 125
Harty, John Mary, archbishop of Cashel and Emly 45, 85, 101, 109, 155, 170, 183, 192, 210–11, 216
Hayes, Patrick Canon, PP Ballylongford, PP Berehaven 110–11
Headford 125, 145, 229
Headley, R. M., OP 72–3
Hoare, Joseph, bishop of Ardagh and Clonmacnoise 19, 157–8
Hobbins, Thomas, CC Arklow 148–9
home rule 3, 5, 15–17, 26–7, 31–3, 81, 97
Hoolihan, Garry 149–50
hunger-strike 28, 62, 114, 127, 173–4, 186, 214
Hurley, John, CC Bantry 70–1

Irish Catholic 10–11, 38, 42, 67, 184, 207, 221
Irish College, Paris 18, 25, 28, 32–3
Irish College, Rome 18, 21–2, 24–5, 147, 156
Irish Ecclesiastical Record 107, 173–4
Irish Free State 33, 240
Irish Independent 11, 38, 42, 49, 62, 76, 105–6, 113, 139, 186, 191, 198, 205, 212, 218, 232
Irish language 27–8
Irish National Volunteers 15
Irish Parliamentary Party 3, 11, 15–16, 97, 244, 246
Irish republic 30–1
Irish Republican Army
  active and inactive units 110, 115, 127, 141
  'chaplains' to 123–4, 126–9, 244
  clerics as informers for 148–50, 195
  clerics as members 114–17, 126–9
  clerics attempt to thwart operations by 66–9, 73, 139–40, 148, 161, 221–3, 230–2
  clerics opposed to 17, 21, 31, 47, 72–3, 93, 97–8, 135, 140, 223–5
  clerics supportive of 77, 98, 109–17, 119–50, 155, 157, 160, 162, 175
  companies founded by clerics 110
  confiscates arms and/or ammunition from clerics 69–70, 143–4
  courts *see* republican courts and Dáil Éireann 84
  Dublin brigade 149
  East Clare brigade 131, 136
  East Limerick brigade 147
  flying columns 73, 110, 122, 126–7, 130–1, 133, 140–1, 157
  GHQ 8, 68, 117, 147, 149
  impact on of clerical condemnation 91–3, 174–6
  impact on of clerical support 145, 147, 174–6
  intimidation of clerics by 65, 70–3
  Kilkenny brigade 66, 117
  Meath brigade 137
  members executed 119, 234
  members given shelter by clerics 140–3, 183
  members on the run 140–1
  members refused funerals 70, 113
  members use clerical garb as disguise 190
  Mid Clare brigade 133
  Mid Cork brigade 91, 126–7, 133
  Mid Limerick brigade 126
  Mid Tipperary brigade 112
  North Cork brigade 91
  North Kerry brigade 72, 132
  North Mayo brigade 68–9
  North Roscommon brigade 69
  North Tipperary brigade 117

policing duties 111–12, 114–16
protects clerics 111, 190
radicalisation 3–4, 48, 98, 103, 110, 117, 121–2, 127, 141, 244
religiosity of members 91, 154
requests clerical presence at killing of 'spies' 138–40, 195
respects clerical status 72–3, 222
role in parishes 109–14, 244
selects suitable clerical collaborators 77, 130–1, 134–5, 137, 140
South Tipperary brigade 43, 73, 132–3
spiritual support for 122–4, 126–40, 160, 164, 244
Waterford brigade 142–3, 160
West Connemara brigade 84, 133, 135
West Cork brigade 61, 92
West Limerick brigade 129
West Mayo brigade 72
see also Irish Volunteers; violence by republicans
Irish Theological Quarterly 170, 173–4
Irish Times 11
Irish Volunteers 4, 8, 48, 110, 126–7, 155, 194
see also Irish National Volunteers; Irish Republican Army
Irish White Cross 232–3

Jesuits 27, 98, 161–3, 168–9, 182, 220–1
Joy, Sinéad 92
just war *see* theology

Kautt, W. H. 67
Kelly, Denis, bishop of Ross
condemns republican violence 30, 58, 82
condemns sectarian violence 86
criticised by republicans 20, 74
criticises republican clerics 25, 32–3
and excommunication 64
experience of revolution in Paris 28
opposition to Sinn Féin 18–19, 25, 27–8, 30–3
Kelly, Michael, archbishop of Sydney 32, 109
Kelly, Patrick, CC Dunboyne 137–8
Kenneally, Ian 37
Keogh, Dermot 21, 85
Keohane, Patrick 22, 24, 27, 33
Kerry
county 53, 66, 69, 72, 75, 92, 106, 110, 129, 132, 139, 162, 175, 190, 221, 224, 227, 230, 237–9
diocese 166, 237–9
Kilfinane 67, 108, 126, 231
Kilkenny 66, 117, 141
Kilkenny, Archdeacon Patrick, PP Claremorris 106–7
Killaloe diocese 32, 104, 159, 168, 188, 216, 224–5
Kilmichael ambush (28 November 1920) 61–3, 137
Kinane, Jeremiah, professor Maynooth College 107, 174
King's County 29, 67, 75–6, 86, 158, 191
Knockbeg College 103, 105, 143
Knocklong 155

Laffan, Michael 104–5
Langan, Thomas Canon, PP Moate 141, 143
last rites 44, 50–2, 60, 192, 200, 235
see also death, preparation for
Leahy, James 112, 192
Lee, John, PP Kilfinane 108, 231
Leeson, D. M. 50, 189, 203, 212
Leitrim 58, 87, 118, 235
Leo XIII, Pope 172–3
Limerick
city 27, 119, 128, 144, 163, 165, 182, 224, 229
county 18, 67, 71, 101, 108–9, 113, 126, 129, 136, 155, 160, 165, 212

Logue, Michael Cardinal,
  archbishop of Armagh 214
  and Bloody Sunday 62
  and British authorities 138, 212
  condemns republican violence 47,
    82, 159
  condemns sectarian violence 90
  criticises B Specials 212
  criticises Sinn Féin 20–1
  criticises young men who join
    IRA 21
  experience of revolution in Paris
    28
  and lay criticism of the clergy
    168–9
  relief work 232–3
  stopped on road by crown forces
    218–19
Londonderry *see* Derry
Longford 16, 40, 125, 157
Lorrha 25, 49, 52, 55, 71, 75–6,
  135, 167
Loughrea 195
Louth 23, 26, 144
Lynch, Liam 91

McCarthy, Florence, Adm.
  Skibbereen 57, 87, 228
McCarthy, Richard, CC Ballyhahill
  129, 142, 147
McDonald, Walter, professor
  Maynooth College 26, 80–1,
  159, 173
MacEoin, Seán 5, 157
McGrath, Andrew 79
McHugh, Charles, bishop of Derry
  233
MacHugh, Patrick, CC Aughagower
  135, 163–4
Macken, Dean Thomas, PP
  Dunmore 204–5
McKenna, Michael, CC Mullagh
  115, 119, 142, 159, 184n.21,
  205
McKenna, Patrick, bishop of
  Clogher 158, 188
McLoughlin, Paul, PP Islandeady
  136–7

MacNeill, Eoin 74, 102–3
Macpherson, Ian 236, 238
Macready, Sir Nevil 54, 138, 183,
  212
MacRory, Joseph, bishop of Down
  and Connor 53, 197, 217
McSweeney, Eugene, CC Fairview
  126
MacSwiney, Mary 74–5, 214
MacSwiney, Terence 28, 62, 74,
  120, 127, 159, 186, 214, 224
Macroom 62, 198, 209
Magee, John, PP Tober 76, 141
Magner, Thomas Canon, PP
  Dunmanway 197–202, 241
Maguire, John, CC Tulla 224–5
Markey, Patrick, PP Ballinalee 157,
  160, 184n.21
Martin, Diarmuid, archbishop of
  Dublin 243
martyrs, clerics as 186, 189, 192–3,
  218, 226, 241, 245
  see also Griffin, Michael; publicity;
    sectarianism
mass *see* communion
Maume, Patrick 241
Maxwell, General John 16, 155, 194
Maynooth
  First Synod of (1875) 153
  St Patrick's College 5, 26, 32,
    80–1, 97, 107, 159, 169, 183,
    193, 214
  Second Synod of (1900) 153–4
Mayo 24, 32, 46, 68–9, 72, 77, 85,
  105, 134–5, 145, 156–7, 163,
  182, 184, 200, 220, 222
Meath
  county 21, 48, 88, 105, 126,
    137–9, 142, 170, 211, 229
  diocese 211
Meehan, John, CC Castlebar 156–7,
  184n.21
Miller, David W. 3, 16, 35, 239
modernism 159
Monaghan 65, 158
morality 20, 28, 36, 45–6, 51,
  55–61, 65, 74, 76–84, 92–3,
  108, 116–17, 119, 128, 130–5,

138, 140, 163, 167–74, 176, 204, 208, 242–3
  see also theology; violence by/attributed to crown forces; violence by republicans
Morgan, Michael, CSsR 190–1, 193
Morley, Michael, CC Headford 145, 184n.21
Morning News 165
Morrisroe, Patrick, bishop of Achonry 31, 52, 64, 216
Mount Melleray Abbey 142–3, 160, 182
Mount St Benedict school 143
Mulcahy, Richard 162, 186
Mulhern, Edward, bishop of Dromore 98
Mullagh 104, 115, 142, 164, 205, 224, 232
Murray, Patrick 5, 7, 153–4, 175, 240

Naughton, James, bishop of Killala 77, 134
Newsinger, John 5
non-involvement by clerics 38, 226, 244
Northern Ireland 5, 240, 242–3
  see also Ulster
nuns see female religious

Oblates 103, 183
O'Callaghan, James, CC North Cathedral, Cork 201–2
Ó Ceallaigh, Sean T. 74
Ó Conbhuidhe, Colmcille, OCSO 243
O'Connell, Patrick, PP Enniskean 137, 175
O'Connor, Dominic, OSFC 126–8, 134, 159, 175, 186–7
O'Connor, Rory 143
O'Dea, Thomas, bishop of Galway, Kilmacduagh and Kilfenora
  and bishops' propaganda campaign 216
  calls for reparation 59
  condemns republican violence 48, 52, 59
  and Griffin killing 62, 194, 196, 200, 215
  life threatened 196, 215
  and republican clerics 194
O'Doherty, Thomas, bishop of Clonfert 100, 149, 193–5, 216–17
O'Donnell, Captain Thomas 118, 186
O'Donnell, Michael Canon, PP Rathkeale 18–19, 33, 55, 78
O'Donoghue, Florence 128, 134, 159
O'Donoghue, John, Adm. Fermoy 50, 57
O'Dwyer, Edward, bishop of Limerick 15–16, 154–6, 159
Offaly see King's County
Ó Fiaich, Tomás 5, 16, 60, 85, 97, 127, 181, 189, 218, 242–3
O'Flanagan, Michael, CC Roscommon 70, 100, 102–4, 144, 154, 159–60
O'Gorman, Canice, OSA 24, 33
O'Halpin, Eunan 202
O'Higgins, Kevin 103
O'Kennedy, William, president St Flannan's College 101, 188–9
O'Leary, Dean David, PP Tralee 53, 206–7
Omagh 120
O'Malley, Ernie 68, 91, 187, 222
O'Malley, Thomas, PP Partry 200, 203
O'Meehan, John, CC Rahoon 193–5
O'Rahilly, Alfred 170–3
Orange Order, Orangemen 89–91, 191, 212
O'Reilly, Patrick, CC Feakle 136, 191–2
O'Riordan, Michael, rector Irish College, Rome 18–19, 22, 24, 78
Ossory diocese 32

O'Sullivan, Charles, bishop of Kerry 75, 166, 237–9

papacy *see* Vatican; Benedict XV, Pope
parish missions 46, 135, 161
parish priests and curates 41–3, 76, 124–5, 151, 154, 163–5, 244
peacekeeping 113–14, 226–32
penance *see* confession
Pius IX, Pope 172
Pius X, Pope 45, 159, 204
politics, priests in 46, 151–5, 237–9
press 36–40, 42–3, 45, 71–2, 93, 124, 159, 165
  see also Catholic Bulletin and Book Review; Freeman's Journal; Irish Catholic; Irish Independent; Irish Times; propaganda; publicity
Privilege, John 219
propaganda 37–8, 76, 93, 214, 216
  see also press; publicity
prosecution of clerics 118–19, 138, 142, 144–5, 156, 158, 182–9, 224–5, 245
  see also arrests of clerics
Protestants, Protestantism 5, 9, 11, 85–90, 111, 218, 221n.53, 246
  see also Orange Order; sectarianism
publicity 93, 159, 165–6, 180, 183, 186, 189, 199, 202, 205–6, 214, 216, 218–19, 226, 245
  see also martyrs, clerics as; press; propaganda

Redemptorists 90–1, 99, 101, 135, 161, 169, 190–1, 235
Redmond, John 15, 18
relief work 232–5
religious clerics 24, 27, 98–9, 101, 128, 142–3, 145–6, 151, 160–3, 182
  see also Augustinians; Benedictines; Capuchins; Carmelites; Dominicans; female religious; Jesuits; Oblates; Redemptorists; Trappists

reparation 58–60
republican courts 105–9, 115–16
Restoration of Order in Ireland Act (1920) 36
Rockwell College, Cashel 182
Roscommon 69, 102–3, 138, 144, 181, 206–7, 212, 216
Ross diocese 18, 64
Royal Irish Constabulary 39, 132, 165, 183
  Catholic members 4, 45, 49–50, 190, 208, 211–12, 221, 244–5
  clerical condemnation of 210–11
  condemnation of attacks against 44–50, 55–60, 65, 135, 159, 211–12, 215, 220
  contrasted with Black and Tans and Auxiliaries 50, 208, 211–12, 214–15, 219, 221, 244–5
  ostracism 48, 190, 245
  relations with clerics 179, 189–90, 199, 210, 220, 244
  surveillance of republican clerics 99, 102, 157
  unable to protect clerics 111
  violence against clerics 189–90
  see also Auxiliaries; Black and Tans; crown forces; violence by/ ascribed to crown forces
Ryan, Dean Innocent, PP Cashel 54, 81–2, 112
Ryan, Michael K., CC Thurles 46, 58
Ryan, P., CC Bournea 197, 203

St Columb's College, Derry 182
St Flannan's College, Ennis 101, 133, 146, 182, 188
St Malachy's College, Belfast 144, 183
St Mary's College, Rathmines 182
St Patrick's College, Maynooth *see* Maynooth
St Patrick's College, Thurles 183
scandal 131–2, 151, 155–6, 167–8
secret societies 3, 17, 19, 77, 99, 167, 174

sectarianism 85–91, 180, 186, 189,
    191, 196, 207, 227, 245
  see also martyrs, clerics as;
    Protestants, Protestantism
sedition 118–21, 156, 185, 187, 224
sermons 37–8, 43, 45–7, 49, 65,
    71–2, 92–3, 132, 141, 155,
    162, 166, 168, 196, 203,
    219–20, 229, 238, 243
sin see morality
Sinn Féin 38
  aeridheachta 71, 102, 227
  canvasses clerical vote 98–9
  clerical opposition to 16–34, 70,
    78
  clerical support for 21–3, 25,
    33–4, 42, 66, 71, 97–121, 151,
    155–7, 160–1, 165, 174, 190,
    196, 199, 203, 221–2, 244
  clerics as party officials 103–5,
    160–1, 163
  contrasted with IRA 70–1, 97–8
  election victory 3–4, 17–18, 31,
    36, 155
  holds meetings near church
    buildings 20, 99
  officials seek shelter with clerics
    103, 143
  proscribed 102, 120
  see also republican courts
Skibbereen 19, 57–8, 86–7, 228
Slattery, James, CC Annascaul 132,
    144
Slattery, John, Adm. Soloheadbeg
    21, 43–4
Sligo 31, 125, 141, 196, 211, 216
Soloheadbeg ambush (21 January
    1919) 6, 18, 21, 43–5, 61,
    77–8, 210, 215, 241
spies and informers 87, 132, 135,
    138–40, 163, 195, 221–5
Strokestown 212, 220
Sullivan, A. M. 167–8, 232
Swanlinbar 56, 88
Swan, William, CC Moynalty 126,
    129, 140
Sweetman, Dom Francis, OSB 143,
    161

Terenure College 103, 146, 182
theology 4, 9, 28, 41, 46, 51, 56–7,
    65, 77–84, 86, 128, 130, 134,
    163, 168–74
  see also morality
Thurles 44, 46, 56, 58, 112, 183,
    192, 210, 227
Tipperary
  county 18, 25, 29, 35, 40, 43–5,
    49, 73, 92, 100, 104, 112, 117,
    125, 132, 133, 139, 145, 166,
    192, 197, 215, 222, 227
  town 44, 78
Tobercurry 31, 52, 211, 216
Townshend, Charles 7, 140
Tralee 53, 72, 75, 162, 168, 206–7,
    223–4, 230
Trappists 142, 243
treaty, Anglo-Irish see Anglo-Irish
    treaty
truce, Anglo Irish see Anglo-Irish
    truce
Tuam
  diocese 24, 216, 228
  town 27, 54, 57, 74, 89, 217,
    228–9
Tyrone 70, 120

Ulster 15, 26, 34, 81, 85, 89–90,
    104, 111, 181, 212, 215,
    227–8, 240
  see also Northern Ireland
Ulster Special Constabulary 111,
    181, 206, 212, 215, 218
unionists 5, 15, 26, 81, 89, 165–6,
    213, 237, 240, 246

Vatican 22, 151–2, 156, 166, 220
  see also Benedict XV, Pope
violence by/ascribed to crown
  forces
  against clerics 179–80, 184, 187,
    189–203, 245
  clerical cooperation in 221–5
  clerics killed 190–5, 197–9,
    201–3, 245
  clerics urge restraint in response
    to 195–6

violence by/ascribed to crown forces (*cont.*)
    condemned by clerics 47, 54, 170, 179, 195–6, 208–19, 226, 245
    death threats against clerics 163, 190, 192, 194, 196–7, 200
    effects on clerical attitudes 16, 30, 40, 60–1, 125, 196, 208, 215, 244–5
    geographical distribution 199, 203
    see also army, British; Auxiliaries; Black and Tans; crown forces; Royal Irish Constabulary
violence by republicans
    against civilians 138–40, 195
    breaks Fifth Commandment 47, 50
    causes loss of reputation for Ireland 26, 30, 44–5
    chronology 39–40, 125, 140–1
    clerical cooperation in 116, 122–5, 127–9, 147–8, 184, 244
    condemned by clerics 3, 18–19, 21, 25–7, 29–32, 35–65, 71, 74–7, 81–2, 84, 86–8, 91–3, 110–11, 135, 141, 155, 159, 164, 167, 175–6, 208–10, 217, 226, 240, 242, 244
    condemned by republican clerics 35, 44, 111, 125, 159, 164
    counterproductive 30, 43–4, 98
    draws down divine wrath 55–9
    evidence of sliding moral scale 25
    futile 31
    geographical distribution 40–1, 125, 199
    local population not involved 43–5, 53–5
    not sanctioned by 1918 election 26, 36
    popular attitudes to 36, 53–5, 65
    punishment of 71, 223
    sanctioned by clerics 117, 128, 130–40, 155–6, 159, 161–6, 168–9, 175, 219, 244
    stains the locality 45, 56–7
    theological objections to 78–84, 169–74
    see also Irish Republican Army; Irish Volunteers
Volunteers *see* Irish National Volunteers; Irish Volunteers; Irish Republican Army

Wall, Thomas, CC Drumcollogher 101
Walsh, William, archbishop of Dublin 16, 21, 24, 28, 81, 93, 98, 101, 103, 156, 167–8, 181, 214, 216, 220, 233–4, 236
Waterford
    city 180, 186
    county 111, 118–19, 142, 160, 181
Waters, John Canon, president Clonliffe College 25, 33, 174
Westmeath 26, 70, 141, 228
Wexford 23, 29, 55, 68, 119, 143, 145, 161, 166, 176, 211, 231
Wicklow 20, 89, 99, 103, 163
Wiel, Jérôme aan de 15, 22
women 5, 9, 74–5, 113, 129, 149, 182, 192, 201, 231
    see also female religious

EU authorised representative for GPSR:
Easy Access System Europe, Mustamäe tee 50,
10621 Tallinn, Estonia
gpsr.requests@easproject.com

www.ingramcontent.com/pod-product-compliance
Lightning Source LLC
Chambersburg PA
CBHW021850230426
43671CB00006B/336